Norman Jay is unquestionably one of the most respected and popular DJs in the world today. Co-founder of the legendary Good Times Sound System and London dance music station KISS FM, Jay fostered the 'Rare Groove' scene pushing the boundaries of the UK's emerging club culture. Awarded an MBE for services to deejaying and music, he recently compiled his most eclectic compilation to date, 'Good Times Skank & Boogie'. He is currently taking his legendary Good Times parties to selected venues around the UK, continuing to convert generations of clubbers to the cause, championing new sounds, yet never forgetting his musical roots, thus guaranteeing nothing but 'Good Times'.

'Norman Jay MBE has lived a life fuller than most can imagine, having witnessed practically every pivotal moment in UK black culture over the past half century ... *Mister Good Times* [is] the story of his life that also doubles up as a first-hand account of the growth of black music culture in the UK, thanks to the fact that it was Jay who was largely responsible for spearheading said growth. He is the pioneer, the author of the musical blueprint that black people in the industry will follow for years to come' GQ

'Norman's contribution to club culture is immeasurable; his passion for music knows no bounds and it was as a result of his groundbreaking warehouse parties that people from all walks of life came together to enjoy the "rare grooves" that he had spent his entire life collecting. He brought new life to undiscovere~~d~~ ~~~~ ~~~~ d on a whole new g~~~~

Norman Jay MBE

MISTER GOOD TIMES

with Lloyd Bradley

dialogue
books

DIALOGUE BOOKS

First published in Great Britain in 2019 by Dialogue Books
This paperback edition published in 2020 by Dialogue Books

10 9 8 7 6 5 4 3 2 1

A CIP catalogue record for this book
is available from the British Library.

ISBN 978-0-349-70067-0

Typeset in Berling by M Rules
Printed and bound in Great Britain by Clays Ltd, Elcograf S.p.A.

Papers used by Dialogue Books are from well-managed forests
and other responsible sources.

Dialogue Books
An imprint of
Little, Brown Book Group
Carmelite House
50 Victoria Embankment
London EC4Y 0DZ

An Hachette UK Company
www.hachette.co.uk

www.littlebrown.co.uk

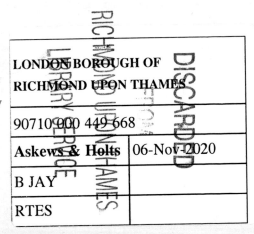

To all my Good Time fans across the globe. Every time I have stood on a stage in front you, be it on the Good Times bus at Notting Hill Carnival, aprés-ski in Alpine snow or on Bondi beach in the blazing hot sun, you continue to be my inspiration to play good music.

Your open mindedness, boundless enthusiasm and non-stop dancing to (nearly) every tune played, even when I have turned 'left' or simply been too 'upfront' in my selections, your positive response serves only to reaffirm a lifelong love of quality music which motivates to me to play on to this day.

To the eternal memory of my brother PAUL and my sister PAMELA.

CONTENTS

part seven: end game

part one:
the notting hill carnival

chapter one: my first carnival

I looked up at this big old house, number 37 Cambridge Gardens, and just knew this would be the place for us. The road was in a turning off Ladbroke Grove just up from the Westway, so we'd be in the heart of the action, and looking at the front garden I had it all pictured in my head: set up my decks there; the amps could sit just there; speaker boxes on each side; run the power line into the house through the front window ... it was perfect, so I knocked on the door. Three white guys answered. I immediately thought they'd be up for it. This was 1980, before gentrification, so a lot of the big houses were squats or low rent properties, where residents had a more open attitude to people like us doing our own thing. I was so sure they'd be amenable that I didn't ask them, I told them. I said, 'I've got a sound system and we're going to set up out here for the weekend.' They didn't really think about it, they just stood there smiling and one of them said, 'Sure! No problem.'

As confident as I thought I had been, I had to work to stop the surprise showing on my face. I maintained this calm demeanour, but inside I was punching the air and screaming 'Yesssss!' I got so excited I told these guys, 'Of course we'll pay you. We'll give you ten bob – 50 pence – to cover the electricity.' They actually looked surprised, and I realised I could have done it for free, but that didn't matter at all. I'd put my flag in the ground. My sound system, Good Times, *was going to play the Notting Hill Carnival.*

This was massive. I was totally aware of the importance of playing the Carnival, but not as somebody who had been taken there since they were a little kid and had its traditions in their blood: the significance for me was as an aspiring black deejay looking to make my mark in London in the 1970s. I had no name as a deejay at that point – the biggest gigs I'd played were my birthday parties at my mum and dad's house – but I was a dedicated clubber and knew the only place that we black deejays could properly express ourselves was the Carnival. It was our platform, somewhere we could make statements that we could truly call our own. At that time it was the only place we could play to a *big* audience on our own terms and be properly creative with our music. I knew what a big deal it was, I felt ready for it.

Cambridge Gardens was right on my manor, too. Although I'd lived in Acton since I was a baby, I'd actually been born in Ladbroke Grove and spent my first few months there. I still looked on it as where I was from because I had a lot of uncles and aunts up there so I was around there all the time – my dad spent his first night in England, in 1955, in a house on the corner of Blagrove Road and Acklam Road, number 1 Blagrove Road, W11. I'd always felt a powerful connection to the area.

Playing the Carnival with so little experience wasn't just a mad idea. I knew I had the music, my brother Joey's equipment was second to none in terms of quality, and my birthday parties were big affairs, so I was mentally prepared to do this. Setting up our sound system to play there was, I realised, a moment I'd been building up to for four or five years.

It was when I went home that the hard part was about to begin. I had to sell the idea to my brother Joey. It was his gear, he'd built the sound system about five years previously as Great Tribulation, a full-on roots reggae sound system, and that day he was anti the idea from the moment I charged in shouting 'Joe! *We've got a spot!*' and I could understand why. With Great Tribulation he was very much a part of the traditional reggae sound system world and knew all the risks, especially at an event like the Carnival where there were hardly any regulations, meaning sound systems could set up where they liked and it was survival of the fittest. Joe was very aware that any newcomer, especially a small sound like ours, was easy pickings and could have been pushed off their patch or, worse still, taxed, which is essentially getting mugged and having equipment or records taken. He was right to be worried, and I'm sure that only my enthusiasm carried it through – there was no way I was even contemplating not doing it.

Back then Carnival used to run all through the bank holiday weekend from Friday evening until Monday night with no curfews. I didn't want to wait a minute more than I had to, so on Friday afternoon we borrowed our dad's old Mk 2 Cortina to get the gear down there. This car was terrible – it kept breaking down, you could start it with a hairpin or a front door key, and it had been nicked so many times that

Dad had put this massive chain through the steering wheel, round the brake and clutch pedals and fastened with an enormous padlock. Not that this mattered to me, as once we took the back seats out there was a huge space, and, wary of Joey's concerns, we took the bare minimum of gear, meaning myself, my brother and Percy Henry, our great big mate who was our muscle, could all pack in. It was raining, Joey was still moaning, but nothing was going to bring me down.

We got there and found other sounds were already playing, so we set up in that front garden, plugged in and we were off. I could hardly believe it, this was a serious dream realised: Good Times was at the Carnival, blasting the best soul and funk in London. I was so caught up in the moment I told my brother that we weren't going to take it down that night, that I was going to stay there all night, sleep there, outside in that front garden, so there'd be no risk to the gear.

It was a good thing we stayed because the next morning, from practically first light, it was a free for all as loads of sounds turned up, driving up and down Cambridge Gardens looking for spots and plugging in anywhere they could. Although our place was secure, a few of them did try to intimidate us, telling us to move, and I had to front them down. With Percy standing next to me I was all, 'Nah, we're here and we ain't moving!' Or if they looked too much for us to take on I'd tell them it was my mum's house, that my parents live there so they can't set up there. Essentially any old cock and bull story so we could hang on to that spot.

As Saturday afternoon went into the evening and things were getting into full swing, with more and more people coming down, I realised how much we'd got away with it on Friday. Now, as a new sound system and one playing jazz/funk, we were getting a baptism of fire, as we were at the sharp end of that time-honoured London soul vs reggae rivalry. How it worked on a day-to-day basis was we, the *soul 'eads*, saw the reggae scene as backward-looking and unimaginative, we would talk about their blues dances as 'dungeon sessions'; in turn the reggae boys reckoned our clothes and dancing were effeminate and our music not black enough – which is putting it far more politely than some people were that afternoon. This is what made the idea of Joey and me sharing a rig all the more remarkable, and I'm sure it would never have happened if we hadn't been brothers. The soul/reggae rivalry was usually harmless, good natured even, but through some of the elements they attracted rather than the sounds themselves, large reggae sound system events too often ended in violence. Now, at the biggest reggae sound system event, that traditional hostility was intensified by Carnival being essentially a Caribbean festival with the music on offer being soca, reggae and calypso, with hardly any American soul or funk. My music wasn't what a lot of people expected or too many of them wanted.

When it really got going, it was madness along Cambridge Gardens, you could hardly hear your own music because it was a cacophony of sound and noise – there was a sound system opposite us, another two doors down the road … there must have been a dozen sound systems playing on a hundred-yard stretch of Cambridge Gardens. They're all playing reggae, and I'm banging jazz/funk and a little bit of disco! People are coming up asking 'Have you got any soca?' and I'm telling them '*Nah*, we don't play that. Ever!' I was adamant! My logic was if they wanted any of that they could go practically anywhere else in the entire Notting Hill Carnival. Then there were those who treated it as an affront and stood there cussing us: 'Wha' dis shit?' ... 'Tek off dis batty bwoy music!' We got booed down a few times, but a little crowd did start to gather, with hardly any white people.

It was quite a funny situation because Joey was at the front of the sound, he's a Rasta with dreadlocks and all the red, gold and green, so every Rastaman that walked past him gave him a nod. Then there's me at the back of the front garden, proper soul boy, nobody knew me, I'm playing this jazz/funk and the same people are cussing me! I'd come back from New York a few days before and I'd brought a suitcase full of tunes back with me – it seemed like a million records, all brilliant, all for Carnival and I was completely buzzing. I was such a militant soul boy and so excited I wasn't going to have anything else, these were the tunes I was going to play and I will admit there were a couple of weird ones in there. Or that was how I planned it, but the reality of the situation was that it was too much of a culture shock for so many of the black people who were there. They wanted to hear their reggae; they wanted to hear their calypso and so on – in fact some of the tunes I'd brought back with me were so upfront even the soul fans around us weren't ready for them! Once we realised the soul thing wasn't really going down too well, Joey and I shared the deejaying. We alternated, he would play for about an hour, playing reggae, with quite a lot of Studio One, then I'd come on for half an hour or forty-five minutes.

It hadn't quite turned out how I imagined, but I don't

think I even noticed, I was totally on cloud nine! All I could think was 'We've made it! We're here . . . we're in the Notting Hill Carnival!' It didn't matter about some people giving us a hard time because I'd put my flag in the ground! Joey, too, was secretly enjoying it as he harboured the same ambitions for the sound, and now he'd set up on the street and played the Carnival. For a sound system it doesn't come any bigger than that.

This was why it was so important for us to play there: to establish our credentials. Good Times had arrived.

chapter two: the significance of carnival

The funniest thing about how determined I was to play at Carnival was that not too long before that I used to hate the *idea* of Carnival. As a black kid trying to make my way in London I was an anglophile and I'd always figured that there had to be a way to be black and British, as this was where I was born and was going to live. Because of that I used to pretty much reject Carnival thinking, 'A bunch of old people following a steel band. What does that mean to me?' I was a young teenager so there was a fair bit of inter-generational rebellion involved, which was particularly acute among so many young black boys and girls of that time because we felt much more London than we did Caribbean. This isn't to say we were disrespectful of Carnival or would have been rude about it, we completely got how it was important to so many people, it just wasn't for us – I'd rather have gone to football or played football than gone to Carnival. In fact I probably did.

When I was a little kid, my mum and dad used to take me, although I honestly thought they could take or leave it. Up until recently they went to Calabash the night before, which was a traditional celebration for people from Trinidad & Tobago and Grenada – they're from Carriacou which is one of the Grenadines – but I always got the impression they went to Carnival itself more out of a sense of duty than being particularly devoted to it. Maybe if they'd still lived in Ladbroke Grove like my uncles and aunts, they'd be more into the whole thing, because they were actually a part of Carnival history: they'd been at the event that is often hailed as the first Carnival. It was organised by the black activist Claudia Jones in St Pancras Town Hall in January 1959, it was London's first Caribbean carnival-type event and it was so spectacular part of it was broadcast on the BBC.

Even if the Carnival tradition was lost on me at that young age, there was a lot about it I did enjoy. I liked going out with my parents as a family, and *loved* going to Ladbroke Grove from where we lived in Acton, because that was where my aunts and uncles and cousins all lived. I'd get together with my cousins and their friends and play football in the street, but if my mum and dad were with me it usually meant I could stay out later.

At the Carnival itself I loved street parades. I was a Cub Scout and sometimes we'd march down the High Street with a little band and people would stand along the side of the road watching. I'd always find the Carnival exciting because it was the first time I'd seen so many people in the streets, and predominantly black people – in other parades we were mostly onlookers, here we *were* the parade. That left an impression, particularly as these were the first times I'd seen so many black people of my mum and dad's age out there enjoying themselves. All the same, ten minutes or so of that was usually enough for me. I'd get bored with it, let them do their thing and sneak off to play football.

It was when I got to my mid-teens that Carnival started changing: not only did it suddenly make sense to me, but I also came to understand what it meant to my parents' generation. This was around 1973 and 1974, when the sound systems made their mark on the event and it became as much about them as it did the parade and the steel bands – maybe more so. That was something I and so many black kids of my age could understand: this was *our* thing, playing *our* music in a way we could relate to! Which was brilliant – it was like going to a club but it cost no money! Bring your own drink or smoke a spliff and it was completely free. Now the Carnival made sense to me. Although I had thought I knew what it meant to the older people, I didn't really until then: it wasn't just about hearing your own music, it was about taking over part of London and celebrating yourselves in a way that the rest of the city couldn't ignore. This was the thinking behind Claudia Jones's original Caribbean Carnival in 1959, to show what we were really about in the face of all the racism and problems black people faced. It was a tradition that had continued, and now we were taking up that baton with sound systems and reggae and soul blasting out on the streets of Ladbroke Grove over the bank holiday weekend. Previously, I just couldn't connect to it because there was no element of it I could properly connect to.

It was also particularly significant to me in the mid-1970s. Although I wasn't really deejaying at that time, I was going to clubs all over London and the suburbs, which, particularly out of town, were adopting door policies that stopped black boys getting in. I believe that whole racism thing in the clubs contributed to the way Carnival evolved so rapidly, as we all felt it and we were all pissed off about it – me in particular. I really was an angry young man and my thinking was, 'You know what? Fuck you! Keep your clubs! Keep your Caister Weekenders! This is how *we* enjoy our music, this is how we do things on our own terms.' In many ways that attitude wasn't unlike the spirit of Claudia Jones, who was basically saying, 'Try as you might, you won't hold us down.' Then if black boys weren't getting in as punters, you knew there were never going to be any opportunities for black deejays, in spite of these places billing themselves as soul or funk clubs. Or never going to happen anywhere other than the Carnival, where we controlled the environment.

The Carnival was just a chance for the prospective deejays to show themselves off early – what you saw and heard over that weekend, the rest of the country saw the next year. Practically all of the emerging street trends in music, street fashion, or dance begin there, because for ages the Carnival has been London's largest catwalk. It's the one platform for all the creatives because it's free, and those showing off down there know the international news crews and tourists will take what they see all over the world. The first jungle records made their first public appearance at Carnival. Up until then jungle was just a localised idea on pirate radio and raves up in Edmonton, but it was at the Carnival before the music media and the music industry picked up on it. The first house records in the UK were played at Notting Hill Carnival by unsung black deejays well before the Summer of Love happened. It was the same for hip hop, the same for electro – I know because I was there when each of those styles showed up.

As the first platform for so much black culture, it has become a conduit to the mainstream. The first time I saw jazz dancing was at the Carnival. All those boys had their new styles and moves they'd been doing all through the year in clubs to tiny audiences of like-minded people, but they were all peacocks, they wanted to perform and they knew at the Carnival the whole world could see them. There's a picture on one of my album covers of a guy break dancing and popping and locking outside our sound system and the whole of the street is standing and watching. That was the sort of attention black culture could command down there every August bank holiday.

I owe my whole professional life to the Carnival, because when we took Joey's sound system down there that was my first big gig – I didn't start deejaying in clubs because those clubs wouldn't give me a squeeze, I started on the street because the Notting Hill Carnival gave me my squeeze. I learned all my skills there, I learned everything about how to be a soul sound-system deejay there, about how to entertain crowds or how to play different sorts of music at different times. By the time you've played the Carnival for a few years, you don't need ten different deejays to come and play ten different styles because you learn how to do it for yourself.

I knew years before we actually took the sound system down there that I *had* to play down there – that's what I meant when I said earlier that I'd been building up to it for about five years. Once I started playing I was a complete convert, as evangelical about it as the older people had been about the steel bands and floats. I'd live for Carnival inasmuch as my whole year would be arranged around it. It was like my homecoming, then as soon as it finished we'd be thinking about the next one and spending the following twelve months getting ready for it. I'd do some amazing gigs during the year and travel to some amazing places to play, but Notting Hill was my Cup Final.

chapter three: continuing at the carnival

Of course we came back to the Carnival in 1981. Although what we'd done that first time out wasn't anything too big, we knew we had left a mark with a few dozen people, maybe a hundred, who had stayed around our sound. They were dancing to the very best soul music, tunes they'd never heard before, because I hadn't even broken the cellophane on them since bringing them back from New York a week or so previously. And they were listening to them on a sound system that was perfect for that, because Joey understood exactly how to set it up and balance it so that my music sounded crisp when played out in the open air. When I was playing, which I did more and more as the weekend went on, this was a *proper* soul sound system. This was important as a few sound systems played soul when they came to the Carnival, but they weren't soul sounds *per se*, they were reggae sounds playing soul for the weekend and were kind of bluffing their way through it. Back then there were a few soul sounds, but I'd done my homework during the years before we went down there and checked them all out – I knew that some of them just didn't sound good out there, and I could murder all of them for music.

We sounded so good that even though it was a bit touch and go when we first set up in Cambridge Gardens, in the end the reggae boys and the other soundmen gave us respect. That in itself was quite funny because it was always such a grudging respect – like they were having teeth pulled by just so much as acknowledging a soul sound system, let alone admitting it was any good! Quite a few dreads used to come around and tell us things like 'Y'know, your sound sound good, yout' man!' or 'Come in wid dat, yout' man!' Never anything overly enthusiastic like 'Wow! That's wicked!', but it didn't matter because I knew that even to get these low key, practically side-of-the-mouth comments was a huge compliment.

They used to surreptitiously check out our music too. I never really knew what was going on elsewhere in the Carnival because I was always too concerned with every aspect of what we were doing, but Joey used to go all over to get his fix of reggae. He knew all the soundmen too, so he could hang out with any of them, and he'd come back and tell me that now they were all playing the big tunes I was running at the previous year's Carnival. That used to make me smile, but it didn't surprise me, and it sums up the 'rivalry' between us and the reggae boys – they love what they love, but, ulti-mately, they know their sound systems are there to entertain people so you have to give them what they want. And, espe-cially at Carnival, playing a little bit of soul isn't going to kill them! But they're only going to play the tunes they know will work, they've got no room for experimentation, so they'd come round by Good Times and clock the reaction we'd get to certain tunes to know what they needed to be going for.

*

For the next couple of years it all went really well. Our crowds grew each time, because that spot in Cambridge Gardens was a little bit out of the way so it was safe, and the people could stay there dancing without causing a major roadblock. We were making a name for ourselves and I felt we had got to a point at which we had become a *destination* – the soul boys and girls were coming to the Carnival and going specifically to 37 Cambridge Gardens because Good Times was playing. Then maybe they didn't go any further than that because Good Times was delivering on all levels and people knew they weren't going to get that anywhere else over the weekend. They had come to dance and we were going to make sure that happened, so I knew they'd be back the next year and probably tell their friends.

Joey was really good, he supported me as our thing was getting bigger, so the sound could physically grow with it, and he definitely saw the potential crowd-wise. For him and his rig this was a great step up from playing dances in church halls or at christenings and he was embracing it, but what he also wanted to do with all this success was test his sound system against others, flex his muscles a little bit.

Joey and the original sound system, Great Tribulation, are from the reggae sound system world, where it's all about competition and sounds playing off against each other in *sound clashes*. Two or three sound systems set up in the same venue and take it in turns to play, with the winner being determined by audience response – bragging rights of being an area's top sound are worth a massive amount and there are even trophies awarded at some sound clashes. Sound systems are judged on how their rig sounds as well as their selection of music – having another version of an opponent's killer tune can be what decides a contest. I never had time for the sound clash. Of course I'd go and support Joey when he was involved in one, but on the whole I hated sound clashes. They could get stupidly competitive and become more about spoiling the other sound's music than you playing your own. To me you should stand or fall by your music, not because the other sound is making noise or spinning back while you're playing, or their people are chopping up your cables.

With that as a background I think the Cambridge Gardens spot was a bit too safe for Joe as there was no competition for us. I, on the other hand, liked it precisely because of that! He wanted a clash, and all I wanted to do was play records and make people dance, but I totally understood where he was coming from: the sound system was his and he wanted to prove what he had built against others. He was agitating for a move and the other boys in the sound system weren't adverse to it and were putting me under pressure. In 1982 I reluctantly let them talk me into it. Obviously we would have to go up against other soul sound systems, which meant going into The Cage.

The Cage was the area under the flyover between Acklam Road and the bridge over the railway; it was an area of concrete not quite as big as a football pitch and completely enclosed with a wire fence, hence the name The Cage. There was a footpath down the outside from the bridge to Acklam Road, and The Cage itself had a gate at either end. Until Good Times began to get established in Cambridge Gardens, this was where the soul music would be found at the Carnival, with the Mastermind, Six-By-Six and Winner Roadshow sound systems. And while that meant a more easy-going crowd, The Cage was notorious for getting attacked by steamer gangs as there were only two relatively small gates, one at either end, and crowds could get trapped in there. I wasn't happy. My brother wanted to set up at the back, down towards the railway, but I said, 'No, Joey, we need the exit!', and I made the boys set up in the top corner, right by the gate that led out to Acklam Road. If it was going to kick off in there I wanted us to be the first to get out.

My mood didn't improve as the day got going. The big tune of the day was Afrika Bambaataa's 'Planet Rock', and that seemed like all anybody was playing. We'd come down there hoping to find out what these other sounds had to offer, but everybody was playing 'Planet Rock', wheeling it back and starting it again. I found it so frustrating that all I was hearing was that, a bit more of some sort of electro like Warp 9 or the Peech Boys or even D Train, then back to a bit of reggae. I hated it, absolutely fucking hated it. Everybody's playing, you can't hear properly because it's under the flyover and next to the tube lines, so everybody's cranked up their volume without too much regard for quality. The music's predictable. People aren't there for us, they're just there. I was thinking about where Good Times was as a sound system by then and how we'd grown to get to this point. Carnival was the highlight of our year, so we had been building up to it and had spent all our money on it – new tweeters, putting in new boxes, painting our boxes ... Plus Good Times had now got a little following from Acton, about fifty of our people had come down to support us and this was what we'd brought them to.

We carried on and did what we did, regardless of what was going on around us, as we were going to keep up our own standards, busting some new tunes and working to entertain the crowd. We'd kind of settled into it, then after it got dark, about 10 or 11 o'clock, suddenly I'm hearing girls screaming and glass breaking. I look up from the decks and the air is full of bricks and rocks and bottles because it's all kicked off at the back, by the footbridge over the railway where Six-By-Six was playing. I climbed up onto one of our boxes to see what was going on and it was pandemonium up there, people were running everywhere and there were a few white-shirted policemen caught in the middle of it, who had lost whatever control they might have had and were overwhelmed, they were getting battered with bricks and rocks and bottles.

I started shouting to Joey, 'Switch the sound off, it's gone mad!' when I realised most of the crowd was stampeding towards us, because we were right by the gate that was away from the violence. It was chaos – at one point I saw this big black guy with what looked like a Samurai sword, waving it about. And all I could think about was saving our gear, but it was far too late for that. *Crash!* Our stacks went over, and I'm thinking, 'I fucking knew this would happen! This is why I didn't want to come in here in the first place!' We did our best to protect our gear, the amps and the decks, and our lot from Acton rallied round to help, but a lot of our gear got smashed or stolen. They took the bullet tweeters and those things cost serious money.

At that point I said I was never coming to the Carnival again, then I realised that was a bit over the top, so I modified it to never again in The Cage: if I play it's on the street to my crowd, no more of this sound clash. When we got home, me, my brother, my dad and my uncle – who were part of what we were doing – had a debrief, discussing what went wrong, and I said, 'Sound clashes.' I said they were a recipe for disaster in an environment like that because they set so many people off against each other. I said no more sound clashes: it's OK, if Joey wants to do his reggae boy thing then he does it without me, but if I'm doing Good Times then the only person supplying the music is me. I was still mad about what we'd been put through, so I was adamant.

It took us the best part of a year and a lot of our money to repair the sound system, but we did and in 1983 we went back to Cambridge Gardens. I think the other soul sound systems went back to The Cage, in fact I know Six-By-Six and Mastermind did, but in 1983 it kicked off again in there. This time the steamer gangs came through spraying CS gas and snatching chains and watches, people got seriously hurt in the stampedes to get out, and I'm pretty sure that after that the police closed it off during Carnival.

chapter four: the riot of 1976

Of course, disturbances at the Carnival were nothing new. In 1975, nearly ten years before that disastrous year in The Cage, there had been a number of confrontations between black boys and the police. The following year, this same conflict blew up into a full-scale riot on the Monday. This was around the time when, as a teenager, I had started going, but on a very casual *ad hoc* basis.

I hadn't been in 1974 and '75, there was no particular reason why not – as I've said, I didn't take it *that* seriously, and my mates and I had probably gone to some seaside town like Margate or Southend for the bank holiday. I know I'd gone to Margate on the bank holiday Monday of 1976, then almost inadvertently ended up back at the Carnival, so I was there when the first big riot happened.

We'd gone to Margate for the day, where we got in a huge row with a bunch of National Front-supporting skinheads who took objection to a group of London black guys having fun in what they saw as 'their town'. We were easily a match for them and seriously hurt a few of them. This big guy with us, who we called Jabba, took a few heads off – figuratively – and threw one guy through a plate glass window. It meant we had to get out of town a bit quick, because we knew there was no way Old Bill would have believed that we didn't start it, and we would have got charged with all sorts of things. That would have been after they gave us a beating in the van.

We got back to London around mid-afternoon, and the choice was go back to Acton and do nothing or go to the Carnival, so of course we chose Door Number Two. This was before mobile phones and twenty-four-hour news, so we had no idea what was happening up there, but when we got to Ladbroke Grove it was properly going off. Stepping out of the tube station and into the thick of it was mad, like nothing I'd seen before. Gangs of black boys were running all over the place, throwing anything they could find at the police, who had no protection – this was before riot shields, so the best they could do was pick up dustbin lids and milk crates. Any police car that came through was attacked, and if it was forced to stop the kids would swarm all over it, kicking it, rocking it, trying to smash the windows. It was mayhem, literally! As near to total anarchy as you could get because, and I'd never seen this before, the police had totally lost control of those streets and it was mob rule. It was impossible not to get sucked into it. Like the football thing I'll talk about in Part Two, some primeval thing took over. I know for me the red mist came down and we were immediately swept up in it.

For me, without even stopping to think about it, I clocked what was going on and realised it was us against Old Bill. While I'm not a violent person, a kind of instinctiveness took over all of us, we knew this was the chance to get the Babylon back for all the rubbish they'd been doing to us over the years. We felt as if, suddenly, we were on equal terms with them: no more when you're walking along and they can cosh you; or when they jump out of a Cortina and push you against a window and put their hands in your pockets. *Not today you don't!* That's how I felt, and I know so many other black guys in London at that time felt exactly the same way. I was nineteen years old, and although I'd had it relatively easy for 1976 (I'd only ever suffered two physical incidents of police brutality), I knew all about it from listening to the stories of my mates and other people close to me, so I was definitely an angry young man. I remember that summer two black boys died in Notting Dale police station – unexplained deaths – then there was the SPG, the Special Patrol Group, who were particularly vicious and at that time seemed like an army of occupation in Ladbroke Grove. They had been at the forefront of the Met's heavy-handed policing of previous Carnivals. I was always hearing about all that stuff – every black person in London did – which is why that rioting spread like it did. People were thinking, 'You know what? For this weekend, these are our streets and we're going to pay you back for all that foolishness from the rest of the year.'

That was one of the most important things about going to the Carnival: the environment the music was played in as much as the music itself. Around the streets of Notting Hill and Ladbroke Grove on those three days, everywhere you looked you saw black people enjoying themselves ... *relaxed*. Of course Old Bill was there, but they weren't going pull a person for smoking a spliff, it was like, 'OK, it's Carnival, you've got a pass.' It was like a modern-day version of J'ouvert, the historic start of the first carnivals in the Caribbean, when it was the one time of the year that the slaves were allowed to mock their masters. But from about 1973 onwards, the policing of Carnival had become increasingly oppressive and forceful. That was another reason why I hadn't been for a few years – the 'wilderness years' I called them – because it was too easy to get into trouble through no fault of your own. Now I was back there and in the thick of it.

Because of how things were going down when we got there, with the police definitely on the receiving end, I wasn't at all scared, or not for myself. I was scared because I remembered my mum and dad and my sisters were going to Carnival that day, so suddenly I'm thinking they could be caught up in all of this. I ran round to see my uncle, who lived in Ruston Close, W11 just off the back of Ladbroke Grove, and sounding as shocked as possible I asked him, 'What's happening? Police everywhere? Where's Mum and Dad?' He told me they'd all gone home and everybody was safe, so I breathed a big theatrical sigh of relief and got into a bit of small talk with him about how terrible it was, but really, as soon as I knew everybody was alright, I was itching to get back out there. I climbed over the wall from his back garden and I went straight out into the street and I was straight into it!

As soon as I was back out there, among that crowd going absolutely nuts, all rational thought was gone. I became that angry, frustrated rioter, as much a part of the mob as anybody else. When I look back, it seems that for a while I wasn't in control of my actions and I wasn't in control of my thoughts. While I *thought* I was in control of what was unfolding in front of me, quickly it went beyond that. That was the first time I'd ever been exposed to that sort of naked violent madness – mob madness – and the truth is it doesn't give you any time to think. You just go with crowd, run with the herd, as if whatever they're doing is a good idea and you find yourself going along with it.

I was right in the corner of Cambridge Gardens and Ladbroke Grove with two or three of my mates when it properly kicked off under the flyover, which was about fifty yards away. That bit was cleared, but there were rocks and pieces of brick cans on the ground, there were two or three coppers in short-sleeved shirts, no protection at all, who were pushing people back really violently. The thing was, most of these people weren't rioters, they were just frightened or confused and trying to get out of there, they were women and older people and children and the coppers were practically assaulting them. That was one of the main reasons all of this had kicked off so fiercely – because Old Bill was dishing it out to everybody, regardless. Within seconds they got covered in rocks and bottles, meaning the people could stampede out of that corner. Most of them were terrified. There were a couple of people standing next to me. One of them had a mac on, and in the ensuing melee he'd got knocked to the ground, right in front of us. We helped him up and his mac was filthy, like he'd been trampled. I looked up and see that now Old Bill has recovered and is standing right in front of us, and we're thinking we're going to rush them – us, three teenagers, going to rush these coppers! That was how much we were affected by what was going on around us.

We didn't rush them, and as they didn't move either, we were able to slip away down to Portobello Road, where we're standing on that corner by the Green, and this mad mob comes down from Golborne Road way. People screaming, desperately trying to get out of the way of this gang, and as we looked at them we could see why. It was at that point this whole thing stopped being about getting our own back on Old Bill or reclaiming those streets, it had become something much darker and genuinely scary. As everybody on the pavements attempted to get away, one guy – a bystander – got knocked to the ground and this posse jumped all over him. This was right in front of me, and I can see the bloke twitching as they swarmed all around him, kicking him, and I can see a couple of them with blades and they're stabbing him in the back. Apart from the twitching, he's motionless, out of it, he can't even cover up let alone defend himself – and even then one of them was still hitting him as he lay there. I said to one of my mates, 'Fuck me! They've killed the guy!' Instinctively, I stepped off the kerb to pull him off, and in that moment I knew that if I tried to intervene I was a dead man. For a split second I'd locked eyes with the attacker and I've never been looked at like that before or since – the only way to describe it is murderous, literally. How this guy looked at me was beyond any kind of hatred, he was totally out of control. I pulled back on to the pavement.

Then this scene got worse. While the victim was motionless on the ground, the guy attacking him took his watch. As he's done so, another one of the mob comes back and says, 'What's he got round his neck?' In that moment I'm filled with absolute horror. All I can think is, '*You fucking black bastard!*' How could you? The guy's lying there on the floor twitching, blood oozing out of his head, they've jumped all over him, stabbed him, *then* come back and robbed him. I didn't bargain for this! This isn't what the events of this afternoon are about. People like the guy lying on the floor are not the enemy. *They are* – Babylon! All of us young black men in London in the 1970s had a grievance with the police – as did most of our dads, only they were quiet about it – and I fully went along with that, but this was mob rule gone completely out of control.

I was wandering about in a daze, because at that time I'm believing I've witnessed a murder. When my head cleared all I could think of was that if we got found in the area, we'd get collared for it and then we'd get done, so we slipped off and walked down the end of Oxford Gardens. Although we didn't witness any more possible murders, things were definitely no calmer down there.

We arrived in that street at exactly the time of that famous newsreel footage of the police car reversing at speed up the road and getting bricked and bottled. We got to the corner of Oxford Gardens just as it sped past, so we are just out of the shot. I wish we'd got there a couple of seconds earlier! It was once the car had gone that people noticed the film crew there and I shouted, 'Get the camera off them! Get them out of here!' What we were going to do with that great big television camera I don't know, but it was about getting swept up in the mayhem again. And people responded. *Bosh!* Within seconds the camera crew went down, and when they got up they were chased out of there, just about managing to keep hold of their equipment. This was when I really stopped to think about what was going on. That little incident had all gone off so quickly, started by just one shout, and they could have been seriously hurt. Again, I'm thinking *they're* not the enemy ... this has all gone mad.

It was at that exact moment that the mob tipped over a car in Oxford Gardens and set fire to it and it went off – *bang!* This wasn't a police car, it was just somebody's car, and I think it was that explosion which jolted me back to the sensible guy I usually was. Although I'd been puffing, I was suddenly very, very sober and I knew I had to get out of there – all I could think of was how the hell would I get back to Acton? There were cars burning on Oxford Gardens, cars burning in Acklam Road, posses of black boys roaming all over the place. It wasn't quite *Mad Max*, but I had never seen anything like this. When I took a good look at what was going on around me, there were still a lot of dazed-looking people wandering around just trying to get home, it was like, 'Oh my God! What have I got myself into?'

Old Bill was regrouping by now and gaining some sort of control, and I knew that if one of them had been stabbed or even killed or beaten up like that other guy, then they were going to take it out on us. I certainly didn't want to be one of those victims. What they had done was seal the area: they'd closed the tube stations so nothing was stopping at Ladbroke Grove or Westbourne Park, and had blocked the roads to effectively seal the main area of the rioting – nobody in and nobody out. There were still all these panicked people walking about just trying to get home and being told they can't go here or they can't go there, and by then I'm concerned that my mum and dad will start panicking if I don't get back soon, because as far as they're concerned I'm in Margate, not down here doing all of this.

When we arrived there that afternoon and saw what was going on, we were full of bravado – kill the Old Bill, all of that – but once those things happened so close up, I knew I wasn't cut out for it. Up until that point I'd thought I was a bad boy, but ultimately I was not, or at least not nearly as bad as I thought I was. As I reflected on what I'd seen, I even began to feel sorry for some of those police caught up in some dread things. I had a lot of conflicting thoughts going on. I tried to reconcile the rioting against the police by thinking, 'Well they were doing this and that to us for how long.' But what about the ones that weren't doing that kind of thing to us? And when those black boys were coming at them with bottles and stones, and anything they could grab, to give the Old Bill their due, they had no protection, just truncheons and a few dustbin lids and they fought it out. Then again, I didn't know whether to afford them any respect because I thought there would have been enough of them who were thinking, 'We are white. This is our country, we won't let you blacks do this.' During that fighting they seemed almost fearless, driven by the idea of 'We will win at all costs. You *will not* defeat us.'

It was partly thinking about that mentality that allowed me to justify so much of what had happened – the fighting against the police, not the thuggery – and I know from some of the people around us that afternoon that it had made some kids just want to fight more. Also, what filled us with even more aggression was the behaviour of some of the police once it had all kicked off – they were just steaming in to crowds of black people indiscriminately. These were just regular Carnival goers who were trying to get away from the trouble and didn't know which way to turn, but so many of the Old Bill didn't care. They were whacking black women with their sticks – that could have been my mum they were hitting, that could have been my sister. They were whacking old people – that could have been one of my old uncles getting shoved like that. So that's how I justified it in my head, but I didn't get involved in it on a one-to-one level.

As soon as it got dark, my thing was all about getting out and getting home, and because of the cordon the police put up this became a bit of a mission. I'd grown up around there, coming up to Grove all the time to play football with my cousins, so I knew the manor really well, so I was able to avoid the big roads and by dodging through a few back gardens I was through the police thing and out of there. With the tube stations either closed or with loads of police outside them, I walked all the way back to my mum's house in Acton, where there were still police cars everywhere. They were on the lookout for whoever they could find reason to pick up and I was giving it my best Joe Public innocence as I walked past them: 'What, me, officer? Been to the Carnival? Naaah! I'm on my way home from an outing to Margate!'

When I got home, the *News at Ten* was on and it was all about how the Grove was ablaze. The papers the next day were headlines of the riots, police casualties and how the streets were burning. Part of me was really shocked and scared, because I could now appreciate the full scale of it and the news stories took me back to the mayhem of actually being there. Then another part of me was thinking this is good, this needed to happen. They won't fuck us over any more – this is where it all changes. I remember thinking, 'This is where all of that shit you've been doing to us stops, but if you want a war, I'm glad there's some kids out there that will give you that war.'

Of course what happened was that the next year, due to how things had gone down in 1976, the police were out for revenge. They got it too, because naturally it kicked off again and this time they were so much better prepared. They put it down really efficiently and left a lot of casualties and arrests among the black youth. Then in 1978 they had shields and knew how to use them and they're directing things from this mobile headquarters on the flyover above Ladbroke Grove station. I was wondering how the Old Bill could get so organised so quickly ... then I found out it was the same riot control techniques and equipment they'd been deploying on the streets of Belfast, which they'd brought to the mainland to use against us at the Carnival. While it was good to let them know we weren't going to lie down and take it, I now realise we were never going to win – but I was young and fearless in those days.

chapter five: the move from cambridge gardens

Back to the 1980s, and although Good Times was getting bigger and more popular at Carnival, by the end of the decade I had become so disillusioned with the whole thing I was on the verge of pulling out. The Cambridge Gardens spot had served us well, but with the crowds we were attracting we'd outgrown it, and we were realising the limitations of being on the street like that. There was always a flow of people just walking past us, which wasn't ideal for the increasing number of people that wanted to stay around us for our music, plus the steamer gangs were causing all sorts of grief. Both of these things were symptoms of what I saw as bigger problems with Carnival as a whole at that time, and I have since realised that was why I was losing faith in it.

During the second half of the decade the Carnival crowds were becoming much more inclusive, as a reflection of London and clubbing in London at that time, plus the Notting Hill Carnival had become a major tourist attraction – a bit like New Orleans's Mardi Gras – so both of these new crowds needed to be accommodated. It was a massive change, as significant as the way things had changed during the mid-70s, when my generation of carnival-goers shifted the event from essentially a procession to something that incorporated the static aspects of the sound system. Once again, in order for Carnival to represent its city it couldn't carry on with the old ways.

I believe that mid-70s change happened because people were left alone to get on with it – nobody stopped the sound systems just setting up and playing. This time Carnival was more structured and it needed those running things to take a positive stance regarding any such evolution. The problem, however, was the traditionalists within the Carnival organisation, who I saw as a bunch of old dinosaurs – they wanted it to be an exclusively black thing and saw this new crowd as 'too many white people'. That approach might have been OK in 1969, but this was 1989 and it made no sense to me. By that time London was an obviously cosmopolitan city, and black performers were far more visible to the mixed public. To encourage those new people, though, perceptions of the Carnival had to be changed.

I'd talk to girls and a lot of my white friends and say 'Why don't you come to Carnival?' They'd tell me it was too dangerous, too risky – they simply didn't feel safe. The reality was that while Carnival had up to two million attendees over the weekend, there were more arrests at Glastonbury each year, where tent robberies at music festivals were becoming widespread, yet it was Carnival that had this reputation as being unsafe. For things to get any better the organisers needed to be seen to be making an effort to change this idea, and I believed to do this they had to embrace the sound systems, which traditionalists hadn't fully done, and create safe, attractive environments for us to play in.

In 1989 I simply couldn't see that happening – in fact I could only see things getting worse. This wasn't my vision of what Carnival should be evolving into and I felt like it was completely incompatible with my whole ethos, my whole attitude. What a contemporary Notting Hill Carnival meant to me was – as well as the procession, obviously – static sound systems, with their own crowds that they've nurtured, whether it's a hundred people or a thousand people, they're *destinations* and people are coming to Carnival because of them. I needed to establish this as a way forward, but because I couldn't see it happening, in 1990 I opted not to take Good Times to the Carnival.

During that year I tried to kid myself that I didn't want to do this any more, that I was over the Carnival, but come August I was like a bear with a sore head. Of course I went up there, and, unsurprisingly, that just made things worse. I walked around, went down to Powis Square and sat on a wall for a bit, where a succession of people came up to me asking how come I wasn't playing that year. Then I went to support my mate Ashley Beedle, a really talented deejay who was up there with Shock Sound System, the only other proper soul sound there that year. I found that so many of our old crowd had ended up there. I was really pleased for them, but inside I was dying. Completely selfishly all I was thinking was, 'This is shit! This should be me! I *need* to be doing this!' That was when I knew Carnival was in my blood – unconsciously and consciously I knew my future as a deejay and our future as a sound system lay with Carnival. Whatever problems there might have been, there was still no other platform of expression for us, so, love it or hate it, I was coming back in 1991. I was going to find a new spot and put our sound system back where it belonged.

As luck would have it, this was the same time that the Carnival authorities appeared to be addressing the issues that concerned me, so they had decided to expand the available sites for sound systems. It was as if they had finally acknowledged sound systems' importance to the Carnival and they called a meeting to allocate new, specifically designated sites. I went to the meeting with my brother and my dad – Dad always used to come to these things with us because he was a great supporter of what we were doing. The meeting was packed. There must have been representatives of sixty sound systems there, everybody buzzing with expectation, but when they announced the proposed new sites, which were further away from the epicentre of Carnival, the room erupted with this groaning and kissing of teeth! 'Rahtid! Mi nah mek dat move!' Then I stood up and declared, 'I'm Norman Jay from Good Times and I'll go. I'm willing to move.' My brother looked at me like 'What are you thinking?', but I'd definitely had enough of what had been going on before.

It all seemed to be going so well, but then I left Joey to sort out the pitch. I can't remember why I couldn't do it, but he went to the allocation meeting. I met him back at my mum and dad's house afterwards and he told me he had got this spot at Ledbury Road and Talbot Road, near Powis Square. It was by a pub called the Ledbury Arms, which wasn't nearly as chi-chi as it is today, and I knew exactly where it was in terms of the Carnival – too near the centre. This was because he still wanted to compete. I exploded! 'What were you fucking doing? Didn't you learn *anything* from that year we went in The Cage? . . . Sound clash isn't a thing you do at Carnival, it's the sort of thing you do at Club Noreik in Tottenham or you do in a hall, *not* on the road. It doesn't work!' I stormed out, yelling at him, 'If you're thinking of setting up there I certainly won't be doing it with you! That's it! If you don't want to do this properly, you're on your own.'

We had to be somewhere safe, somewhere our crowds felt secure enough to enjoy themselves and where people couldn't be rushing past us upsetting our equipment. I wasn't going to jeopardise the opportunity Carnival gave me, which was a new blank canvas to bring London clubbing to the street. I totally respected the roots reggae sound system culture, it just wasn't for me. As I've said, I couldn't have been less interested in sound clashes. I wanted to define Good Times by the quality of the music we were playing and the quality of the equipment we played it on – that's what I believed would distinguish us as a true sound system of the modern era. And I believed deep down Joey knew I was right.

After ranting at my brother I went straight out to my car and drove up to the Carnival office, where, although it was about seven or eight in the evening, I figured somebody would still be there. Sure enough, there was Claire Holder, a young black barrister who, as chair of the Notting Hill Carnival Trust, was always very easy to talk to and appeared sympathetic to most issues. Although I was still boiling up inside, I'd calmed down a bit on the drive and could ask her quite calmly if all the spots had been allocated. She said, 'Well, your brother ...', and I just cut her off, told her to scrap all of that and I'd take the spot by Sainsbury's at the top of Ladbroke Grove, which was such a plum site I knew in my heart it would be gone. Sure enough, Herbie from Mastermind had taken it. I was gutted. I didn't know what to do. The one spot I would have moved to from Cambridge Gardens had gone, but I was determined not to go further into the Carnival.

I came out of the office, which is at the top of the Grove, walked a few yards down, then turned left towards the Ha'penny Steps. I don't know why, I think I must've been trying to clear my head, but I walked under the arch, down the concrete steps towards Southern Row, and I looked around and thought, 'You know what? This is perfect!' It was one of those light bulb moments, and standing on the corner of West Row and Southern Row I could clearly visualise us setting up here. We would be well away from the Carnival's epicentre – it was exactly a mile away from Cambridge Gardens – and we'd be opening the north end of Notting Hill and Ladbroke Grove. It was tucked away so nobody would be able to find us except our own crowd, who I knew would look for us. It could be perfect. This was a radical step away from what the Carnival had become and towards what I was looking for – it felt like leaving London for the day and relocating to somewhere like Newcastle.

I rushed back to the office, with my head close to exploding with all the potential I could see for Good Times on this spot. By now it's about nine o'clock, Claire's about to go home, and I charge in shouting, 'Give me Southern Row! . . . Give me that corner! . . . That's where Good Times is gonna go! . . . Make it official, put it in the book!' She was more than willing to give me that spot because nobody else had shown any interest in it, for, as I would find out, the very same reasons my brother and my dad weren't at all keen.

I knew I was going to have to justify why I wanted to move there, so before I even got home I'd made a list in my head of why it was just right for us. It's safer and because there will be no trouble, more girls will come there and everything will be calmer. There'll be no sound bleed so we won't have to worry about that sort of interference. And, ultimately, the crowd we'll get in front of us will be there because they *want* to be there, they support us – we won't be one of those sound systems just plonked on the road with a transient crowd that walks past, does a little shake then moves on to the next. This is our chance to establish ourselves as *the* destination sound.

The next day I sat down to a reasoning session with both my brothers, my dad and my uncle, and I told them we're not going to the spot Joey got, we were going to go to Southern Row, at the back of the Carnival office. Immediately my dad and my brother started objecting, telling me how it was too out of the way and nobody would come there. Really, their objections played into why I liked the spot so much: people would just have to walk over the canal bridge and they'd be in Kensal Road, five minutes away, but at the same time missing all the nonsense that had been going on elsewhere; then if they want to go it's back over the bridge and you're in

Harrow Road. Totally easy access – some of my posh friends even came down there on a canal boat straight from Camden Lock, tied up outside the old Lynne Franks PR building and stepped straight across the road down to Good Times! Yes, it was 'out of the way', but at that point there would be no other sound systems there, so it would be strictly our crowd and we could shape the experience how we wanted and build our own thing.

Also, there was another important reason why this location was good for us: Carnival took place across three London boroughs. It was mostly Kensington & Chelsea, the top of it on the north side of the Harrow Road was Brent, and bits to the south and to the east were Westminster. This particular spot was Kensington & Chelsea, and while none of the councils were particularly easy to deal with when it came to Carnival, they weren't bad – the lesser of the three evils! Westminster was a nightmare, according to other sound-men, and it's a good job we never went to the Ledbury spot because that was part of Westminster.

As for nobody finding us, I said they were going to have to trust me because it wasn't going to happen overnight and I had a five-year plan. The first year we'll be establishing ourselves and it won't matter how many flyers we put out or much I talk about it on the radio – I had my Kiss FM show by then – people will still go to the old spot on Cambridge Gardens. First year we'll get maybe three or four hundred people, then they'll talk about it and we'll have another year to build it up and we'll get double that for the following Carnival, and in four or five years' time you won't be able to move in there. Which is exactly what came to pass, and we stayed there from 1991 until we stopped playing the Carnival in 2013.

The first time we set up, my uncle, who was a carpenter, came down and built us a little stage. He'd do that every year until we got the bus, and for three years we had the spot to ourselves. That was great, and in 1994 we were joined by another sound system, Sancho Panza, which was run by two English guys, Jim Angell and Matt Brown, who went on to become pretty big before they quit a year or two after us. They played mostly house music with a Latin tinge in there and were set up on Middle Row opposite the old bus garage, by the school wall, which was close enough for us to complement each other but far enough away that there was no interference. Then a year or so later, an old school roots reggae sound was set up on East Row, Aba Shanti-I. They were from east London and deeply Rasta – I always saw them as the spiritual successors to Jah Shaka.

I loved the fact those other sound systems were there. I used to go round to them and a lot of the white people who came to Good Times used to check out Aba Shanti-I as well. Officially, this was the Northern Quarter of Carnival, but I dubbed that little plot the Bermuda Triangle, because it was somewhere people disappeared from the rest of the Carnival! It was brilliant having three sound systems along Southern Row, with the architecture that was there before the redevelopment making a kind of amphitheatre, so we all sounded crisp and there was virtually no sound bleed between us. All of us were in there doing something different and it was a one-stop shop for London club culture-style entertainment, of the more grown-up end! There was a whole spectrum of music, from soul and funk to house, to hip hop, to a tinge of Latin, to traditional reggae, to white-boy house ... whatever you wanted. This situation was everything I imagined the Carnival could be, and quickly became the epicentre of almost an alternative Carnival, a New Carnival, a Carnival for the twenty-first century.

chapter six: growing

Life was good for Good Times in our new spot, and by the middle of the 1990s we were becoming so popular our little homemade system couldn't cope with the size of the crowd. We knew this was coming for a while and, really, had been delaying doing anything about it because as a group – as well as Joey and myself there were three or four others – we had been very reluctant to hire a PA system from a regular hire company. As much as possible, we wanted to keep our money circulating within the black community; we felt strongly about Carnival being a black endeavour and money generated from it should stay that way. By that time we felt the whole event was under increasing attack from commercial entities who wanted a piece of the credibility or the fame that came from sound systems like ours, but were never going to give us any money, or not enough to make a difference. We'll discuss sponsorship in depth later on, but as we wanted nothing to do with an outside PA company and we knew we needed a bigger rig, we opted to rent some equipment from another sound system and borrowed more speakers to augment what we already had. At least that way we could keep the money among us soundmen.

Incidentally, the first thing I did when we got those other boxes was get my uncle to build front panels for them, just a frame and scrim we could put over them so nobody would see the boxes came from two different sound systems! Although it was a lot of effort to go to for just a couple of days, in my mind presentation was a big part of who we were, and I was rigid about how we had to look right – not only did Good Times have to play the best music, but it had to be played on the best-sounding sound and best-*looking* equipment. This was our stage show and I wanted to blaze a trail that others would follow.

We used the other sound system equipment to supplement ours for a couple of years. The first time wasn't too bad, but by the second year we'd grown even more, so we were back to struggling and realising the old school way could only reach so far – by then our crowd was so large we weren't getting the coverage. In 1995 I decided that was it, the last time we were going to do it that way. Ultimately it wasn't what anybody wanted, but to me Carnival had to be perfect, we had to pull it off *exactly* how I imagined it should be. If putting on that level of set meant sacrificing a principle then so be it, we'd kept it going the other way for as long as we possibly could. We were growing and reaching the point I always wanted us to get to at Carnival, and we couldn't allow ourselves to be limited simply by our choice of equipment, so I took the executive decision that we needed to bring in a specialist PA company. Hey! Good Times was my thing, so of course I could decide these things!

Every night after we'd played the Carnival we had a debrief. We'd sit round the kitchen table at my mum and dad's house and go through everything that happened during the gig. These sessions could last all night, my mum and my sister would usually go to bed leaving me, my dad and my brother up talking about what we did right, what we did wrong, what ideas worked and what ideas didn't, and, most importantly, how we could improve things ... I wanted to make sure our crowd got the best gig they possibly could and that Good Times continued to get better. These sessions could go on all night, because I was always buzzing from the day and there was no way I could have gone to sleep. After that Carnival I announced we were going to hire a PA for the next one, and there wasn't really any objection because they knew we hadn't been at our best for the size of the crowd we were pulling in. Most of the discussion that followed was about cost, whether we could guarantee something that sounded like we wanted it to sound, and what to do about the Good Times logos, which were on all the speaker boxes.

I was very confident on all those fronts. Joey knew how to talk to sound engineers to get exactly what we wanted, I knew we could absorb the cost of PA hire from other gigs we did during the year, and by then we had the bus so that was all the Good Times signage we needed. The question I got asked most frequently about that changeover was whether it made a difference to me as I played to the crowd – I think people thought it would be more like a music festival than a sound system event because I was using a regular PA. I could see their point – kind of: when I'm at music festivals I'm just a deejay like all the others, just doing my job and the best I can to make people dance and get the most out of the music. The reason it appears so different is because I never use a mic when I'm at one of those things, I just play. When I'm at Carnival, however, it's my show and the people are there for *me* not the bands – I'm there looking out at the crowd and thinking, 'You all know me and I know *you* and I know *you* ... I know hundreds of you out there! I'm one of you! You see me on the street ... I see you out shopping ... I see you in record shops!' There's a relationship I have with my own crowds, especially at Carnival, and unlike some of the bigger festivals, you're not just this person who's miles away or who is surrounded by an entourage or security.

That was actually the case in practice too. Looking out from the bus I used to see faces I'd recognise from previous years, and the same people would come back each year – I'll swear there were people coming just to take a selfie in front of the Good Times bus. It had become something of a meeting place, especially for a lot of old clubbers, more so on the Monday when I played more jazz/funk. The Sunday crowds tended to be younger, more energetic and I used to play a lot of jungle, a lot of upbeat stuff and *bang*, they'd go mad, but Monday was the old fuckers who couldn't be arsed to do the going out thing during the rest of the year. They were quite happy to come to Good Times at the Carnival because they knew they'd hear all the music they knew and loved, meet all the people they wanted to meet, and find themselves in a safe environment. I genuinely got to know people who came to Good Times at the Carnival: there were the ones who came over every year from New York, there was a posse of fifty or sixty Belgians who would come over on coaches, regulars from London and from all over Great Britain in coach parties. It was the greatest feeling to know these people came back every year for Good Times and I used to work hard to make sure everybody felt welcome. We'd decorate the bus with bunting of all the different flags from around the world, and shout out to all the different nations, *everybody*! 'This is for all my brothers and sisters from the motherland! Say Africa! *Waaaay!* ... This is for all my friends from Germany! Say Germany! *Waaaay!* ...' And so on.

Everybody was welcome, and not just from the point of view of different nationalities. What Good Times meant to me was it was totally inclusive, *nobody* was told they couldn't come in – black, white, Asian, people in wheelchairs, all my gay and lesbian friends, everybody felt included. This was what Good Times stood for and you wouldn't find that anywhere else at the Carnival. It was my utopia and it wasn't an accident either: we worked hard to create this safe environment and to encourage the same sort of crowds I'd get at a Shake and Fingerpop event. I would tell the crowds, 'If you want to go to Glastonbury and wallow in six inches of mud, fine, but if you just want to dance to the best music in the world – non-stop entertainment – this is the last great free street party going!'

This meant I had a very mixed crowd, which in turn meant I took a lot of stick from the 'too many white people' lobby, and although at no point did I agree with that way of thinking, I could understand why it was levelled at me as a criticism. What I had noticed when we first went to the Carnival was that our crowd was predominantly black, but gradually more and more white people and Asian people felt comfortable to come there and the make-up of it started to noticeably change. This was at a time when you couldn't read any press about the Carnival that wasn't negative and we were working against that to try and change perceptions. This was one of the main reasons I had wanted to move away from the centre down to Middle Row.

Not that I cared about what people were saying. This was my audience, one that came to my sound system – a black sound system – to events in which we made everybody feel welcome. Nobody felt intimidated. Of course that meant white people could and would turn up. The people who were giving me a hard time over it were missing the point – maybe deliberately, I don't know – everybody was welcome, but we, the Good Times black sound system, were in charge and everybody was aware of that and respected that, so now let's just get on with enjoying ourselves. Nobody was compromising anything.

If the weather was good, we'd start playing at about 11 in the morning, but we wouldn't even begin to fill up until maybe 2 p.m. I'd play a lot of jazz, kind of listening music, and white people used to rock up with their kids and sit down! They'd sit down cross-legged and bring out picnics! Little Johnny and little Sarah would be running around, while their mums would be serving food out of Tupperware! I used to love it, it was just so chilled out. Then as the years went by I used to notice more and more young black people doing this, which I thought was brilliant too – it was another way to take advantage of the Good Times vibe and enjoy the Carnival in an unexpected way that echoed how London and Londoners were changing. It was the perfect illustration of how Carnival needed to move on from what it had been in the 1970s and 1980s, and I was so proud we were able to make it happen.

We used to get a lot of celebrities pass through because it was safe. Some would come on to the bus and some would just be there in the crowd enjoying the vibe. Quite a few footballers would come by – Rio Ferdinand was a regular, and his brother Anton, even David Ginola was there one year. One year Joey spotted Trevor McDonald in our crowd. I knew my dad would have loved to have met him, but didn't want to risk embarrassing him on the mic, so I just looked at him when he was looking up at the bus and my dad and I gave him a wave. He waved back and my dad was *properly* made up!

We were the first sound system down there to have internet streaming – ten years before anybody else had it, although I will admit it came about in spite of me rather than because of me! My mate Dele was an early adopter, an internet whizzkid who had been playing about on it since the mid-80s and was continually trying to convince me Good Times needed a web presence. I had no interest whatsoever – at that point I'd only just got a mobile phone, which was about as big as a brick – so when he was trying to tell me about domain-name-this and streaming-that he might as well have been talking French. After three years of this, I was giving him a lift home from the Carnival and he convinced me to come in so he could show me what he could do for us. Dele had a basement flat in Bayswater and as I walked down the steps it was like I was walking into the future.

He had four screens set up, and he went online, told me he'd just been doing a few tests, and showed me a map of the world with pinpoints all over it representing people he'd been talking to or who were talking about Good Times and the Carnival. There were markers in Miami, Buenos Aires, New York ... all over Europe ... and he told me these were my fans all over the world. He typed in 'I've got Norman Jay sitting here next to me right now ...' to start what I now know was a webchat. Within seconds these pinpoints were exploding all over the map, popping up everywhere, and I couldn't do it, I got stage fright! I think I was a bit over-whelmed by it all, but I do know it took me about a minute to realise this was something I had to be a part of, and Dele was a couple of steps ahead of me in that respect.

He told me he'd already taken the liberty of registering domain names, and it was a good thing he had because I didn't even know what a domain name was, let alone the importance of registering it. He'd thought of it all, though, and registered Good Times, Good Times Sound System and Norman Jay, and he'd built me a website. All at no cost to me, because he believed in what we were doing and wanted to be part of it. He understood the bigger picture as well, and was full of ideas of what we could do: some of them pie in the sky, but one in particular was so on the money – live-streaming my set at next year's Carnival.

When we started seriously planning the next Carnival, about March, Dele and I began talking about it properly and because I knew so little about the technology involved, he had to explain streaming to me in really simple terms. I was constantly amazed at how it could be done and how, back then, it was relatively easy to organise, in spite of having to get the road dug up to connect Good Times to the internet that weekend. I went and spoke to Claire Holder from the

Carnival Trust again, who had no problem with what we wanted to do. I had to talk to the council about digging up the road, then it was a matter of making arrangements with the Post Office – this was before British Telecom. They told me I needed permission from the factory opposite, which they gave, and then it cost me five hundred quid for the Post Office to lay the connection lines and we were off! Dele came down, set up the screens and all the other hardware on the bus, and Good Times had a live stream.

No one really had streaming or broadband back then. The bandwidth was very, very narrow, just about wide enough for a dozen people to listen at once, but people were listening! All over the world! My aunt, my dad's youngest sister who is just a few years older than me, lived in New York and because of her job with a bank she was another internet kid. Unbeknownst to me somebody, probably my dad, had got in touch to say what we were going to do, so she'd got the New York end of my family round the house to listen. We're rocking the set from the top of the bus and a message from her came up on one of the screens! *Whoa!!* That was it for me! I'm playing the Carnival in Notting Hill and they're hearing all the music I'm playing live in New York! How cool is that? I got Dele to type out a message back to them and if I hadn't been sold on it by then, that would have been enough to sign me up for life.

This was years before anybody else was doing anything like this and it cost them a fortune to do it. I know I've been incredibly lucky because I've always hooked up with really good people who saw what I was trying to do and wanted to help. They connected with the Good Times vibes and ideology, saw the significance and the symbolism of what we were about and wanted to be part of it. Just like Dele did those first live streams and set me up online, this other guy Terry Walshe, who became a friend, approached me and said he wanted to make a film about us. Again, it wasn't going to cost us a penny. He saw the importance of it and wanted to record our story – he filmed us at the Carnival, in New York ... all over the place. The documentary, *Good Times*, came out in 2002, and it's a great film. As I said, we were very lucky, but I also think the vibes we've always tried to put out went a long way towards attracting this sort of goodwill from so many good people.

I've been making quite a big deal about the 'safety' element of where we had moved to, but it was incredibly important because we wouldn't have been able to establish the situation I've described had we not created such a secure environment. It was one of the reasons our crowd grew so quickly: we could demonstrate that it was possible for *anybody* to come to Carnival and their biggest concern be how much fun they were going to have and not whether they were going to get robbed or assaulted. With the perceptions of Carnival routinely put out by the press and broadcasters, I knew it was vital to get this message across on as wide a level as possible. Over the years I had become a sort of unofficial spokesman for the Carnival – the MBE definitely helps – and I used to get my twenty-second slot on the *News at Ten* in the run up to the weekend. I knew how short these windows were. I had to extol the virtues and the positive side of Carnival before the rest of the media started with their 'Close this thing down ... nine hundred arrests ... drugs and violence on our streets ... ', so I'd come prepared with as many facts as I could reel off. I'd bone up on this stuff in the week before and I was ready to go to war for the Carnival, reminding them of things like the amount of people arrested at Glastonbury for drug-related offences and tent robberies etc. Then I'd give them the positive PR soundbite of how the previous year was the biggest, safest Carnival, with over two million people, and how there were no arrests and not even a hint of trouble where we were.

I used to phrase this last bit like that so people thought about the whole event when I said 'not a hint of trouble' – the rest of the media used to embellish things, so why not? – but it was the truth that nothing ever went off at our spot. In all the years we were on Middle Row we had not one recorded incident of violence or robbery or anything. This was down to how we policed it ourselves, and because it was my reputation at stake, I took it personally, so I wasn't taking any chances or leaving it up to the Old Bill. Essentially we used shame to prevent anything from breaking out, and because our crowd was so invested in the whole Good Times experience – this was their piece of the Carnival as much as it was ours – they helped us carry it off. With the top deck of the bus raising us up so high we could see the whole crowd, we were constantly watching for any little thing that looked like something might be about to go off. If one of the group saw anything they'd tell me and I'd stop the music, then once the groans had died down, get on the mic. 'Oi! You!' and I'd point right at them. 'What you fucking doing? This is Good Times! That sort of thing don't happen here!' I'd put it right on them by telling the crowd, 'Look, this is the wanker who thinks he's having more fun than you lot!' The crowd would boo him and start hissing and the chances were whoever I'd taken aim at would just disappear. One year I got a red card and red-carded this idiot, people were laughing at him as he slunk away. We could turn it into fun, but the result was that we never had any badness go on at Good Times, while avoiding the same oppressive atmosphere that heavy-handed police or security might have created.

chapter seven: the expense of playing the carnival

The early years of doing the Carnival were pretty carefree, and although the just-turn-up-and-play way of doing things didn't last through most of the 1980s, it remained pretty relaxed. Once we got into the '90s and we'd been doing it about twelve years, there were rumours all over the place that the major political parties, the Greater London Authority, the three local councils and the police wanted to close it down. Although nobody came right out and said it, between those bodies they started to impose more and more rules and regulations, most of which had a cost involved. So many of these new controls were being applied to sound systems, and I don't believe that was accidental – sound systems had long been at odds with the older Carnival organisers, who saw them as having no part in the traditional mobile parade. Also, by their very nature sound systems were fiercely independent and a bit rebellious, so the authorities probably thought they were at the root of any trouble. Things moved to a point where we were having to comply with the same rules and regulations that govern Glastonbury and other festivals on greenfield sites, which is ridiculous because we were nothing like that: we were an urban event on city streets completely open to the public. When we argued that, saying we should be a special case, we got hit with a completely different set of criteria – ancient byelaws and Victorian-era regulations that we never even knew existed. Essentially, the authorities were trying to price sound systems out and introduce regulations to bring Carnival down to a more controllable event. Me being me, that just strengthened my resolve to be there.

By September 2002 they had got rid of chief executive Claire Holder, who helped me get my spot back in 1991 and who had become a key figure in standing in between them and us – the authorities and the participants, respectively. She was of Trinidadian heritage, and she had been involved in the Carnival since she was a child, volunteering in the office as a teenager, so she understood the ethos of event, and how it was all about freedom and creative expression. She was so protective of it that at one point Kensington & Chelsea council claimed she had declared war on them. With Claire gone, though, the establishment could be much more heavy-handed, and started bringing in all these new rulings under the blanket of 'health and safety'. No more of the ragga-style roll up, play what you want and sell what you want, the authorities' tactic was not to say no, but to make it prohibitively expensive – 'Yes, of course you can do that, but here's what it's going to cost you.'

During the 1990s you had to be licensed to get one of the allocated pitches, while the cost of those permits was rising rapidly. You had to have public liability insurance in order to get a licence and that went up every year, and the council decided how much cover you needed related to where your pitch was. Because they knew we'd attract a big crowd we had to have £5 million worth of cover for the weekend. It used to be at Carnival any sound system or anybody with a front garden would buy a few cases of beer or Coca-Cola and sell them off a table for a decent profit, or rig up a barbecue and sell jerk chicken or grilled fish. The street hustler would get to bank holiday weekend and think, 'Bwoy! I mek a money at the carnival yuh know!', go to the cash and carry, then him and his mates would be pulling their wheelie bin full of ice and coining it selling cold drinks. Carnival used to be treated as a special case, and people were allowed to break certain rules that a 'regular' market trader would have to abide by, but then the council teamed up with the police, and people were getting shut down when previously everybody had turned a blind eye. Again, if they wanted to sell then they'd have to pay upfront for a licence, be restricted in what they could sell and only trade during the times that the licence allowed. This was particularly bad on the sound systems who were running makeshift bars, because none of them made a penny from playing the Carnival – Good Times never did – so this was the only way they could get back any of what it cost them to be there.

The authorities even brought in noise abatement people – *to a sound system* – but the biggest skank was the stewarding. For years the Carnival itself had supplied stewards, for free, so it wasn't anything you had to worry about – most sound systems came with their own security anyway, we did. Suddenly, Kensington & Chelsea were telling the sounds that this wasn't enough and that they had to use council-accredited stewards, this was how many they would need and as they'd now have to pay for them, this is how much it would cost. If a sound couldn't pay that upfront, then they didn't get a licence and they weren't allowed to play. I went along with it, but I deeply resented it because I felt they were putting an extra squeeze on me with the amount of security I was being asked to hire – there had never been any trouble at Good Times, when in comparison, a mile down the road at the Colville Gardens stage there were reports of violence and a stabbing incident. I always figured this bit was the thin edge of the wedge that would lead to sound systems having to pay a share of the costs of the police, like football clubs do, with the council backing all of this with their ultimate sanction: if you don't pay you don't play.

Another massive 'health and safety' cost was fencing or security barriers. Most sound systems knew how all of this worked, how to protect themselves and their gear and create their own spaces. It had all worked well in the past, but now they were telling operators what fencing they had to have and to what standard, and each sound system was going to have to hire it themselves. Because it was a bank holiday the hire was always for three days, even though the sound systems were now only allowed to be there for Sunday and Monday. As it was going to the Notting Hill Carnival, hire firms bumped their prices right up, saying it was due to high insurance premiums.

All these costs were rising exponentially year on year, and I saw several well-established sound systems just give up and say they couldn't afford to be there any more. I, however, was totally driven by the fact that I didn't want them to force me out: those fascists at Kensington & Chelsea council, they're not driving me out; the police, they're not driving me out! I was of the mindset that I was here before those people got involved and I'll be there after they're gone. There was no way Babylon was going to beat me down. I understood my place in the Carnival hierarchy; we were one of the biggest and most prominent sound systems there and because of that I felt a weight of responsibility. I used to sit in at every Carnival Committee or council meeting I was invited to and urge the other soundmen there to comply with what was being asked of them. I'd tell them there was a bigger picture here, this drip-drip effect of trying to destroy Carnival would be taking away one of the fundamentals of black British culture. I'd appeal to them, saying it was a *cultural obligation* to keep Carnival going. Maybe because I was a little bit older I understood its significance and recognised how it was a platform for new, young, emerging black talent to get noticed on a world stage. No matter what beefs I might have had with other sound systems, we couldn't let the authorities win this one.

The other reality was that I was one of the lucky ones and I could afford to comply with everything, no matter how many rules they put in there, and I felt I had to, too. We were always held up in the media as a paragon of virtue – every August I'd be asked to go on television to talk about the Carnival – so if they got rid of Good Times there would be a domino effect. It would make it much easier for them to start chipping away at the other sound systems and closing down sites.

As I've said before, my whole year was geared up to doing

Carnival, so I bankrolled the whole thing myself. Quite apart from all the costs Kensington & Chelsea were putting on us, the only thing we owned was the sound system itself – everything else had to be hired in and when the Good Times crowd got huge we had to bring in a lot of extra gear. We had to hire in the generator, another three-day hire with a bank holiday and a Carnival premium, as apparently a lot of them didn't get returned because the hirers nicked them or just left them there. That was a big expense but it wasn't worth us buying one, as the size we needed in the later years would have cost tens of thousands for something we'd only use two days a year, and then where do you keep it? It was like the bus – people used to ask me why didn't we buy a bus instead of hiring it, but it would cost a fortune to get a PSV (Public Service Vehicle) licence, not to mention MOT and insurance to be able to drive it down to the Carnival. Then there's garaging costs for the rest of the year. The only thing we could catch a break on was the van to get our gear in and out, which was from a hire service just down the road from my mum's. The guy who worked there knew me and my family so he trusted me, and while he wasn't even supposed to give me the hire, he'd let me take a van without any forms, cash in hand, and bring it back before it was missed on Tuesday. With a full tank!

By the time we stopped doing Carnival it was costing Good Times between £40,000 and £50,000 to play those two days, or really it was costing *me* that much because I stood behind all those costs. We didn't get any funding from any arts organisations as I didn't want to be beholden to anybody – too many times I'd seen people take those grants only to be told what to do and how to present themselves. I wanted none of that, I'd seen we were popular, I'd seen us growing and happily I was in a position to finance that – up to a point. And I didn't mind because I knew I could absorb these costs during the year. In fact, I looked on it as an investment as a lot of the big gigs I got, especially the overseas ones, were a result of being at the Carnival and showing off what Good Times was about.

There were ways we managed to offset some of that cost, but they weren't cheap. I always looked upon the Good Times operation at the Carnival as the Gold Seal, the sound system against which other sound systems would be judged, so we set very high standards for *everything* else that we did. We could sell beer quite legally, because I was one of only four people who had a liquor licence for that weekend, but we didn't want lukewarm beer, or worse still lukewarm beer mixed with ice, wanted to sell proper *cold* beer, so I brought in a freezer truck the night before. Our beer was stored frozen so that when we sold it, it was still so cold sometimes you dropped it. I was the first to do this at Carnival, and yes, it cost me but it was worth it because the beer we sold was as good as the music we played. Same with the food – we wanted to avoid all those things people hate when they go to festivals, so the food would be properly cooked and it would be tasty, no burnt offerings. Too often at Carnival the jerk chicken is more like jerk puke! That's not food! We had our thing branded The Good Times Soul Kitchen, run by my older sister Gloria. She and her husband are chefs, who for years had a spot in Stoke Newington where they cooked authentic delicious Caribbean food. Again, that sort of attention to detail meant we weren't making as much from the food as we might have, but we'd get queues for the food two hours before we'd played the first tune. My afterparty helped too: every year I'd book Subterrania, under the flyover at Acklam Road, where I could charge admission and the 600 tickets would sell out immediately.

Because we were so well presented and obviously well run, we managed to attract some outside sponsorship. I was very wary of drinks companies, which is the easiest sponsorship for somebody like us to get because they don't want to give you any money, they just want to give you beer. *No!* I didn't need beer, I needed finance to help me build my infrastructure for the weekend. Fifty cases of whatever cost them nothing, and the politics of the whole thing meant it did them more good than me as it gave their beer the cred from being associated with Good Times, plus there might be new people trying it. Then, the first year we had the bus, this rickety old thing that the crowd loved as much as I did – we'll get on to me and red buses later – we hired it and the whole weekend went so well that Budweiser approached us and offered us proper sponsorship for the next year. Not beer, actual money. Initially they offered about ten grand, but my management negotiated with them and got them to pay for the refurbishment of the bus plus getting it there, as well as the rental of the generator – our biggest single cost – and all my other expenses. And they gave us some cash on top of that, with which we bought new kit and built brand-new speaker boxes! It was fantastic!

That year, 1996, we looked and sounded at the absolute

top of our game, the crowd were loving it even more than the last year off the bus, and that show of faith in us really seemed to energise the whole Good Times crew. Then, as it happened, one of Budweiser's bigwigs from America was in London and he came there – probably wanted to see how the UK office was spending his money! He absolutely loved the whole thing, thought this was the exactly the sort of association their brand needed, so he extended our deal for five years and upped the money. This was very handy, as at that point, after their first dealings with us, Budweiser UK didn't want to know any more. But that didn't matter! We were sponsored directly by Budweiser in America! Head office and nobody could argue with that. That money helped us immensely and when it ran out, I realised how much Carnival was costing me.

So although I wasn't as badly off as some of the other sounds, who were losing money they were going to struggle to make back, and although for me it was always a culture thing, I couldn't continue to ignore the rising costs. Or at least I could have, but my accountants couldn't. There came a point when they were telling me, 'Norman, you *can't*, this is unsustainable.' Then my younger sister, who is really good at figures, did all of Good Times's number-crunching and said, 'Bruv, I'm putting my foot down, you're not going back next year!'

The truth was, even for somebody who never looked at the numbers, I knew the writing had been on the wall for about three or four years. I had some pretty decent contacts within Kensington & Chelsea council and I'd been told that the area Good Times's pitch was on was due for redevelopment, so I knew I wouldn't be there much longer and it was highly unlikely they'd be handing out any new pitches. I was feeling creatively frustrated too, because I wanted to put on some live acts, but the council had a million rules and regulations for live performance, and of course you had to pay for this and pay for that. I felt like I was being put in a straitjacket, because we were operating at capacity – we'd have 8,000 people in front of the Good Times bus – and although I wanted to move it to another level, I felt there was nowhere else to go with it.

Another new problem surfaced in 2012, which meant that something the police planned to instigate from the next year onwards caused the nearest thing we'd ever had to crowd trouble in 2013. Our spot was going to be made into something called a Controlled Zone, which meant the police could control everything in it, but specifically who came in and out. I was very wary of this, because our Carnival crowd were younger than me and not part of my generation from the '60s and '70s, who had been taught by experience to be wary of Old Bill. My crowd were mostly white kids who had never had the police get heavy-handed with them, and weren't used to being told 'No!' I figured this could be a recipe for disaster, but what could I do about it?

I was particularly disappointed because I had very good relations with the Section Commander of that area from the Met Police, whose boss was one of the highest placed black guys in the force. Apparently, he was a Good Times fan, so I would be invited to debriefs.

In most cases they were cutting me a lot of slack because we never had any trouble, but along with that Controlled

Zone, I found out they were about to bring in a rule whereby – and they showed it to me on a graph – you were only supposed to have 2.3 people per square metre! I think they were going to calculate it by helicopter photographs. That would have seriously cut our crowd and the whole vibe of the occasion. With the dire warnings I was getting about the costs, I felt ready to let it go, it was time to quit. I talked my sister and the accountant into letting me do one more. 2013 was going to be my last Carnival.

chapter eight: the last carnival

When I was doing that last one, there were times when I was properly choked up – I had tears in my eyes and if I'd tried to speak I'm sure the floodgates would have opened. At that point I couldn't bring myself to tell the crowd I wouldn't be back the next year, and on reflection I think that made me feel a bit worse. I wish I could say I went out on an absolute high, and the last one I did was the best ever, but that wasn't the case – the year before, 2012, had been the best we'd ever done. In that year the weather was fantastic, everybody seemed really up for it, and I've never seen it fill up so early: on both days by half past eleven you couldn't move. Shoulder to shoulder, always good-natured, it was brilliant. It was our peak and the last year before they made us a Controlled Zone, two facts I don't believe are unrelated.

All the fears I'd had from when the police told us this was happening were realised, as they had put a big barrier across the top of West Row. People were rocking up at one o'clock or so, many like they did every year, and the police were telling them they can't come down and quite a few people took exception to this. One of my sons noticed what was happening first, then from the top of the bus I saw it had caused a couple of skirmishes and at one point it looked like it might have kicked off a riot. I was so glad nothing serious happened, because it would have been terrible to go out that way.

OK, so that last one wasn't quite the pinnacle, but I was fiercely proud of what me, my brother Joey and the Good Times crew – including my dad and my uncle – had achieved. And truly thankful for what Carnival had done for me: when I started I wasn't even really a deejay, or it definitely wasn't a career, but this event had singlehandedly elevated me, Norman Jay, to what I became. It gave me a status, allowed me to become a successful club deejay, to have radio shows, to play festivals. And it was on my own ground too – I was a Grove Boy born and took a lot of pride from the fact I made it as a deejay in an area of London I hold so dear. It meant so much to me to be able to do that there, because when I looked off the top of the bus I was just yards away from the Ha'penny Steps, where my mum used to push me in my pram to the clinic in 1958 and 1959. And I came back there fifty years later as King of the Hill.

part two:
childhood

chapter nine: my family

I was the oldest of six children. I had two brothers, Joey and Paul, and three sisters named Carol (or CJ as the family called her), Pamela and Patsy – sadly Pamela and Paul have passed. I also have an older half-sister, Gloria, who I didn't really know about until I was old enough to understand these things. As kids we only used to see her on bank holidays because Mum and Dad would take us all to the fair together, and although we're all very close now, back then I used to resent not being the oldest on those occasions because I'd come to enjoy the privilege it carried!

My dad was a Grade 1 Civil Engineer for London Transport. He had always been very studious and when he first came to Britain in the 1950s, he was going to night classes while all his mates were out partying. He got his papers so when he joined London Transport he could work his way up the grades; he built the Victoria Line – not the physical work, but he was part of the team that planned it and made the decisions. He was a big cheese for London Transport in the civil engineering world by then.

My dad often had more than one job – at one point he was working nights for London Transport, he was studying, he was a part-time janitor in those big houses in Pelham Street off of Earls Court, *and* he was marking up the board in the bookies on a Saturday. This meant it seemed like he was always working, but he had ambitions for himself and, together with my mum who worked for United Biscuits (McVities) in Harlesden as a production line supervisor, they were ambitious for us as a family. I was born in Ladbroke Grove around the time the whole race riot thing was kicking off in Latimer Road, which was only about a hundred yards away from where they lived; not much of that street remains now, Grenfell Tower is built where it used to be. Even without the race riots, Grove was a really rough area back then and various factions were always trying to stoke up tensions between black and white people, but it was where my parents could afford to live and both of them had brothers and sisters in the same area.

One of my dad's brothers, Uncle Tyson, lived at number 7 Rillington Place, three doors down from the serial killer John Christie, who strangled his wife and at least six other people *in that very flat*! My uncle moved there in the '60s, about ten years after the murders, but I still love telling people the story. After we moved to Acton I was always going up to Grove, and us kids played football in that street, as it was a blocked turning with the old brickworks' big wall at one end. We kicked about outside what had been Christie's flat – probably broke the windows more than once – and played marbles on the same manhole cover they pulled up looking for bodies.

I was only a kid so of course I didn't know anything about any of that. The street had been renamed Ruston Close because nobody wanted to live on Rillington Place. I found out about it when, completely by chance, my wife, my mum and dad and I were watching *10 Rillington Place*, the Richard Fleischer film of the murders starring Richard Attenborough as Christie, and I recognised it. 'Isn't that Uncle Tyson's street?' Mum and Dad just nodded and smiled knowingly and I was all, 'Why didn't you tell me? We used to play in that street!' The film had been shot in the actual road, using number 6 as number 10 because the house itself, right at the end, had long since been boarded up. The street was demolished in the early 1970s – it was run down even by the standards of the whole run-down area – and my uncle was moved to Mary Place, just round the corner from Grenfell.

How we ended up in Acton, according to my mum, is that one day a brick was thrown through one of the flat's front windows and some of the broken glass fell into my cot. My mum blew up! She told my dad, 'That's it! That's enough! We're getting out of here!' Then my dad took over the story and told me how he borrowed a scooter, a Lambretta or a Vespa, put my mum on the back and drove two or three miles from home, which put them in Acton, and just rode around looking for houses for sale. They came across the one we moved to and Mum said, 'This is the one, I want to buy this house!' With help from my mum's sister's husband, Uncle Melvin, my dad's brother Uncle Sam and a money lender, they got a deposit and a mortgage and sixty years later still live in the same house, a great big three-storey Victorian.

When Dad told me this a couple of years ago the vision of my mum and dad on a scooter was so funny I almost died laughing – of course I was looking at him then and can't remember the young, cool version of my parents! But they'd had all sorts of experiences and adventures, and they'd never make a big deal out of any of them, like my dad used to come out with things he'd tell Joey and me just straight out of the blue. One night we were doing a party in a house in Blagrove Road, on the corner of Acklam Road, practically under the flyover. The house was empty and we'd broken in, and my dad came in with a big smile on his face. He told us he had spent his first night in England sleeping in the attic of that very house, then told us the stories of what it was like to actually be in the situation he'd been in, young and in an environment so far removed from where he'd come from. It was brilliant.

At a time when there seemed to be an intergenerational stand-off between Caribbean immigrants and their born-in-Britain children, I was very fortunate to have parents who were so understanding and supportive of me and my five siblings.

For example, when we were running the sound system Dad would get involved and always come and help, and I have to give him real props for that: I can't think of one other black father who would have encouraged his sons to do something like that: 'Get a proper job ... don't waste your time with that sound system business!' Dad's brother would do his bit too, because he was a carpenter and so much of it seemed to involve those skills – I can remember Joey and my uncle outside in the garden in the snow trying to get some speaker boxes finished.

He used to show up at a lot of our functions, because he worked nights and could delegate work as the boss, so when he knew we were playing out he'd often rock up at our parties, show his face for an hour or half an hour, then go back to work. He actually became quite a well-known face at our events, but he was never intrusive, he would always stay in the background. He came because he was genuinely interested in what two of his sons were doing and really supported us in that. He and my mum were pretty distrustful when Joey started building the sound system, but as soon as it was finished and he was playing out my dad would show up to support him. We used to have to borrow his car quite a lot and he was always good enough to allow it, provided we put petrol in it. My mum and dad never interfered, my dad really was a man of few words, an observer. The only furious rows I can remember between Dad and Joey was when Joe locksed up – he was natty from when he was at school in 1973 – and then that was only because my dad was concerned he'd never get a job looking like that.

In many ways they were like practically anybody's parents, inasmuch as once they understood we were trying to do something positive, they realised they could trust us. We could have been out there getting up to all sorts – my mum used to say, 'They could be doing bad t'ings, instead they're doing goodness.' Where my dad wasn't much like anybody else's parents is how he used to help us. When we were doing a party and he came round, he'd always ask if we needed anything and that could be a real life saver, as he'd get food in for the crew – *patty runs* we used to call it. More than once we had him take bags of cash out of a party and drop it home or at our co-promoter's flat, because we didn't want to be left holding it right at the end. Then if we were running out of drink he'd go to this all-night shop in Willesden Lane in Kilburn, Airey's, and come back with his car loaded with drink. That in itself led to another surprise about my dad.

Mr Airey was a Jamaican who ran one of London's first twenty-four-hour shops by exploiting a loophole that meant as long as he closed for two minutes from 11.59p.m. to 12.01a.m., he could sell alcohol the rest of the time. There was a lot of talk that he had an illegal card school in the back, but everybody in north and west London knew of the place. In the '70s, the patties he sold was about the only late night food you could get outside Soho, or if a party ran out of drink he would be open – all roads led to Airey's and in the early hours of Saturday and Sunday cars would be two deep outside the shop. Everybody was kind of scared of Mr Airey because he was so gruff and uncompromising, his prices were always massively inflated and if you queried them he'd always tell you the same thing, 'Am I asking you to buy it? . . . If you don't want it . . . *Next customer!*' He never seemed to have time for anybody, and from us it was all, 'Yes Mr Airey, no Mr Airey!', then one night I've gone up there from one of my parties with my dad, we walked in and Dad casually says, 'Hensley, y'alright?' It took me a minute to realise he was talking to Mr Airey! I didn't even know he'd been in the shop before! Then, at the same moment Winston walked in, the legendary doorman at the Wag, and he was going through to the back room, but stopped and said to my old man, 'W'appen, Luke?' *To my dad!* Wooooaaah!!!! I couldn't believe it, all these really cool people on first-name terms with my dad! Then Mr Airey, who didn't seem to trust any-body, is saying to my dad, 'How much you need? What you want?' And my dad could take what he wanted. 'My God!'

I thought. 'This is wicked!!' and all I could do was wonder how many more levels there were to my dad.

In many respects we were like a regular black Brady Bunch family. I was the adventurous one, the more colourful outgoing one, I would take risks and I was always the one that saw the bigger picture. Paul was studious, he was very good at school, never truanted, and became a high-ranking signals engineer with London Transport. Joey and I were very close as kids because there's only fifteen months between us, and although later we had separate lives defined largely by our musical choices, when it came to doing things that would mutually benefit us we were a team, a strong team – a strong family unit with the old man backing us. Joey was always very focused on the sound system, although I was always the one that came up with the plan – 'This is how we'll do it, this is what will happen', and then go on and organise it. More often than not, things would pan out the way I described them and he was perfectly happy. Joey was the most socially conscious of all of us: as a black man, a Rasta, he was very big on black history, repatriation, all the different cultural strands. He was very outspoken and would wear his heart on his sleeve. Compared with him I was a rebellious, football-loving, dandy soul boy, but neither of us cared! My sisters used to tease me quite a bit, dismissively calling me a soul boy because they were into reggae and lovers rock, I guess more traditional in their way, but they were always supportive of what I wanted to do as a deejay. My last sister Patsy was the brightest of all of us and worked in a law firm for many years, doing corporate law – she wasn't a lawyer, but she worked in a high-level corporate environment and is very smart.

Actually everybody in our house was pretty smart and I used to love the lively discourse that went on about politics and what it meant to be black in London. Everybody said their piece, Joey was always the most militant, far more so than me, because, maybe from the side that I saw it, I wanted to get along – I wanted an easier ride. I was usually much more *forgiving* because I felt I wanted to operate in the white world and I believed I understood how it worked. My mum generally listened to all of the discussions that would go on and agreed with certain views, but was always fearful that Joey and I might end up getting involved in something and getting hurt, especially when all the rioting was kicking off. When the rioting was going off in Brixton in 1981 she was all, 'You children shouldn't go down deh. Make sure you don't go near Brixton this weekend.' Little did she know we'd long since made plans.

My dad tacitly supported all of the uprising that was going on around that time, but never outwardly. Privately he supported the stand that black people were making, which he admitted to me years later, but at the time he kept quiet – thinking back he could have lectured us, or he could have stopped us, but he didn't. Dad was always very aware, always very informed, he wasn't one of those parents that stuck his head in the sand. He may not have known precisely what Joe and I were up to, but in the wider community he was always up to speed with what was going on. I have no idea how he knew, because every time I saw him, he was reading the *Sporting Life*! I used to nickname him Andy Capp, after the newspaper cartoon character, because he was always reading the racing and the sports pages, but when it came to that kind of politics, he was on top of it. I was shocked! 'How do you know that, Dad?' My dad's not really a talker, he's a listener – he'd be invisible in the room until you asked him a question, then he'd give you the most eloquent answer with well thought-out reasoning. We used to have long reasoning sessions. Sometimes his views would be misguided, or not always based on fact or research, but that's what reasoning is all about: so much of it is born out of personal experience, and you can't argue with that.

If you spoke to my mum and dad they'd tell you I was different from my brothers and sisters in how I looked at the world, and early on I realised I had a different mindset to the others as, for want of a better description, I knew how to play the game. I knew the language of the white people around me, I understood the body language, understood the euphemisms – I even knew cockney rhyming slang! I think I had a better understanding of my surroundings; of the people that I mixed with; of the people that I was at school with. I had a really good understanding of the way the white mind thinks from very early on and I never had a problem and I've never really suffered racist abuse. All I knew was that I wasn't an idiot, I mixed easily, I made friends easily, I assimilated easily and I never had an issue. Maybe my blackness didn't intimidate anybody, didn't threaten anybody, but I never suffered the kind of negativity a lot of my peers or my brothers faced. As I mentioned, Joey had dreadlocks at a time before they were a fashion and he suffered for it far more than I did. Me, however, I *always* had a lot of white mates, from back when I was in school – I was the black kid who had a lot of white mates; I was the black kid who went to white things. I never saw myself as being odd because I was black. In fact I was never conscious of it unless somebody went out of their way to make me feel that way, to remind me that I'm a nigger, and to be honest, this hardly ever happened.

When I was growing up a lot of my white mates were the first wave of skinheads – peanuts we used to call them. There wasn't the same stigma attached to them as the ones that came later, these were really just the kids who grew up in the same working class areas I did, like Grove and Shepherd's Bush. It was actually a bit of cultural exchange for me, because they seemed to like the same music I liked, black music, and I liked the way they dressed. I could just about relate that look to the rudeboy look of my black friends' older brothers or the newbies who had just got off the boat from Jamaica in 1964 or '65, but really to me it reflected the street fashions and the football terraces of the time so I also thought it was really contemporary. Today, I'm amazed at how many of the original skinheads there are still about who have stayed true to it. You see these seventy-year-old blokes wearing Harringtons and brogues with little badges that say 'Trojan Forever' or 'Spirit of 69'. I ride with some of them in my scooter club and they love their black music, reggae, Motown, Stax, Northern soul and can still do the dances. To me I think that's a mark of how enduring this subculture has been – it never died. Punk went mainstream, but this is Britain's last true underground movement.

At school the whole skinhead thing fascinated all of us boys, and the first book I ever read that I didn't have to was Richard Allen's *Skinhead*. *Everybody* I knew read that book, and when this battered, dog-eared copy doing the rounds at school eventually got to me I devoured it, it was like my bible. Now I'm older I understand that it was pap and that the author, James Moffat, had just done his research very well, but when I was fourteen all I knew was he had got it so spot on. The football I went to, the people I knew, the clothes I wore ... he even mentioned Acton and Ealing and described them – *that's where I live!* It was so real to me I felt as if he had been following me and my mates around. My little circle read all the others, *Suedehead*, *Skinhead Escapes*, *Boot Boys* and so on, and we could recite passages out of them. We had a standing joke that if one of us got pissed up or did something stupid, suddenly a line from a Richard Allen book would come out. Thirty years later, when I first hooked up with my wife Jane, I told her they were the first books I ever read, and as a present for me she sourced the whole set of first editions and surprised me with all of them. It was genius. Looking back at it now, if you want to know what my life was like when I was twelve or thirteen years old, pick up a Richard Allen book and read a few pages, because that was what I wanted to be like and what I wanted to do – without the violence, obviously.

My dad wasn't what you'd call a disciplinarian. He didn't need to be because we knew he trusted us and we respected him – the last thing I wanted to do was cross any lines that might betray that trust. Also, like so many black kids of that time there was the matter of bringing shame to your parents – I wasn't scared of getting nicked, I was scared of my dad finding out! It doesn't matter what the police do to you, they could break your arm or bag you up and throw you in the back of a van, but none of this comes close to what you'll face if you bring shame or dishonour to your dad's house. I never crossed that line; I came close and pushed the margins a lot, and as a result took the belt a few times, but looking back, when I did take it I fully deserved it. No question. I can't think of an instance when my dad gave me a hiding simply because he could. You can lie to everybody, but you can't lie to yourself: the times I got licks, and they were rare occasions, I fully deserved it and now I can tell him that.

Today I appreciate my mum and dad in a way you can't imagine. I'm so grateful I've got them here still and for everything they did for me in the past. It was their ambition that inspired me to be as fiercely driven as I was – the sound system was going to be the *best*; the music was going to be the *best*; the parties were going to be the *best* ... I'm forever grateful to my mum and dad for never discouraging me from anything; whatever venture attempted there was never a question, there was always support. Unconditional support. No matter what I tried to do my mum and dad had faith in me. On the rare occasions I wanted advice from my dad he'd give it, but never lectured me on 'I don't think you should do this', or 'I think you should do that'. As a young man making your way in the world that sort of situation cannot be overvalued.

I wanted to be that sort of father to my own two sons, Mark and Russell, and they have both grown into fine men, but in the beginning that was down to their mother and my former partner Maria. I was absolutely made up to become a dad, but at the same time I knew I was much too young – when Mark was born I had only turned twenty a few days earlier – but thankfully Maria was a brilliant mother. We were like teenage sweethearts thrust into being parents. For the first few months she was living with her mum, I was living with my mum, and the baby spent his time between us. Getting a flat became a priority and we eventually got a council flat in Shepherd's Bush, moving in together sometime in 1978 just before Mark's first birthday. Although I saw myself as a baby making a baby, I knew enough to know that I had to get a regular job.

I'd been through my second period of unemployment when I did draw the dole, because in spite of my previous reservations I was a dad now – I justified it internally by telling myself it was no more than I was entitled to. It wasn't right, though, I had a young kid and a partner and I wanted to step up and look after them, so I knew I needed to clock myself on. I did a few menial, shit jobs that never lasted long and I wouldn't have taken on if I hadn't been a parent. Then, some time in 1978, as I'd trained as a litho printer I landed a job in the stationery department of Quaker Oats, printing all of their stationery. That was the first time I'd ever been put on a monthly salary, which was great because it helped me to save and didn't make it nearly so easy to go home on Friday via the record shop! By then I had a serious record-buying habit so getting paid week to week in cash, my God it was a nightmare! I kept that job for about three years, and after that I went to work at a print shop in Denman Street round the back of Piccadilly. This was much better because it was in the West End, where for me so much was going on, and as I eventually became manager of the shop, I had use of the van.

My second son Russell was born four years after Mark and we lived together in that flat as a family unit until I bought a house for house for us in 1991. I wanted to get us out of the council flat, not that I had anything against council flats – I'd shared one with some mates when I was younger – but as a family we needed more space and after growing up in my parents' house, owning my own home was the natural thing to do. I'd applied several times for a mortgage and would get turned down, either because I had no regular income or my income wasn't enough, but then I got the job as an A&R man at Gilles Peterson's on the Talkin' Loud record label, which was backed by PolyGram. It was amazing – as soon as I got that job, I showed the same mortgage lenders the contract and they gave me a mortgage straight away, they practically jumped down my throat to give me the money! That was one of the main reasons I accepted the offer from PolyGram – it gave me the security of tenure to get a mortgage.

Although we were all living together for quite a while, it was Maria bringing the boys up. Thankfully, she was an absolutely fantastic mother and made a brilliant job of it when I was really an absent father. For a while I'd put my ideas on hold to step up, worked the nine-to-five and supported my family, but as that went on and I started getting deeper into music and records and clubs, making a living from music became more of a viable situation. I was bored of doing the litho thing and was sure the best thing for all of us would be for me to make a career out of my passion, and once we started playing the Carnival I knew there was never going to be anything else. As an example of how bored I was with the print, the reason I left Quaker Oats was because I wanted to go to football match! I had been to watch Spurs play Manchester City at Wembley in the 1981 FA Cup final, which had finished in a draw to be replayed in the middle of the week. That first game was brilliant so I asked at work to take the time off to go to the replay. I was told no, and if I went not to come back as I'd be sacked. Guess what happened! Nobody was telling me that! I went to the football, Spurs won, I absolutely loved it, but I had no job to go back to.

My music thing was just starting to take off. Joey and I were doing some parties, I was hustling records – selling obscure or as yet undiscovered imports to club deejays – and while I knew I was getting something going, at this point it was subsistence level. I was barely eking out a living and Maria, who had mostly been a stay-at-home mum, would get part-time jobs. That's when I went to work in the print shop in Denman Street – I knew the kids were my responsibility and they came first, even if it did mean a day job *and* working the sound system. If I needed any convincing, I just had to think back to the hours my dad put in when he was getting his civil engineering certificates, so pursuing a career as a deejay while I managed a print shop was never going to be a problem. And we had a van for the sound system!

As I got more successful as a deejay, I spent a lot more time with the boys and to this day we are all very close. I did my best to make up for the time I wasn't there and I think overall, obviously with everything their mother did for them, we did a really good job. Maria and I split up in 1994. It was all very amicable, we were just too young to be parents, and as I got older I realised we wanted different things and we grew apart. Russell and Mark, though, are testament to how we definitely got something right.

chapter ten: buying my first records

My earliest memory of real excitement at the prospect of buying records was one day when, completely out of the blue, my dad gave me some money to go up to Shepherd's Bush. I was only ten, going on eleven, but I'd always been an adventurous child – the last thing I wanted to be was like some of the kids round my way, who were so parochial they didn't want to go past the end of the road. I had a thirst for going to new places, I was confident about travelling on my own, and my dad used to encourage me. I was sitting watching television that day and he said to me, 'You want to go to Shepherd's Bush?' I loved Shepherd's Bush market, so I'm up on my feet *'Yeaahh!!'* Then he took out a five-pound note and said, 'Here you are, go and buy some records', and I realised he wasn't coming with me! My mum wasn't at all keen, 'You can't send the child . . . ' but Dad is all, 'Let him go . . . Go and buy some records.' I had to carefully fold the fiver up – this is when they were enormous – put it in my pocket, and set off down the road.

I knew exactly where I was going. I was going to go to Webster's, the black record shop where all the big boys went, which sold mostly reggae and ska but a lot of soul as well. I'd

been there before with my best mate from school, Donny –
we'd go up to Webster's on a Saturday to hang around
outside, fascinated by the comings and goings. Occasionally
he'd get brave and say 'Let's go in', but I'd never been in there
by myself or actually bought anything.

I get the 266 bus to the high street and I'm *buzzing*! I can
hardly hold it together! At the high street I jump on a 207,
can't wait, and get off outside Shepherd's Bush tube station.
This is so exciting. I go in, a bit sheepish, and I'm hit with the
music playing and guys just chilling and nodding their heads
in time. Then panic grips me, this money's burning a hole
in my pocket, and I'm suddenly paranoid of getting taxed by
these bigger boys as they did back then – I felt I couldn't take
my money out and I was too scared to go up and buy records
because somebody would have took it. 'Wha' dis likkle yout'
man doing with all dis money?'

In the end I just stood at the back of the shop and waited
all day until the crowds had drifted away and he was getting ready to close up at about six o'clock – I'm sure my
mum must have been worried sick. The thing is, I wasn't
bored at all, I was just hearing the music on this great shop
sound system, and watching people come and go. Skinheads
coming up there, kids in parkas, loads of black boys from
Shepherd's Bush who I didn't know ... quite a few of the
older guys I recognised from Grove and I saw some of the
boys who played football in the same park as me. I was in
awe of it all, then just as Webster was packing up I went up
to the counter and said can I take a copy of this, can I take
one of those ... and so on. I got about a dozen records and
spent the whole five pounds and he must've thought it was

Christmas. Just about to close the doors and this yout' man pops up to buy all these tunes! I can't remember all of them, one was Johnny Nash's 'You Got Soul' on the Major Minor label, and there was 'Sitting on the Dock of the Bay' by Otis Redding, because I didn't want to buy them all for myself so I'm trying to think of records my dad or my mum would like. I got Desmond Dekker's 'Israelites', the first time it was issued on Pyramid, there was a Motown record I'm pretty sure was the Temptations ... I bought mostly reggae and I can still see the labels, Big Shot, Pyramid, Swan – I was a nerd even back then!

I got home and, understandably, my dad's a bit jumpy, 'Where you been all day?' I think he thought I'd just run off with that fiver! I held out the bag and said Dad, I've bought all these records and he just smiled and started to put them on the gram!

It was an amazing feeling! I'd bought records before, one or two from a pop shop in Ealing or at Woolworths on the high street, but nothing from Webster's, *a black record shop* – just carrying the bag home on the bus made me feel like a big man! I wasn't buying Top 20 tunes, I was buying soul and reggae and I felt like a real music man. Then, best of all, my dad let me keep them – these records were mine.

There was another record shop Donny and I used to go to. It was in Harlesden and we'd jump on the 266 bus going the opposite way, get off at Willesden Junction then walk up the High Street past the clock tower. That in itself was a thrill because we weren't supposed to be up there by ourselves, but the record shop right on Harlesden High Street was something else. It was bigger than Webster's and the guys in it looked bigger – *big Harlesden men!* Funnily, we thought we'd grown a bit just by being there. When we got the courage to go in, the shop was packed and of course we didn't talk to anybody, we'd literally spend hours just watching people buy records and, when we remembered, nodding along to the music. To me, it was mesmerising watching people buying records, there was a real swagger about it all: 'Give me one a dem, sah!' . . . 'Let me tek dat' . . . blokes were coming in, 'You have the new this . . . You have the new that . . .' I'm standing there taking it all in and thinking, 'One day I'm going to be able to do that.'

That was why actually buying the records at Webster's was so important in my story, because I think I was building a relationship with records and record shops before I'd really settled my relationship with music – it's no wonder I became a deejay not a musician! To me, record shops, the black ones anyway, weren't simply exciting because everybody there was so much older, I also totally understood they were a social place, a hub. It was where people came together, and I must have made the connection that it was the music that brought them there in the first place. At that age, the only other place I knew like that was where we played football in the park, ninety-a-side games that became the real meeting place for us kids – especially in 1966 when England won the World Cup and *everybody* was football crazy with World Cup Willie and all of that.

There was music involved there as well, with the older black boys and their white mates who were latter-model mods and the original skinheads. Mk1 Skinheads I call them, who to us were like big men but they were probably only about fourteen or fifteen, although I remember a couple of them had sideburns! At least one of them would bring a battery-powered Dansette record player to the park, and others would bring their records, mostly reggae and ska, plus a bit of Motown, and in between you'd hear mod stuff like the Small Faces or the Spencer Davis Group. I remember after the games people would crowd round the record player, especially the girls. Second to the match this was the hub, and whoever had the records or the record player was at the centre of it. The perfect combination for me, as music and football would both become really important in my life.

While I know I was too young to make the conscious connections that I can make now, I do remember records having a certain importance for me from age three or four, or maybe even earlier, because my dad always had music in the house. He had his Bush radiogram, which he'd play every day or at least every other day, and for the first years he had it my brothers and sisters and I weren't allowed anywhere near it. *Absolutely not!* Which meant it took on this kind of iconic status amongst us kids. His records were similar, but my dad was so generous he'd lend anybody anything, and he'd obviously never heard the old maxim 'never lend books or records'. My aunts and uncles and cousins would come round with 'Luke, can mi borrow this?' and if my mum was there she'd always say '*No!*', because my dad would let them take anything. If they took something and ended up forgetting to give it back my mum would always tell him, 'See I tol' yuh ... But you wouldn't listen.' I know I learned from that because when I began to get records on a fairly regular basis I never lent them out – I'd lend you anything else, but records? Nah! They're mine!

My dad used to mark his records as well, which is another thing I must have picked up from him, as I don't remember anybody telling me to do it. Because I was so obsessed with records, any time my mum and dad were out I'd pull all his records out of the radiogram and just look at them. I was fascinated by the labels, what the companies were called, the design of them, the information . . . To me it was all part of what made records so special. What I also saw was that Dad had neatly marked his initials, MLJ, on the label of every one; consequently, as soon as I got my records I'd put my initials on them. Like my dad I did it neatly, then later on I would scratch them on the run-out groove, because I worked for a printing company when I left school where I'd scribe plates, like a lithographer, and my eyes were so good I could write in really tiny letters. So small in fact that only I knew, so if anybody took one of my records I'd look straight in the run-out groove and immediately know if that tune was mine or not.

It was around the time I bought those records at Webster's that I was able to really get into the record-buying habit because I blagged myself a paper round. I was underage – you had to be thirteen to do a paper round – but I was fiercely independent, I wanted to have my own money and my mum and dad didn't mind. I was so happy because I was getting ten shillings a week – fifty pence – which meant I could buy one single a week (they were 6/8, six shillings and eight pence, or 34p each), and still have cash left over for other stuff. Or, if I saved for two weeks I could buy one of those budget price albums, like *Club Reggae* or *This Is Soul!* or a *Motown Chartbusters*. I knew about the Trojan *Tighten Up!* series, and although they had by far the best reggae tunes on them, I had seen the albums in the shops with those risqué pictures on the sleeves and there was no way I'd bring them into my house at the time. Perhaps my mum and dad would have been alright about it but I was never going to take the chance. If I wanted a tune on one of those LPs I bought the single! At the tender age I was, that was pornography as far as I was concerned.

chapter eleven: the red rover years

As I said earlier, I was always an adventurous kid, and one Sunday I was literally given a licence to roam. I was in my mum's road on the way home from my paper round, and I saw this white kid who lived about halfway down the street. He was a couple of years older than me and, if I'm honest, I didn't really trust him. I'd never ever spoken to him, but he's coming out of his house, he's looked around and started across the road towards me. I was very wary and had no idea why he'd want to bother me, then he said, "Ere, mate, you know about Red Rover?' I had no idea what he was talking about, so he pulled out this little orange card and started telling me that I could go on buses for free, all day long with it. Then he said I could have it. For nothing. Basically, I'm thinking, 'Fuck off, nobody gives away anything like that!' Because I loved buses I figured if it was half as good as he said it was, it would be fantastic, and why would he give it to me? He said, 'Go on, test it if you want', and although I didn't believe him I took it. He looked around furtively and ran back into his house.

My mum and dad weren't in, and I sat there looking at it, thinking I've done my round, I wasn't going to the park to play football until lunchtime, and he'd said the card was valid until five to midnight ... On the other hand, I'm thinking it's too good to be true, the only people who could go on any bus they want for free was my dad and my uncles and aunts who worked for London Transport. It looked official, it had 'Child' and 'Three shillings' and that day's date on it, and I had nothing else to do so I thought I'd give it a go. I put some money in my pocket just in case.

I got on a 226 going towards Hammersmith and my heart was pounding! It was one of those things where every time I got on a bus by myself I was very nervous about meeting other black people in case they knew my mum or dad or they just started questioning me about what I was doing on my own, and now I've got this ticket with me that may or may not be dodgy! It was still quite early, there's nobody on the bus except this black conductor and it took him five minutes before he came up to ask me for the fare. I bottled it! I completely lost my nerve to try this ticket out and took out my money to pay him! I was expecting the fare to be tuppence, but he's charged me the full fare stage of sixpence, which is all my money and we're nearly at Hammersmith. All I can think of is I have to try this card on the way home and it better work or I've got to walk.

The bus turns at Hammersmith and I get on another one to get home. My heart's racing! Is this thing for real? The conductor came up and it was now or never – what's the worst he could do to me? Throw me off? When I held out the pass I didn't even dare look at him, I looked out of the window as casually as possible. And he walked straight past me! *Unbelievable!* This thing really works! Naturally I didn't get off at Acton, I stayed on the bus and went to North Acton. From there I made my way to Kensal Rise, because I had an aunt who lived there so I knew there were a load of buses I could choose from outside Kensal Rise station. There's the 6, the 36, the 46, the 52 ... *Waaarrrgggh!* It was like overload! I just jumped on a number 6 and went to Oxford Street! Sunday buses, mostly empty, and I'm hopping on and off all the time – even the surly old black conductors and clippies are not questioning me! I used that thing all day!

I came back about seven, eight o'clock that night. My mum and dad are going mad and my brother Joey just wants to find out where I've been. Of course I'm still buzzing – 'I've been on a Red Rover.' I'm practically shouting! They're asking me 'What's a Red Rover?' I showed them and my dad had heard of it so that was in my favour, and I'm pretty sure I got licks for being out that late, but it was so worth it just to have ridden round London on buses like that.

Then the following week, almost as if he was waiting for me, the same thing happens. He gives me the exact same thing. This time he gives me the pink one, the Twin Rover, which I can use on the tube as well. I knew it worked, so I'm completely confident this time, but all the same, when I went to get on the Central Line, showed the ticket and the guy walked me through I still couldn't quite believe it and I'm like *woooaaah*!!! But that was it, I didn't really want to roll around on trains all day, just a short hop on the tube then back on the buses because I understood you could see more of London from the buses. I was gone! I go up to Trafalgar Square on the number 12, first time I've ever been there.

Then I go to Dulwich, which is the end of the line for that route in the other direction – first time I've ever crossed the river. I'm all over the place! Hampstead on the 159, never been there before, then back down south again before I went home. *Unbelievable!*

When I went back to school after that first day I took the ticket with me and straight away began blagging my mates to come with me. It took a few weeks to persuade them – as I had been, they were highly sceptical about travelling on any bus you wanted for three shillings, but they came round, and sometimes it was just me and my brother. We didn't bother with the Twin Rover because we only wanted the buses, and suddenly we've got a great day out! We didn't have to worry about food: all anybody needed was a shilling for a bag of chips, and you could nick a pint of milk off a doorstep. Then it was all about 'Where shall we go? Let's go to the end of this line and see what's there. How far can we go out of London on a red bus?'

By the time I was eleven or twelve, my working knowledge of London was phenomenal – I had like a cab driver's grasp of where so many landmarks were. It was funny, so many of my lot had never been further than Ladbroke Grove, Shepherd's Bush was their world's end, yet I was travelling all over the city, finding out what places I'd read about actually looked like. What drove me on was I had a real interest in it – I was a London geek! I'd always been interested in the city, through books or things my dad showed me, and now I knew I could get *anywhere* in London on this ticket I got to know *everywhere* in London. It just opened up to me, which to a ten-year-old kid was magical.

I saw these landmarks I'd only ever seen in books or on television, and standing there looking at them I was so proud that this was my city.

I loved the randomness of it too, the idea that if I go there something might happen. My wife Jane says I'm still the same now, she's always telling me how hopeless I am with a prescribed itinerary, but the truth is I feel stifled. On those Red Rovers I was always free, I'd end up on marches or tagging along with something that was going on, quite by accident – 'Yeah looks interesting, I'll join that.' Although today it's more like, 'Oh look, there's a record shop . . . '

I went to the Tower of London . . . the Planetarium . . . Madame Tussauds . . . Trafalgar Square . . . the British Museum . . . London Zoo . . . I never went in to any of these places at the time, many I still haven't visited to this day, but just standing outside clocking them was enough for me. I remember going to the Post Office Tower (now the BT Tower), which had only been open a couple of years, and just walking around the surrounding streets looking up at it and being amazed – I was only a kid! I went to the river for the first time, and had no idea we lived so close to Hammersmith – for years I was trying to figure out where the Thames was in relation to our house. I'd been getting on and off buses at Hammersmith for ages, and on the map it looked like the river was only a couple of streets away, but I'd be walking around going '*Where* is the river?' If I'd followed the people or followed the signs I would have found it, but I didn't think of that. When I finally did find it, it was because the 266 used to run a special extended route to Hammersmith Bridge on Boat Race day and I was on one of those – up until then it had never occurred to me to cross the road and walk down there. I loved all of it. I got to know my city inside out through seeing things on those Red Rovers, and developed a love affair with London I'm still enjoying today.

It was on a Red Rover that I went to Spurs for the first time, or should I say *almost* went to Spurs for the first time. This was months before I ever went to a game, when I was probably about ten years old. I had this fascination with Spurs from when I was a very young kid, I think because everybody else round my way was QPR or Chelsea and I just wanted to be different. I'd just jumped off a number 11 at Liverpool Street and was thinking about where to go next, and for no reason I can remember thought 'Why don't I try and find out where the Spurs ground is?' I jumped on a 149, I think, at Liverpool Street and it headed up through Shoreditch and Dalston to Tottenham. It was pouring with rain. I went on the upper deck where the windows were all steamed up and there was hardly anybody on it. The bus got up to Tottenham, with the conductor announcing the Town Hall and other stuff and I'm trying to see out of the window. 'Where's this ground then? I should be able to see the flood-lights.' I was starting to get nervous, thinking I must be on the wrong bus because it can't be on this road, and I got off at the next stop after Bruce Grove, thinking I couldn't find it, crossed the road and got another bus back to Liverpool Street. I found out a few months later that if I'd stayed on the bus another two stops I would have seen the stadium because I would have been practically outside it.

I used to be fascinated by Oxford Street, and as I used to get off at Marble Arch it didn't take me long to discover Speakers' Corner and I was absolutely spellbound by what went on up there. The idea that just anybody could get up on a soapbox and spout about anything they wanted was simply brilliant – then when people started debating it got even better! All sorts of mad people up there banging on about stuff I didn't have a clue about, but I loved the theatre of it all. Also there would be a lot of black people up there, mostly Africans, I think, although I found out much later that Marcus Garvey used to speak there in the 1930s. This was brilliant because there were no serious black people on television in the 1960s, so this was the first time I'd ever seen people who looked like my mum and dad being so assertive.

Coming down from Speakers' Corner one time in 1968, I almost found myself caught up in one of the biggest London news stories of the time. I was walking down Park Lane and could see loads of police. I was following the sound of the sirens, seeing police horses and hearing a real lot of noise from a side street. That was enough for me! All I could think was something was going on down there and I can't get involved because I'm on my own and if my dad finds out! That was always my default fear – my dad finds out and I'm for the belt. It was years later I found out that the American Embassy was just down that side street and I'd almost wandered into that big, violent anti-Vietnam War demo which became known as the Battle of Grosvenor Square. I was so close and I had no idea.

*

The places I used to visit left such an impression on me that years later, when I used to have to look after my siblings because Mum and Dad were at work, I used to take them out for the day on Red Rovers and Twin Rovers. We'd ride around on trains and buses, and spend my own money taking them into the places I just used to stand outside – I'd take them to the museums, like the Science Museum, the Natural History Museum or the British Museum, we went to the Tower, I took them to the London Planetarium . . . they loved it as much as I did, which really made me feel gratified about what this city has to offer.

chapter twelve: my first proper job

Somebody else who was a huge influence on my young teen-age life was this old guy, Ernie Gadsby, who used to drive an *Evening News* delivery van and became a mentor to me as I worked with him running the papers after school. Back when London had two daily evening papers, the *Evening News* was the other one, and 'running the papers' was literally that – running with a bundle of papers! I had to jump out of the van's sliding door, dash into a shop or to a street ven-dor's pitch, dump them, then run to catch up with the van. Because it was all about getting the papers out as quick as possible, especially the late Saturday edition with the classi-fied football results, the van would never actually stop unless it absolutely had to, it just slowed down a bit for me to jump in and out. In between drops I'd be sitting back with my feet on the dashboard and the door slid back; it all looked so cool that this was the job every young lad in London wanted, and how I got it was I just went and asked.

About half a dozen of the *Evening News* vans used to park up by the park we played football in, to wait for the truck to come out to drop off the bundles of papers for their rounds in west London, and one day I got up the courage to talk to one of the drivers. All Yosser Hughes-ish I said, 'I could do that, mate, could you give us a job?' I tried to keep it casual and was expecting a 'Fuck off, black boy', but he looked at me and said, 'You wan' to run the papers on Saturday? What's your name?' ... 'My name's Norman.' ... 'Well, Norman, meet me by the park where we pick up the afternoon edition and we'll see.'

That whole week my head was spinning. Is he for real? Is this thing really happening? Come Saturday I'm not supposed to meet him until 1.30p.m., but I'm there in the park from 10a.m. playing football and this game is going *so slow*! I haven't told anybody playing about this, because I'm still not convinced it will happen, then I see Ernie's van pull up – I'd remembered the serial number, 390. He got out and called 'Norman!' and I think I had the ball and just left it and sprinted across the field to the vans. There was another kid in the van, a big kid who was sixteen when I was not yet twelve, and it was him that said to me, 'If you want to run the papers on a Saturday, I'll give you ten bob a time.' I couldn't believe it! Ten shillings for an afternoon's work? It took me a week at my paper round to earn that. As it turned out, this guy was an Arsenal fan and wanted to go to football every other week so he needed somebody to cover for him – this was before I went to football myself – so now he could shoot off to Highbury.

On those Saturdays, rain or shine, I was out there working with Ernie and I absolutely loved it. We had two editions to do, the early racing edition and the one with the classified football results in it – that was the big one because the *News* prided itself on getting that edition in the shops before the

Evening Standard. We'd be sitting in the van, all calm, waiting for what seemed like ages, then the depot van would turn up from Carmelite House, the offices and printworks for the *News* on the Thames by Blackfriars, and all hell would break loose. The matches would have ended at twenty to five, the results would be printed on the front and the depot van would have them up to us about half an hour later, then we had to have the papers in the shops and the round finished by quarter past six! It was mad! Ernie used to do Acton, Hangar Lane, part of Ealing and Greenford, and I'm sure he used to break the speed limit, or that's what it felt like, he'd break red lights like this was an ambulance, hop up on the pavement sometimes – maybe the police gave those vans a pass, because we never got stopped! All the time I'm sitting in the front with no seatbelt, they weren't compulsory then, and the door open. I'd run the papers in – *bosh!* – then back in the van for the next one. It was no wonder this job was so coveted – it was one of the most exhilarating things I've ever done.

Ernie and I used to talk in the van all the time, and he would give me all this great fatherly advice about life in general, which I soaked up like a sponge. It was nothing to do with church, which was about the only other place a young black kid would get advice outside the family. I was still going to church and I *hated* it. Ernie was a guy who kind of filled the spaces that my dad couldn't, because my dad worked nights so he was always asleep during the day, and although I knew he cared sometimes he literally wasn't there. Ernie was a guy who had great life experience, but it was a very different experience to my parents, He fought in World War Two, and was in the Battle of Anzio, a big decisive battle in Italy that lasted for months, and when I asked about it he'd quietly say, 'I saw some terrible things there, I can't really talk about it and that's why I'm a peace-loving man. You grow up and you live your life a peaceful, decent way, that's the most important thing.' When I first started with him he used to talk to me about the other lad he had, the big kid who Ernie knew I used to look up to, and he would tell me, 'He's only a young lad, but he's a hooligan, don't you follow him or do what he does.' It was later on I found out that this kid was one of the top skinhead boys in the Arsenal North Bank and he got stabbed fighting at football – he showed me the plaster over the wound and I remember thinking 'Boy! Arsenal's dread! I'm never going over there!'

Ernie had a pivotal role in my timeline, as he took me on and looked after me. I'd say he gave me a really good grounding. I knew he wasn't my father but he was a father figure, a mentor, and even though his wife was very ill at the time – which I didn't find out until later – he always seemed to have time to talk to me. He got to know my parents because he would always bring me home at the end of the round and my mum and dad knew that if I was in Ernie's company then I was OK.

Ernie was always telling he knew I would 'amount to something', that I was trustworthy and reliable, and one day, out of the blue, he proved what he thought of me by giving me my own *Evening News* pitch. It was outside Acton mainline station, down the end of my mum's road, and he just told me if I wanted to I could run it, every night after school. It took me by surprise and I had to ask 'Are you sure?' He was, and I could start on Monday. This was a real big deal, because it had the potential to pay up to eight bob – forty pence – a night, if I was good at it. Big money, considering I was only about thirteen by then.

I didn't tell anybody at school because I was much too young to be doing this and I didn't want to risk being stopped. I told my mum and she said I was too young, but my dad thought it was great! That first evening when I set up on the pitch, my first customer was my dad – he walked up and bought three papers off me, I'll never forget that. My uncle came down later to give me some sale, as they say, and I never looked back after that. When Ernie came round later, he counted all the money out on the seat of the van, took the cost price of the papers, just that, pushed the rest towards me and said, 'That's yours.' I was staggered, there was over six shillings there! He just said, 'You've earned it', and that was it for me, it completely turned my head! I was no longer remotely interested in school, I would just sit there waiting for it to finish so I could get to sell my papers outside the station. I can remember having conversations with Ernie after that where I'd tell him how much I hated school and all I wanted to do was work for the *Evening News*, and couldn't understand it when he'd pull me up on that and tell me go to school, because he worked for the *Evening News* and I couldn't imagine doing better than him.

I did that for ages, going on to pitches in Perivale and Ealing Broadway – Ernie would always pick me up at half eight or so and drop me home – and I loved working for the *News*. A long time after I stopped, I still hated the *Evening Standard* after they took it over when it went bust. I was actually a bit confused because when I was selling it, at the beginning of the evening my pile of *Evening News* would be three or four times as high as the *Standard*, which people would only buy when the *News* was sold out. Not so long ago somebody posted online how their first job was selling the newspapers outside Ladbroke Grove station, and he put up a photo of his old newsboxes. I don't post much, but I had to reply to that saying 'That was my first job too!' because I really did come over nostalgic.

chapter thirteen: school

If anybody ever asks me, my natural reaction is to say I was hopeless at school, but that's not really true. Yes, I left school with no qualifications, but that was because I couldn't wait to get out of there to earn money. I wasn't thick, but I wasn't a brainbox either. I read a lot of books in those early days – up to this day I still do. I was always good at English, in fact I'm still pretty good at grammar, spelling and punctuation and I like to think I'm articulate. Maths was a non-starter for me, I just couldn't be bothered with it, which was funny because when I was at school I had an evening job that involved handling money and doing all the mental arithmetic that involved.

I used to argue a lot in school, in any lesson that had some sort of discussion. For example in history I'd always be arguing 'Why don't we learn black history?' This was real teenage stuff, as it wasn't as if I particularly wanted to learn black history, it was just that they didn't teach it so it was something I could take a stand about. Also, it gave me the excuse to pout and say, 'Well, if you're not teaching me that then I'm not interested!' Really I think it was all a bit of a cop-out on my part. When I was there all I thought about was leaving and getting a job to be able to earn my own money, and then virtually as soon as I was old enough that's what I did.

Even at that tender age I knew I had to get a job – going on the dole wasn't *a thing* then like it became later on – and I didn't want to be a villain, like some of my pals who got involved in various nefarious activities, because I knew I couldn't be locked up. I was about sixteen then, and as far as I was concerned that old adage of 'If you can't do the time, don't do the crime' really rang true – since I was a kid I'd been as free as a bird and there was no way that was going to be taken away from me. What really rammed it home to me was the first time someone I was close to got sent to borstal, as young offenders' units were called then. He was on remand for burglary, I think, and he ended up in Wormwood Scrubs prison, about a mile from my mum's house. He sent me a Visiting Order, which is what prisoners have to send out and get approved for people to come and visit them, which I'd never heard of up until then. I went to see him and the whole experience of the loss of liberty shook me up so badly that I vowed I would never end up in one of these places. I would never have my freedom taken away from me.

I often think that if kids had that experience at a young age, just visiting a prison and seeing how really grim life in there is, then potential criminals would think twice about breaking the law. It's also interesting that I didn't think about crime as a way forward – as a career option – the most important factor to me was the prospect of getting caught and punished. Even in my mind I was never a real criminal because the ones that I knew – and I knew quite a few – never considered that they might get caught, or if they did it didn't seem to bother them. I've also got to give my mum and dad huge props for this: as headstrong as I was, they instilled their strong right-from-wrong values in me. I'm eternally grateful for that. They gave me a great deal of freedom, but I wasn't completely running wild as they gave me restrictions as well. I was no angel, and I used to come right up against those boundaries and push them or cross them whenever I could – I'd feel the wrath of my dad's belt, he'd say, 'You're too harden! ... If you don't hear, you will feel!' But all through that I knew they were there and supporting me, and even when I might have got really angry with them I still knew that subconsciously. I believe I always had a sense of what I should and shouldn't be doing.

Underneath all of this I must have felt secure in the fact that even if I was being punished they were showing interest in me, in all of us kids, because I believe the worst thing you can do to kids is not show any interest in them – it's a fine line between giving freedom and not caring. My dad giving me the money to buy the records was a great example of this. I don't know for sure if he knew that I had any real interest in music, but he understood that as long as I was interested in something I wouldn't be up to any badness, so he thought about something I *might* be interested in and that related to something he was into – records. Looking back now, I'm amazed. My dad gave me my head at that really young age, and that's stayed with me my whole life.

With Mum and Dad as really strong characters behind me, I was never going down the wrong path, and I thank them every time I see them. I tease them a lot too, because there is always a lot of laughter in my mum's house. I call them immigrants and during the Windrush scandal in 2018, when people who had come from the West Indies perfectly legally in the 1950s were being detained, I would tell them that if it wasn't for me they would have been deported! But I also thank them for me being born here because the opportunities I've had in the UK I wouldn't have had anywhere else. In the mid-1970s there was talk in the family about us all migrating to America, and I have no idea how that would've ended up – probably with me doing some no mark, dead end job. Instead, though, they opted to stay and in the late 1970s and '80s I found myself doing some really creative things, meeting some really inspiring people who were about changing things and challenging things. I loved that and it's down to my mum and dad that this was able to happen.

chapter fourteen: football I

Before I became obsessed with records, my biggest passion was football. Sure I loved music – music and girls – but once I discovered going to football I felt I'd found my calling: I was a Spurs fan. When so many of my mates were doing boring things on a Saturday, or doing nothing at all, I had this whole ritual of getting up early, going over to White Hart Lane, meeting up with all these people who I didn't see at any other time, then taking in all the emotions that supporters go through at live football matches.

I loved that, but what I loved even more was going to away games. By the time I was able to do that it was the 1970s, when the football violence thing was just becoming prevalent, and I just found a thrill in that even though, and I've said this in loads of interviews, I was never a *hooligan*. I was never a person that went round smashing things up or beating people up, but I loved the exhilaration of being in a gang – running with the herd somewhere foreign. What I used to go through in one of those days was something else: in the morning, on the train to wherever you're going, you're really happy and everybody's cracking jokes; then when you get off you're suddenly in a hostile environment and you're filled with fear – real fear. Come quarter to five and the final whistle it's even worse: 'How am I getting out of this situation? How am I getting out of the grounds and back to the station?' Sometimes it was literally a stroll, other times it was like that old film *The Warriors*, when a New York street gang had to fight their way through the city and back home. It could be scary.

When I was very young I would be playing football practically any time I got a spare five minutes – I was a pretty useful number 8, an inside right – then in the summer of 1966 I'd just watched England win the World Cup and I'd become a fanatic. Practically everybody round my way supported Queens Park Rangers as the local team. Kids at school would chant '*Rod-nee . . . Rod-nee*' for Rodney Marsh every time somebody did a bit of skill in the playground. I was desperate to go and see a football game, but my dad wouldn't let me and I didn't have anybody to take me, so one Saturday afternoon I got brave!

I didn't know where the Rangers ground was, but I knew it was on the way to Webster's record shop in Shepherd's Bush because sometimes I'd be on the bus and I'd see everybody in blue and white scarves and rosettes, then they'd get off two stops before me. They'd walk down the side streets off Uxbridge Road, so I figured it must be down there, but didn't have the bottle to go on my own. Some of the kids that went down there were quite rough and being a black boy I thought I might get picked on – I was only eight or nine, but I understood not to put myself on offer going to those things. As it turned out, the first time I got up the courage to go in to a game that was exactly the case.

One afternoon I made up my mind to just follow this crowd and go to a game, so I made up some fib for my mum about where I was going, my dad worked nights so he was asleep, I got off the bus before Shepherd's Bush. Oh boy! I'm going to my first football match! When I saw the stadium wall I remember thinking how it looked so big, and how I could hardly believe it was so close to where I lived. It was only a reserve game, QPR versus Chelsea reserves, and there weren't many people there, but once I was inside it was, 'Woooah! I'm actually here! So this is what all my mates are talking about!'

I stood at the Loftus Road end and walked right down to the front behind the goal. My first impression of my first game is how big the players looked. I'd only seen football on television, now it's live, only a few feet away, and I was really little, they looked like giants. They were massive, I couldn't believe how muscly they were, and the noise I could hear when they went into tackles seemed like gladiators in combat. To a little kid it was absolutely thrilling. But I had to keep my wits about me because I noticed some kid in the schoolboys' enclosure – back then all grounds sectioned off part of the terraces for kids – who I recognised as a Grove boy. He was a couple of years older than me, I think his dad had a stall on Portobello Market, and he was patrolling this area like he was the boss. He was bullying the other kids, who all seemed to know his name, and I realised pretty quickly that this was the guy who ran things and best not to cross him. There were no other black boys in there and suddenly I heard someone shout, 'What's this nigger doing in here?' It came from behind me, I didn't look round but

I was sure it was that kid. I pretended I didn't hear as I was on my own and didn't want to get into anything. I made my way to the back of the stand and I thought this isn't for me, I like it, it's exciting, it's my local team and I did try to support it, but if that's what's going on here then I won't be coming here again. It was a long time before I went back to Loftus Road, and that first time might have had something to do with why I ended up supporting Spurs.

The first time I can really remember Spurs as a team is the 1967 Cup Final, Tottenham against Chelsea, which I watched on our rented DER television that we had to keep banging to make the hissing stop! Back then Jimmy Greaves was an absolute icon and as he played the same position as me, he was my hero. Also, I was so pleased Spurs won that match because all the kids I hated at school seemed to be Chelsea supporters. That year at school, suddenly there were a lot of Manchester United fans, because they had just won the European Cup and the kids were attracted to it as a glory club – which hasn't changed in the last fifty years! So everybody I knew was either QPR (who had become the first Third Division team to win the League Cup so their stock was high), Chelsea or Manchester United, and as I never wanted to be the same as everybody else, when I was asked 'Who are you then?' I'd say Tottenham. 'What do you mean you're *Tottenham*?' This was before I'd ever even been there, and I loved the fact I supported a team that *nobody else did*, a team that was miles away.

I'd made up my mind I was going to go to a Spurs game, but remembered when I hadn't been able to find the Spurs ground on a Red Rover trip, so I knew I had some work to do. I thought about it for ages, then got prompted into doing something almost by accident. A family friend was round at our house, I don't think she was a relative but she was a close enough friend for us kids to call her 'Auntie', and I heard her say she lived in Edmonton. Just out of curiosity I looked up where that was in the A-Z London map book, and saw it was down the road from Tottenham. It took me a few weeks to pluck up the courage to ask my mum to let me go and visit her. This wasn't an unusual request, as I was always jumping on trains and buses and turning up at relatives' houses, greeted by 'Norman? How did you get here?' Getting to Edmonton, though, was the big prize! There was no Victoria line (it didn't open until later that same month, and when it did it only ran from Highbury & Islington to Walthamstow), so I had to plan this like a military operation. I got up early, got on a Piccadilly line train at Acton Town, went all the way up to Finsbury Park and caught the W3 bus, a little single decker with turnstiles, to White Hart Lane. Not the stadium, but the road White Hart Lane, which is *really* long and I wanted the far end – that was a bit confusing, because the bus had turned in to White Hart Lane, but there were no Spurs fans on it! I needn't have worried – as it got closer to the ground more and more people wearing Spurs colours were getting on.

When I got off the bus at Tottenham High Road everyone turned right for the ground. What I remember most is seeing the floodlights and more people than I'd ever seen in my life. When I had gone to QPR they were still in the old Third Division, and their crowds were only about five or six thousand; this crowd would have been ten times that as they used to get over 60,000 in before it was made all-seater. But I wasn't going to the game, I had to turn left to get another bus up to my mum's friend's house. This was just a recce but it was enough – I was definitely coming back, I was going to pick a game then beg my mum to let go to visit this family friend again.

Getting my mum's OK was easy, and as we didn't have a phone she couldn't ring up to check that I'd been there. It was October 1967, I was ten turning eleven the following month, I was in the top year of primary school and there I was, going to Spurs with no parental control, no one telling me what to do and I'm just *lost* in this sea of fans. I'd done it, I'd made it to Spurs! We were playing Nottingham Forest, it was a 1-1 draw and I've still got the match-day programme.

It was only about midday by the time I arrived at the ground. The match didn't kick off for another three hours but you had to get there at that time to get in the queue to be sure of a good place on the terraces. The gates were just opening but I was entranced, I just wanted to walk around outside. I was by myself and I was so in awe that I must have looked a bit lost, as all the blokes were going, 'You all right, sonny?' . . . ''Ere, go in 'ere, go in the schoolboys' . . . ''Ere, let this little boy in the queue!' There's me, a little black boy, in my littler blue anorak, with my City of London badges sewn on the sleeves – I used to love badges and being in the cubs, I earned all my badges and used to sew them on myself, such was my sense of pride – and never before had I received that sort of treatment from white blokes. This was nothing like my experience at QPR, so I was instantly put at my ease and made to feel welcome. From that moment on I knew this was my club and these were my people.

I paid nine pence or a shilling (four or five pence in today's coin) and went through the turnstiles. Back then you could walk all around the ground and choose where you wanted to stand, and the kids all used to try and get behind the goals so I followed. It was getting packed in there, but I was so shy and scared to try and get down the front because I didn't want to push in in front of all these white kids, but the grown-up Spurs fans helped me out again. 'You alright, mate?' ... 'Can't you see, son?' ... ''Ere, get this kid down the front.' And they lifted me up over their heads and passed me right down the front. *Wow!!!!* Absolutely amazing.

I guess I was revelling in the fact that I was the only little black boy there, and that might have been why those around me would make sure nothing ever happened to me. Maybe they were looking at me as some sort of lucky mascot, because in those days old white blokes would rub black boys' heads for luck! I don't know what it was but I can never remember suffering any racism at Spurs, and I was going ten years before the bananas used to get thrown at black players. I've sat on panels discussing racism in football, Kick It Out and all of that, and have honestly said that of my own experiences at Spurs, where there were very few black faces around when I started going, it was as if they took me in and embraced me straight away. It could be a different story when we went to some away games, but we'll get to that later.

I loved that club from that moment on and I took great pride in the fact that in my primary school I was the only one that had been to White Hart Lane, when for everyone else it was the local teams. Through Sunday I could hardly wait to get into school, I was so excited I wasn't thinking straight and nearly let myself down when my mum asked how was it at Auntie's! I'd momentarily forgotten that was where I was meant to be, but managed to blurt out a 'Yeah ... yeah ... It was great!' and seemed to get away with it. Then when I walked in to school on Monday with my Tottenham programme I was like a conquering hero! First of all my mates were asking where I got it from, and I told them 'The game!' because *I go to Spurs*! QPR? ... Chelsea? Fuck that! I'm a Tottenham Man! I was overlooking the fact that I was only ten years old. Then they're asking how did I get all the way up there – back then, from where we lived, Tottenham might as well have been the other end of the world. I enjoyed my celebrity status as the kid who had *seen* Jimmy Greaves in the flesh, *seen* Mike England and had *seen* Pat Jennings, who is my all-time goalkeeping hero. Straight away I was planning how to go to my next game, and the planning had to be just as meticulous. I knew I could do my paper round and make enough money to get to games, but because I couldn't let my mum and dad find out where I was going I had to go through all the same sort of subterfuge.

For a year or two I was going up to Spurs on my own, because it took a while to convince any of my west London mates to go, but that never bothered me. I've always been affable, I make friends easily, even though for a while as a teenager I was really shy with girls – *properly* shy. I never had a problem going anywhere on my own, and Spurs was no exception. In no time I'd made a lot of friends, schoolboy friends. This was great because it gave me another reason to look forward to every other Saturday. I'd go up there, meet these people, they didn't know anything about me, I didn't know anything about them, all we've got in common is Tottenham. I used to think that was brilliant, it was so completely different from the times I would go to QPR and practically everybody I met went to my school. A lot of these kids at Spurs were locals from Tottenham, Walthamstow or Edmonton and they'd ask me where I lived: 'I live in Acton.' . . . 'Where's that?' So I'd tell them Ladbroke Grove, and they'd all heard of that. Then it was *'What?!?* You come all the way from Ladbroke Grove to go to Spurs?' I used to love that.

Although I was a sociable little kid, I suppose I was really a bit of loner because I was always very single-minded – some people will say I still am – and if I couldn't persuade anyone else to come with me I wasn't scared to go and do things on my own. I did, however, get a great sense of belonging from going to Spurs and being part of that whole common cause football supporter thing. This happened immediately, as I felt a kinship with what was going on at White Hart Lane as soon as those guys took to me and made sure I could see and I was OK. They used to call me Titch, in the beginning, as I was so small – 'Oi Titch! Over 'ere!' – but thankfully the name never really stuck. They seemed to genuinely like me and I looked up to these big lads, white lads and black lads. As time went on there was one black guy they used to call Brixton, who was a face over at Spurs, he was one of the few black lads there, and I naturally gravitated to him and a few others who I quickly got to know because there wasn't that many of us. Going there in the early days, though, I felt immediately accepted, not that I was consciously looking for it, although maybe deep down I was seeking that but not realising it, I just felt at home. Yeah, I love this, this is what I want to do.

I'd never attached myself emotionally to QPR either – even though I liked them, they were my local team and all my school mates, all my mates down Portobello Market, everyone went, I just didn't connect with them in my mind. When I started going to Spurs they were just a bit past the 'glamour years' of winning the League and FA Cup double – Manchester United had taken over as the exciting team – but Spurs were the glamour team for me. I was always a fan of Jimmy Greaves, and watching Spurs on the television a few times I remember that Brian Moore on *The Big Match* on a Sunday afternoon usually picked out Jimmy Greaves for special praise. I didn't want to support a club that everyone round my way did, I wanted to be different. I don't know why, for some reason I just felt better when I was the odd one out.

chapter fifteen: leaving school

I actually left school around Easter 1974, just a few months before I should have done my exams. Three of us left that Easter; the rest of my mates stayed on for their exams then left straight away in the summer. I suppose it would have made sense for me to hang on for a bit longer and do my exams, but I couldn't wait to start earning money. There was never any talk about going on to further education among anybody I knew, there was only one kid from my year who went on to college and my attitude was '*What!?!* Who goes to university? Black kids don't go to university.' Which was actually very much the case in 1974, although I'm sure that had I had the option for going to some sort of creative school, like art college, and my school had been more geared up to that, I would have flourished. Unquestionably. Back then, in my circumstances, you were either academic or you weren't and no provision was being made for anybody that might be creative in another way. The schools address that sort of thing *now*, but back then you'd end up being groomed to be factory fodder.

For me all it was all about getting my first proper wage packet, that moment when the first thing you do is pull out your allowance to give to your mum – I'd always give her half my wages. It was a truly amazing feeling of being able to pay my way, I felt properly grown up to be helping my mum and therefore the whole family. This was kind of ironic, because I'd get paid on Friday afternoon and then be skint by Wednesday – to get me through the rest of the week I'd have to borrow back the money I'd given my mum a few days before! I was always broke, and constantly subbing, Mum used to tease me about it all the time. If I'd come in with a bag from Contempo Records, the shop that sold American imports, she'd drily say, 'So you're going to eat your records then?'

I don't think my mum and dad were too happy about me leaving school like I did, but as long as I got a job they weren't going to try and stop me. The problem was that actually meant getting a job – a real job. I wasn't workshy by any means, but what was scaring me at that time was that I didn't know what I wanted to do, but I was going have to do it all day for the rest of my life. My brother Paul followed my dad into London Transport and I thought about doing the same because I loved trains and buses. I also liked the idea of being a cab driver because I'd never be out of work. Some of my older mates were in the first year of an apprenticeship, but I knew being an electrician or a plumber wasn't for me. Most of all, I just knew I didn't want to be factory fodder.

When I was working on the *Evening News* I harboured ambitions of working for them in the print room, but Fleet Street was a closed shop and such a hot bed of racism there was no point in even thinking about that. However, when I went to the meeting with my school's careers officer, he offered up a job at the litho printers working in the dark room, and I jumped at it for three very important reasons. I could start the very next Monday, so I could be out of school without being out of work; it was in Park Royal, which is about a mile and a half from Acton, close enough for me to ride my bike up there; and it paid pretty decent money. The fact that they trained me to be a lithographic printer was a bit of a bonus!

I had for so long relished this idea of going to work as a rite of passage and here was a situation that was making it incredibly easy for me. I stayed there for a little over two years, until the beginning of summer 1976, and then I only left because the foreman was such a bastard. He was quite openly racist and in the beginning I took a lot of it, kind of accepting that was what went on in the workplace. As I grew up there, I used to walk into work thinking I really don't want to be doing and taking this sort of shit until the gold watch days. It began to really get to me, I couldn't see any possible way forward there so I ended up hating that job – sometimes I'd literally be talking to myself, wondering out loud, 'What the fuck am I doing here? Come on, Norman, you can do better than this!' I even had fleeting moments thinking I should have stayed on at school, but those moments were always fleeting!

I had a furious argument with my dad when I walked out of that job. He had such a strong work ethic and really blew up when I told him: 'Why yuh leave that job? ... It a good job ... ' I had been becoming politically aware in the way that younger people do, so I told my dad it was different for my generation, that we weren't going to work somewhere until we were sixty-five and then they give you a watch and tell you to go! I was telling him, 'Why do we – black people – always have to be the ones who have to go and get the job? Why can't we be the bosses? Why can't we run things?' I remember hardly believing that I was actually saying these things, especially as my dad ran his own team, but I was saying to my mum and dad, 'The trouble with your generation is it was always about getting a job, always about going and working for *The Man*!' Of course by then I'd been listening to all these records like James Brown, Curtis Mayfield and so on and I'm using terms like 'The Man', and I'm sure all of that had influenced my thinking.

The conflict went on while I didn't have a job, and the root of my intransigence was that I thought my dad was giving his all to London Transport, but they weren't treating him right. He worked really hard to get to where he was as an engineer, but once he had an accident at work and was off for a long time all he got from them was a tiny little letter, and then when he left after years of excellent service, all they gave him was a photograph of a train! *A fucking train!* That incensed me and it fuelled my general sense of injustice and rebellion. Nobody was going to do that to me, I was going to live or die by my own efforts and not allow anybody to let me down like that.

Of course the reality of it was that I was unemployed and using this spirit of rebellion to make all the excuses about why I shouldn't get another job. That year, 1976, the summer was brilliant and the music coming out at the time was fantastic but while that was a great distraction, I was pissed off because I didn't have the money to finance the things I'd come to enjoy. I didn't even sign on – I found it too much like hard work, filling in all those forms to get what? Then you'd have to go to every pointless interview they sent you to or you wouldn't get anything at all. Also, I was of the opinion that, as it was before computers, if you don't sign on, they don't know you're there, they can't trace you. You know, The Man can't find you!

At this stage in my life, the temptation for crime was there again. I had no money; I was used to doing and buying pretty much what I wanted; I wanted to rebel against what I saw as the straight world; and by now people I knew were moving up in the criminal world to stealing cars and stereos. I won't deny it, I could get envious of my mates who appeared to be living an easy life and would turn up in 1600E Cortinas or even some battered old Jag, like they're living life large, but then I wouldn't see them for a few months. 'Where you been?' . . . 'I've been doing a stretch!' What a ridiculous way of living your life! That was just far too short term for me – I always knew I was cleverer than that and I didn't need a certificate from school to tell me I was smart. I was streetwise enough, too, sufficiently worldly to understand my surroundings and successfully navigate them. Really, though, it was my mum and dad's work ethic and their whole approach to life that stopped me going down that route. It had left its mark on me so indelibly that I couldn't even consider crime.

I was always broke, desperate for money most of the time, but I never tipped over the edge to go and steal, because somewhere in my subconscious I knew that turning criminal wasn't just about money. Firstly, I knew guys who had loads of money but they still did crime, but mostly it was because of my parents. When I was younger we never had much in our family, but they had standards and they had ambition: they showed me the value of working for something and how what you ended up with could be worth much more than its material value. They were the first in the family to own their own home, and when they moved us out from Grove to Acton, they impressed upon me – without actually saying as much – how much it had been worth the scrimping and saving to buy that house. It became the home of everybody in my extended family. All of the weddings and christenings and big birthdays of all my aunts and uncles and cousins who came to England were held at Mum's house. *Everything!* It was the centre of our family's community and I could see how proud my mum and dad were of that. Although now looking back I know it was great, back then it was kind of a pain in the arse to have our house always full of people I didn't know.

As a result, I wanted to work for what I got, as opposed to robbing it or robbing the money for it. Although I'd see these guys in flashy cars, I'd think, 'When I do get a car, that car's going to be *mine* from the efforts of my own toil, nobody's going to be able to take it away from me as stolen property. And, as a result, I know I'll appreciate it all the more.' For as long as I can remember I've always worked for everything I've ever owned.

chapter sixteen: football II

I will always remember my first away game. 12 September 1970, West Bromwich Albion at the Hawthorns ground – once again, I've still got the programme. I loved it. It was like going to a game but somehow *concentrated*, a much more intense experience as away fans are super up for it, no way was theirs a casual thing. Then there was the journey to wherever we were going, two or three hours of just Spurs fans building themselves up for the afternoon ahead. This was around the time that British Rail started running Football Specials, trains dedicated to individual club's away fans with reduced price tickets – the carriages weren't in the best condition, and they'd be held up to allow any other train through, but we didn't care. This cheap travel meant there would be thousands of fans travelling to away matches, although my lot usually bunked the fares as we saw it as a challenge to get all the way to Manchester or Birmingham without paying! Even if I did have to buy a ticket, a pound usually covered the whole day: ten bob for the train, a couple of bob to get in the ground and a shilling for a horrible pie or a Marmite sandwich.

I loved the ritual: meeting everybody at Euston or

wherever, having a laugh on the train, coming out of the station at the other end and wandering round these northern towns, if there wasn't a police escort to the ground. That was something I enjoyed, because away from the football I was getting to see so many of these northern towns as the remnants of old Victorian or Edwardian England, especially the mining towns before they disappeared or were changed for ever. The thing that struck me most of all was houses with no front gardens, not something you saw in Acton or Grove!

You had to be on alert on these walks from the station to the ground, because suddenly the other team's mob would be in front of you and often, even if we did have the police with us, it would all kick off. When I say 'it would all kick off', nearly all the time it was never as bad as most people imagined. Most of it – in fact all of it for my lot – was just running around and shouting, real mob mentality stuff. The media used to hype it all up to sell papers. I was running with the herd, and it was usually relatively harmless, all bravado and posturing. It was just what kids of my age in my generation did – it was normal. We were all fourteen, fifteen or sixteen and we weren't hooligans – 99 per cent of the fans weren't bad people, they were just regular kids who were at school or first- or second-year apprentices. I got chucked out of quite a few grounds – not properly arrested, just ejected – and that was always along with a bunch of others and never for anything more serious that pushing and shoving. I wasn't hitting or fighting anybody, I wasn't smashing windows, I wasn't damaging property, but being in a gang, *a giant gang*, for a few hours on a Saturday afternoon was my kicks, that was my thrill. And I loved it – I'll make no bones about that.

The tribalism of the singing and chanting was brilliant. The whole thing of several thousand people giving it their all, in unison, is enough to move anybody. The creativity was amazing, a song would be on *Top of the Pops* on Thursday then it would be adapted and on the terraces on Saturday – out of your team's players, you could always find one name that would fit in. It helped that the 1960s and '70s were a golden age of pop creativity, and most of the songs had choruses that lent themselves to adaptation – Slade, the Beatles, Elton John, the Kinks ... Gary Glitter records were perfect for it: *'Hello! Hello! Tottenham aggro! Hello!'* Most of what you hear today in grounds aren't *songs*, they're chants – repetitive samples – and the actual songs are ones going back to the 1970s that never went away, they just keep getting rehashed.

The appallingly un-PC rivalry between football fans used to appeal to me too. It was a product of the times, because hardly anyone would carry on like that these days, but back then it was part and parcel of going to football. We'd call northerners 'bin dippers' and we'd wave five-pound notes and chant, 'We've got jobs ... we've got jobs ...' Or 'Sign on, sign on with a pen in your hand/Cos you'll never get a job ...' to the tune of 'You'll Never Walk Alone'. Nowadays how deeply offensive some of this stuff was makes me laugh, but it still used to happen on a widespread level and every club seemed to have something all other fans would make a point of picking on. There was the perception that Spurs was a Jewish club and other fans, particularly Chelsea and Manchester City, would start hissing, *'sssssssssss'*, which was meant to be the sound of the gas chambers. These days the

Spurs mob own it and call themselves 'The Yid Army'; it's still wrong on every level but back then we'd be just as bad. As an example, when we used to go to Manchester United and they started with their anti-Jewish songs, we'd start singing, 'Who's that lying on the runway? Who's that lying in the snow?', in reference to the Munich air disaster of 1958, where eight United players were killed when their plane crashed on an icy runway. There were quite a few chants I wouldn't join in with, but most of them I did even though I knew they were wrong. It was just part of being a young football fan in the 1970s.

My recall of that era is almost perfect. I can remember the games, I can remember the stations we went to, I can remember what happened, I can remember whether Spurs caused a ruckus that day, or whether the Spurs fans got properly served up. It made quite an impression on me, and to this day if I go to Spurs I still see people I remember from going to these games as a kid. I couldn't tell you their names, but they'll come up to me and say, 'Alright, Norman? I remember you when we went to Derby, in 1974!' or 'I remember you were the only coloured boy with us when we went up to Middlesbrough . . . ' It's like old war veterans, and although most of the time I don't know them from Adam it's great that we've got that in common and can acknowledge each other's history.

Of course it wasn't all completely innocuous. I knew some real hooligans, everybody on the fringes knew who had the reputation for being a bit naughty and knew who to stay clear of. I had to be careful in the circles I was moving with at football too. Kids were always getting chucked out of grounds if anything began to go off – the Old Bill just used to put you out and that was it, sometimes you'd get nicked and maybe a £20 fine and no criminal record. Some of the more hardened fans, though, were moving up to a more serious level and actually getting jailed for football offences. That seemed so ridiculously pointless and it used to totally confuse me – how can you go to jail for a football offence? But they did.

I did get arrested once, during a row at Euston station after we'd come back from an away game and ran into Liverpool, who had been at Crystal Palace. I wasn't seriously involved with it but I was there. The British Transport Police bagged up a load of us – notably all the black boys – and took us to Kentish Town police station, which is the only night I've ever spent in a cell. I was charged with affray, then bailed to appear at Highbury Corner Magistrates Court, where the lies the arresting officer told the court absolutely staggered me! The charge was bogus because it wasn't even a fight – it was them running away from us without a single punch thrown – but what was being trotted out by Old Bill about what had happened was ridiculous. I couldn't do anything about it other than think, 'I never trusted you before this, and you've just proved why none of us should.' I was given six months' probation.

I had to report to a probation officer every week and tell him what I'd been doing since he last saw me, which was really boring but not much of a problem. Worse than that was having to sign in at Ealing police station every Saturday at three o'clock so I physically couldn't go to Tottenham. *It did my head in!* It so inconvenienced me that it was worse than doing community service or anything – I *lived* for Saturdays and going to Spurs!

As far as my dad was concerned – which was probably what worried me most – I muddled and lied my way through it. I didn't really explain it, just kind of mumbled about wrongful arrest and racist police and spun a yarn out of that. Basically I got away with it. In spite of Old Bill's lies and the fact that I shouldn't even have been charged in the first place, I didn't end up with a criminal record, or if I did it didn't last long, because when they gave me the MBE years later, they would have done all the background checks and I must have come up clean.

Perhaps because I was a bit older, or, dare I say it, a bit more intelligent, I didn't carry on that way. They were volatile times, the late '70s early '80s, when the football thing was changing from boot boy to football casual and there was a sinister undercurrent of violence that I really couldn't get my head around. I still went to a lot of games, but I'd pick and choose which ones they would be, because it was starting to get frightening – a sizeable element seemed to be taking it too seriously. Of course I loved all the shouting and the insults and so on, but enough of the Spurs mob would carry it on way beyond the game. They'd be at some boozer in the West End or they'd wait for another mob to come back to Euston or St Pancras and ambush them. For years those London stations used to be a nightmare between six and eight o'clock on a Saturday: Spurs fans would be there waiting for Arsenal to come back from somewhere, or Arsenal would be waiting for Millwall, or Leeds fans on their way home from Crystal Palace would get ambushed ... I didn't mind the rivalry while the game was happening, but an hour later I wasn't going to go to some pub and carry it on. No, I liked music and I liked girls, so my interest in football finished not long after the final whistle and I was off to the record shop.

I think it was pretty significant that as I got older the football/music balance shifted in my life and going to Spurs wasn't my *whole* life, like some of the guys who lived it continuously. It was one of the things I dipped in and out of, and my personality was never going to embrace it as a lifestyle – I'm convinced the big difference was that I didn't drink, so I'd be preparing to go out clubbing, not *pubbing*. My approach after a few hours of Spurs on a Saturday afternoon was, 'You know what, that was brilliant, but Greg Edwards is on and right now I'm not really interested in anything other than *Soul Spectrum*.'

chapter seventeen: football III (liverpool)

When I was going to football in the late 1970s, when black players were coming in and the whole throwing bananas and monkey chanting thing was going on, it didn't happen at Spurs. Maybe we really were a Jewish club so wouldn't get into all of that, and we didn't get any black players for ages so the opposing fans didn't do it at White Hart Lane. All the years I was going to Spurs, from when I was a little kid, I can't remember any racism among fans – I'm not saying it didn't go on, but I can't think of one incident when it was directed at me. Even when I went away as part of the Spurs mob, I never felt I was being singled out – the other fans wanted to rip *all* of our heads off. The exceptions were Leeds United and the two Merseyside clubs, Liverpool and Everton: those three grounds were terrible as there was a real hateful, vicious racism among those supporters that went far beyond football. The first time a little gang of us went with Spurs to Anfield, Liverpool's home ground, it was my most terrifying football experience. And we didn't have to wait until we got to the stadium. It all kicked off the moment we arrived.

It was the 1973/74 season, the year I left school, and we'd

heard all these stories about what happens up there, how all Scousers are thieves and they'll take your clothes, how they carry Stanley knives and love to stripe Cockneys – to cut them down the cheek. We even heard they put two blades next to one another in the Stanley knives, so that the cut is wider and leaves a really horrible scar. Because I'd heard all of this, I didn't go up there in my first years of going to away games, but as I'd so enjoyed going to the smaller places and felt pretty much invincible as part of the Spurs mob, I saw no reason to avoid going up there. I went with four of my black mates, two mixed race kids and one white guy, and that was the big mistake – not going with a white guy, but going up there looking like a black posse.

As this was a big game, there were three or four trainloads of Spurs fans going up from Euston. We were on the first train so that we could get up there early and see what was happening. We figured there was safety in numbers, so we weren't too bothered about the stories we'd heard. When the train pulled in to Lime Street station, it was the same as any other away game: you could open the doors before the train stopped, so people jumped out and started running along the platform, with the big 'Tottenham ... Tottenham' chants going up immediately. To me, that was a big part of going to these places – jumping off the train and immediately announcing our presence. As often happened, the home team had a firm waiting at the station, so there's a couple of hundred Liverpool fans on the concourse jeering and chanting, but when they saw us it all changed. They're ignoring the white Spurs fans and have properly started on us. 'Nigger ... nigger ... fookin' nigger ...' They were pointing at us and miming throat-slitting, or this particularly horrible gesture: they'd jerk their closed fists up close to their necks, as they flopped their heads to one side. I'd never seen it before but it didn't take too much to work it out – lynching.

So much for being part of the Spurs mob, too. We look around and everybody's hiding their scarves and somehow just melting away, *we were on our own*! The police were almost as bad, herding us towards these buses by whacking us with their truncheons – the liberties Old Bill used to take with football fans were the same liberties they tried to take with black people at Carnival four or five years later. They had these double-decker buses lined up to take the Spurs fans to the ground so we couldn't roam around Liverpool, and they're screaming at us, 'Get on the fookin' bus!' We jumped on a bus and ran upstairs, but the white kids who had been trying to hide their scarves wouldn't get on the same bus as us, so we weren't getting the safety in numbers. Then it really kicked off. The Scousers came charging out of the station, Old Bill has done nothing to attempt to stop them, and they're running across the bonnets of cars shouting 'Get those spooks … Get them fookin' darkies!' Everybody else had fled, and they were only after us.

I was terrified, and knew I had to keep my wits about me – they couldn't all get up the stairs, but we couldn't let any of them up. Some of us in that posse were pretty handy, especially my mate Ceophus – he'd done his leg in and was hobbling along with a walking stick that day, so as they tried to get up the stairs he was knocking them down. There were even a few of them who had got on the roof of the bus, jumping up and down on it, which is when I realised this was nothing to do with football – this was a race thing. The hatred on those faces was something I'd never experienced before. We got out of there in the end. The Scousers weren't getting at us up the stairs, so may have just given up – I very much doubt Old Bill came on to pull them off – and they figured they'd wait for us at the stadium. The bus took us up there, where things didn't get any better.

My most vivid memory of being in that stadium that day is the security – *security* – telling us, 'You're not going to get out of here alive . . . You'll get done in here!' That kind of set the tone – it was horrendous. We ended up standing at the back of the Spurs fans, so we're taking slaps on the backs of our heads, and the Scousers were pissing on us. Literally! It's called a hot leg, and whoever is doing it just stands behind you and just pisses down your leg and there's nothing you can do about it. Ceophus is getting a bit lively, but we were on a hiding to nothing so we made a collective decision. At half time we went to find some stewards, told them we needed to get out and we had to practically beg them to let us out – I think they thought our discomfort was funny. After a lot of haggling and pleading they agreed to let us out, and if we needed any further proof that we'd made the right decision, they took us out through the front of the stand, walked us past the famous Kop end and all I can hear is ten thousand Scousers singing *'Who's the nigger in the hat?'*

We got out of the stadium and didn't feel any happier. It was all these little alleys and narrow cobbled streets and we're crapping ourselves – *absolutely*. We don't know where we're going, we could get turned around and end up back at the stadium or we could get attacked from anywhere. We got on the main road and thought, 'Let's get a bus! Liverpool isn't that big, Lime Street can't be that far away and the buses have to go there.' They did, but none of them would stop for us. Even at the bus stop! So we knew what was going on, and it confirmed our view that this went beyond football rivalries. We were all young and fit, even though some of us were smoking, and it was important we kept moving, so we kind of trotted it back to Lime Street, practically carrying Ceophus along with us.

It was just over two miles to Lime Street station and we made it in about thirty-five minutes, getting there about half past four, totally knackered. We sat down in this old school buffet they had up there, drinking tea or Coke, and had this overwhelming feeling of relief – the game was still going on, we figured we'd get on a train in the next twenty minutes or so and we'd be safe. We were talking about what a close shave it was and how we feared for the rest of our lot who would be there at the end – never mind they deserted us earlier, because right then we saw ourselves as the lucky ones. Just as we were saying that, we hear this almighty 'Liverpool ... Liverpool ...' and hundreds of them flooded the concourse.

We were spotted almost immediately and as they came rushing at the doors we figured they couldn't all get through the only entrance, so our best bet was to try and hold them off there. We ran at the doors, jumping over tables, smashing plates, chairs going over, cutlery all over the place, and we chucked anything we could pick up at them. The first lot got properly leathered as we threw tables, knives and forks, chairs, glasses, plates . . . anything! We were crapping ourselves, but we gave it everything as we held them off, wanting to create as much of a din as possible so the police would have to get involved, if for no other reason than to save British Rail property. Which, after what seemed like an age but in reality was only a few minutes, they did, and even then they were blaming us for starting everything! We were fighting for our lives and all they seemed worried about was nicking us! Old Bill backed everybody off, led us out of there, then didn't know what to do with us because they didn't know who we were. We had to tell them, 'We're Tottenham, up for the game, that's our train over there, we need to get on the football special.' I think they were a bit confused because the game hadn't finished yet, so they weren't expecting Spurs fans back at the station for about another three quarters of an hour. This had caught us by surprise too – we wouldn't exactly have been sitting there drinking tea if we'd thought for a minute we'd be attacked like that! I later found out that this was a marauder Liverpool mob who had come down *specifically* to look for us: after the whole ground had very clearly seen us being led out, this lot left a little bit later to ambush us at the station. That's how much beating up some black boys meant to them, compared with watching their team play.

Old Bill put us on the train – probably as they couldn't think what else to do with us – and we could at last relax a bit. I was privately thinking I would never come here again; it was my first and brutal introduction to *proper* racism at football, and it scared me into thinking, 'I'm not up for this.' Up until then I'd go everywhere with Spurs and if we got chased around some northern or midlands town it wasn't because you were black, it was because you were Spurs – a rival firm. On this occasion no, it wasn't that at all. At the same time, once we'd got away from there our thoughts turned to Liverpool coming down to play at Tottenham – or Everton, or any Scouse team – because just as our walk from Anfield to Lime Street was dangerous, the walk down to our ground from Seven Sisters Road past Tottenham Green could be dread. Even today it is a dark walk, but back in the '70s we would turn it into a nightmare for any away fan, and we all knew the return fixture with Liverpool would be no exception.

On the day of the game, the guys and I went up to Seven Sisters quite a while before kick-off and, as usual, we'd hang out in this black record shop by the tube – Body Music, I think it was called, and it was much bigger then. On this day, the shop is *packed*, it seemed like every young black football fan in London was in there. I recognised faces from Arsenal, there was some of my West Ham mates, this posse from Brixton who went to Chelsea, some boys from Millwall . . . I knew a lot of these boys by reputation, and they could be a bit naughty. Every black kid that had ever been up to Anfield or Everton's Goodison Park had got the same treatment, so any time a team from Liverpool came to London they got together like this for payback. They would wait for their trains to come in at Euston, and then because the Scouse mob would get the tube along to Edgware Road to go robbing in the hi-fi shops, these black guys would ambush them at stations along the way like Great Portland Street or Baker

Street. That day I was told there had already been some skirmishes at Euston, with Liverpool fans chased down the tube.

If the guys from various firms coming together was different from a normal afternoon going to Tottenham, what took it to another level of extraordinary were the dozens of black guys who had nothing to do with football hanging out in the shop. These were some mean-looking black dudes and I thought they were just buying records until I heard somebody say, 'We heard they done some of the brothers up there, we're from The Farm and they won't get away with that round here!' *Farm?* What are they talking about? I hadn't realised it immediately, but this was my first encounter with the guys from Broadwater Farm, this notorious estate in Tottenham. This was just great, there was going to be some serious payback.

The first group of about thirty or forty Liverpool fans came out of Seven Sisters tube and they did the worst thing they could have done – they went and waited at the bus stop for a 279 to the ground! Either they were desperate not to do The Walk, or the half a dozen Old Bill that were escorting them told them not to, but it meant they were just standing there twenty yards away. Suddenly these black guys stormed out of the shop, rushed them, then it all kicked off. They hurt quite a few of them, and the rest scattered.

Then a second wave came out of the station, singing, chanting and wandering everywhere. This is the lot who have been robbing down the West End and along the Edgware Road, so they've got clothes and radios and stereos and all sorts of stuff with them, but these guys from The Farm aren't football fans, they're not just there for a scrap, they're proper *sticksmen*. All they can see is easy pickings as they're taxing the Scousers, taking the stuff they'd just robbed from shops in town. All around me I was hearing, 'Yeah? Come 'ere white boy, gimme dat!' These guys took no prisoners, they *terrorised* the Scousers: 'We're Broadwater Farm and this is Tottenham!' *Whack*. 'This ain't Toxteth, this is Tottenham!' *Whack*. 'Now give me your train ticket home!' They would either burn the ticket in front of them or, to add insult to injury, make whoever they were draping up tear it up themselves. Imagine how much we loved that after our experiences up there. It was all spreading out because the Scousers were trying to get away, the police found it difficult to protect them and they were getting properly served. Try as they might, they couldn't get away because black boys don't get tired – when we're chasing we will hunt you down like a lion going after a zebra. We don't get tired. The white boys smoke and drink and when they get chased they get knackered. We'll run all day if we're chasing them.

After that we knew we'd better not go up to Liverpool for the next two or three seasons, but that really didn't matter. Revenge had never been so sweet and it was made so much better by the fact that it was dealt out by brothers from different mobs and those who had no interest in football, who all came together after we'd been attacked like that.

part three:
raving

chapter eighteen: early raving

When I was about thirteen or so I remember hearing whispers about this guy John Henry who threw really good house parties. He was quite a few years older than me. I played Sunday football with his younger brother Gerald, and they lived in Chiswick in this big Victorian house. The story was that his parents were back in the West Indies and he was responsible for the house, so he used to have regular dances there, once a month or so. I heard about these parties through the girls at school who always knew about such things before the boys – they were a proper social grapevine, the Facebook of their day. They were all talking about how great John Henry's parties were, so I could hardly think about anything other than getting myself to one of them, and Chiswick being only about a mile away from my mum's made it seem possible.

I talked to my mate Ernie who lived round the corner and he was really up for it, then reality set in – we looked like a couple of street urchins! So we left it a few weeks while we saved up and I went to the market and got measured up for a new pair of strides. I was so pleased with these trousers I felt unstoppable, we were ready to go to John Henry's. Although

I knew who John Henry was and I'd talk about him like he was a mate he wasn't, so at football I went to work on Gerald to wheedle our way into one of the parties. I just kept on asking questions about them and talking about how I'd heard they were really good until he had no choice but to tell me to come along.

We got there and it was everything we hoped it would be. There were some of the older girls from school, and the ones we fancied *were all there*! John's playing the music with a white mate of his on this rudimentary set-up, with the valves on the amp being the only lighting in the room, and his taste was impeccable. He's playing all the reggae you'd expect him to play, the John Holt and all of that, but he's playing Al Green, the Chi-Lites, the Jackson 5 and the soul stuff that I loved. All the parties I'd been to before this were reggae – they were house parties with the light on and mum, dad or an aunt standing in the corner! This was like a big people's affair, the light was off and, if you had the courage, you could take a girl you fancied into the corner and slo-o-o-w dance – you couldn't do that if someone's parents were there.

I was *loving* this music. 'Got to Be There' by Michael Jackson was a big tune, as were Al Green's 'Back Up Train' and The Delfonics's 'Didn't I (Blow Your Mind This Time)': these were all records that I'd bought but I'd never heard out before, because they were too slow for those other parties. Now, in a darkened room, I was dancing with *all* the girls to them. I'm in someone else's house, the music is fantastic – apart from the reggae – there's no adults that I need to feel embarrassed about ... this was my introduction to proper parties, and after that first one I *lived* for John Henry's parties. He's passed now, which is a shame, but back in the very early '70s in West London, his parties were famous.

These nights also introduced me to a whole new crowd from Chiswick. I met this little crew from around there that included a dancer called Clive Clarke, who was a year older than me and went on to perform on *Top of the Pops* with the dance troupe Zoo and to become a renowned choreographer. I met Barry Stone, a white guy who was an original skinhead from 1969 and liked all that Trojan stuff, but was also really into soul. He went on to become a deejay on the pirate station Invicta, one of the first all-soul music stations. They used to go out all around Chiswick, to these big pubs that had their weekly soul nights that they'd tell me all about, and I was fascinated, even though I looked too young to get in to any of them. There was an infamous place on Kew Bridge they used to go to, which I was too scared to go near because I'd heard about a big skinhead battle there and some black guys getting cut. The Park Hotel in Greenford was another one they used to go to, and all the girls I used to like at school would go there too, in particular one skinhead girl who I really fancied. The funniest thing was some guys in my class telling me about all the skinheads and skinhead girls who used to go to the Park on a Friday night, but none of those kids could dance! They used to try to get me to go up there because I used to drop a few slick dance moves in the playground!

There was a guy in my class called Dermot, who was always trying to get me to go there, but I was really conscious of how I looked – I looked so young and I was paranoid they wouldn't let me in. He'd tell me we'd be going up with his older brother Seamus, who was the coolest, best-dressed kid around so we'd be alright, and eventually he talked me around. I got on the E3 bus to go up and meet them but I was really nervous because often these things ended up in a fight – I'd heard too many stories about kids getting glassed or bottled or hit with a chair, so I knew the potential was always there. That's just how it was. I was always really mindful of this, it was a lot of the reason why I never drank. I never wanted to be drunk in those situations. I knew of guys who were real wankers, who as soon as they'd had one or two drinks – Dutch courage – wanted to fight the world, and the Park Hotel had such a notorious reputation that I figured I'd be surrounded by people like that. I asked if any black people went up there, they told me, 'One or two, but you'll be alright'. That didn't exactly put me at ease.

I went up there wearing a new Fred Perry shirt, red with the blue trim on the collar, I had ice blue Levis Sta-Prest and a pair of Ivy Shop Gibsons, which had taken me about three months to save up for. I only wish I had a photograph of what I looked like that night – I looked so right, just really young! The music was brilliant, they were playing a couple of James Brown records, and like so many of those places the white kids used to line up and watch the black boys dance. All these skinhead kids would wait for the black boys to show them what to do – like with that Rufus Thomas tune 'Do the Funky Chicken', they'd form a circle to watch the black boys do the funky chicken. It used to be like that back when these guys would bring their Dansettes over the park. I remember these black guys in their pork pie hats showing the white boys what shuffling was.

Back then, if any black kid went to a largely white club it would be assumed he was a brilliant dancer, so practically anything you did would be held up as amazing, meaning we kind of had them beat before we even started. It was the same sort of teenage racial profiling that got applied to the Chinese kids during the kung fu craze of the early '70s: at school everybody was wary of them because we thought there was a good chance they were a kung fu expert – a lot of them used to moody up and get into a fighting stance!

That night at the Park, they played 'The Liquidator' and some other of those pop-a-top reggae tunes, and I used to do all those dances at school – I was light on my feet, I loved dancing, I could shuffle and everything! Then they played 'Moonhop' by Derrick Morgan. I could do the 'Moonhop', so I went for it and I totally won the whole crowd over. I quickly got over my nervousness and was dropping moves, proper showing off, doing steps, leading line dancing, all of that. I'd have circles open up around me and all these girls, because the place was full of skinhead girls, asking me, 'How did you do that?'

That night at the Park Hotel was fantastic, and I believe it's from that moment that clubs became the thing for me. I discovered I really loved the dancing, because that was my way to show off – I wasn't good at anything else, except maybe football, but I could dance and dancing got the girls' attention in a way that football never could. From then on, for me, music and dance went hand in hand, and as soon as I was old enough to get in clubs I was in clubs ... I loved it.

chapter nineteen: clothes I

Like practically any teenager, I understood the importance of looking right in a situation like that, but I'd been aware of clothes and how to dress for quite a while before that. I'd always had a latent interest in style and fashion, and my earliest memory of it was being really impressed by the original mods on their scooters in their parkas, so I couldn't have been much older than six or seven. When you're that age you assume these trends are going to be around forever, so I used to think 'When I grow up I'm going to have one of them, I'm going to do that.' As it was I did both – buying a scooter and wearing a parka – but only after they'd come back as a revival.

When I was ten or eleven practically every kid I knew, black or white, was into the skinhead fashion. I was no different and it was a lot of what motivated me to go for the job on the *Evening News* van. The kid who ran the papers for Ernie before me, Billy, always looked immaculate. He always wore a Ben Sherman shirt, which was the first time I'd actually seen one, although we talked about them at school all the time. He had these brogues that he put up on the dashboard, always immaculately polished, always Levi's jeans or

Sta-Prest, and in winter this big sheepskin – I used to idolise him. When I first went out in the van I used to equate the job with those clothes, and thought 'If I keep this job I can dress like that!', because there was no other way somebody like me would have been able to afford all of that gear. This was in 1967 or '68, when I just used to admire those kids from afar. Apart from maybe Ben Sherman, I didn't know what the brands were, I really didn't know what anything was, I'd just look at these kids and think how I'd love to look like that. I got hooked into this whole style thing from a very young age.

I had what passed for a Crombie among us kids – not a proper Crombie at all but a woollen overcoat from the market that *looked* like a Crombie, and because I couldn't afford a sheepskin I had an imitation, a *cheapskin* as we used to call them. My mum bought me my first Ben Sherman, lime green it was, but at that time all my mates were broke and I wanted to be independent, to be able to buy my own clothes. Then suddenly when I started on the papers I could. I could buy my Ben Shermans, I could buy my Levi's, I could buy my Fred Perrys! I loved that look, because a few of the black mates at the time had it and they looked fantastic. My mate Ernie was one of the original black skinheads and he's got this wicked photo of himself sitting on a swing in the park, skiffle cut with a razor parting on the side, union shirt, bleached Levi's, braces and massive DMs. I wish I had some pictures of myself from back then.

Once I got to secondary school there was even more pressure to keep up. There was Dermot, the kid from my class who I used to go to the Park Hotel with, and he was the style guru in my year, but his older brother Seamus used to help him out, so he had an advantage. The style guru of the whole school, though, was this guy Rudy Weller, and when he came to school it was like a catwalk – 'This is what you'll be wearing next term!' The funniest thing about Rudy Weller was that when I first got to the school and heard about him, I assumed with a name like that he was a black kid, but he wasn't, he was a white kid! He was the double of Jason King, the secret agent on the television played by Peter Wyngarde. He was just growing his hair out from a suedehead, and he always looked like a male model. *Every* girl in the school, without exception, fancied him, but he never went out with any of them – it was like they were not worthy and he only went out with girls from outside the school.

Rudy later became famous as a sculptor. He designed *The Horses of Helios* outside the Criterion Theatre in Piccadilly, and *The Daughters of Helios*, the three women diving off the building six floors above. In the late '60s, though, if you wanted your style cues you got them from him, as there'd be cheaper knock-off versions of the clothes he wore in the market for the rest of us one term or two terms later. Dermot, who genuinely knew about fashion, used to explain to the class what Rudy was wearing because nobody of our age would have the courage to go up to him and ask!

The talk at school was that Rudy's mum and dad had separated, and his mum had a good job somewhere and spoiled him rotten, so any clothes he wanted he got. There was another rumour that his mum allowed him to put bets on and he used to win money on the horses or White City dogs. This could all have been urban myth, but he was getting money from somewhere because he came to school in

Ivy Shop brogues that cost £5/19/6! That was *way* out of the league of the rest of us, who were earning about ten bob a week. Disregarding what he spent, I had no idea where he was getting his style cues from, but he knew about the Ivy Shop in Richmond in any case – the proprietor Johnny Simon had his first shop there before opening in Soho. It was Rudy that told people at school about it, and this was how high the bar was set for me.

chapter twenty: early raving II

In going to these places like the Park Hotel with an older teenage crowd and specialist black music, I'd completely lost interest in what was happening on my own doorstep. I still loved Acton, it was where I lived, but youth clubs like the Priory Youth Centre or St Saviour's, which were meant for kids my age, just didn't float my boat. They were full of things I hated, like table tennis or snooker, plus they were where the deadbeat kids from the Acton Vale used to hang out when they were starting to smoke gear and get into trouble. If these youth clubs ever held a dance, it wouldn't even be as exciting as the house parties where the parents stayed in the room – at least at those I might get to hear some of the Trojan sounds I liked, but these would be pure pop music. This wasn't a case of me having anything against regular white pop music – I feel a real affinity with so much of what came out in the 1960s and early '70s. I was simply a bit discerning and only bothered with the interesting end of it.

I *loved* the Beatles, still do, in fact I consider myself a Beatles Baby because their music was a soundtrack to my growing up. There were so many different aspects to what the Beatles did that it was virtually impossible not to find some part of it you liked. Back then, popular culture was far more popular than it is now because there was so little choice. There was one legal pop music radio station and a couple of pirate ships, and only three TV channels, so everybody heard and saw the same things – everybody knew all the same records and practically everybody watched the same TV programmes. Like if you went to football on Boxing Day, all anybody was talking about was the Morecambe & Wise Christmas show, because *everybody* had watched it; similarly, so many pop songs were turned into terrace songs as soon as they came out, as *everybody* watched *Top of the Pops* and knew them. My love of pop songs of that era definitely help me to recall events that happened or things I did, just remember the music that went with whatever it was, and a lot of the songs I was keen on were white pop songs.

Of course I watched *Top of the Pops*, but I really remember *Ready, Steady Go!*, which had more R&B on it and definitely had a mod attitude. Radio Luxembourg was better than the BBC's Radio 1. Although it could be picked up on my dad's gram, as we weren't allowed to touch that I'd listen to it on somebody else's transistor radio when I was out. One of my favourite songs from that time was the title track from the movie *To Sir With Love*. I had a *big* schoolboy crush on Lulu, who to me had total mod styling – the hair, the dresses, the dancing. It's still one of my favourite songs and Sidney Poitier is my all-time top black actor. Through the 1980s and '90s, because I could afford to by then, I used to style myself on him – suits, clothes, haircut, all of that – he was the original black mod. When we went into the 1970s, quite a few of my mates got into Bowie or Elton John or ELO, but I liked the more soulful side of glam rock or the real anthemic tunes that were just there to make you dance and could be adapted as terrace songs. The first big record I remember from somewhere I began going regularly was by Steam, 'Na Na Hey Hey Kiss Him Goodbye'. I used to love that record, and I still play that to white audiences and they absolutely love it too. I play it with impunity because I remember it new. I didn't buy it back then because I had so much else to spend my money on, but I loved it. Nowadays I play all of my favourite rock and pop songs – I don't care, I think I've earned the right to do that!

Pretty soon I wanted to move on from places like the Park Hotel, which were basically rooms behind pubs that played music once a week, so I started going to the Hammersmith Palais on a Thursday night. I was fifteen going on sixteen when I went up there, and although it was a big, famous nightclub it was also my local disco because it was just a 266 bus ride away. Going to the Palais gave me a real sense of achievement: I was still at school, I was quite small and I looked very young, yet I still got in! It was also quite a watershed in terms of my going-out experience; it felt really grown up.

In reality, the Palais was a real logs disco, but I absolutely loved it. 'Logs discos' were what we used to call the white boy clubs, the Hitman and Her-type discos of their day, and the 'logs' were just general knockabout kids who didn't care about the music or dancing, who were really there for the drinking and the fighting. You wouldn't even want to chirp the girls you'd find in there. There were usually about three or four fights a night – all of a sudden you'd hear screaming and glasses breaking, see tables overturned and there'd be a rush of black and white kids to one end of the dancefloor. I tried to keep away from all of that: basically, I was petrified. I could deal with it on a Saturday afternoon at football, maybe, because you could see it all in front of you and you know it's mostly handbags, just goading and posturing and abuse, but this was properly nasty. I've always hated violence in pubs or clubs or in confined spaces. In fact, I'm not sure how long I would have carried on going to the Palais, because its glamour soon wore off. However, I was about to move up another level in the clubbing world, as within weeks of going to the Palais I was starting to hear about all these other clubs through John Henry and Clive Clarke.

The first place they told me about was West Kensington Bird's Nest – the Bird's Nests were a chain of discos owned by the brewery Watneys and attached to their pubs. They were all over London: Paddington, West Hampstead, Waterloo, Muswell Hill ... This one had changed management and was now called Hunters, but you had to be twenty-one to get in and I was petrified because I looked about fourteen. The first time I went there I got knocked back at the door, and it was crushing! I saw all my mates get in because they were all quite tall and their Ravel platform shoes gave them another few inches! I felt so embarrassed that I wouldn't go back for weeks, then I thought about how Clive was getting in – he'd only been knocked back once as far as I knew – yet he was a little bit shorter than me, so I thought I'd try again. I went with Clive and two girls from school, who were quite tall, and I was at the door *teetering* on my Ravels when the bouncer asked me how old I was. I was dreading this and I'd been practising saying it in my head on the way up there, as there was nothing worse than hesitating, like you don't know how old you are! 'Twenty-one!' I replied. Yes, I said it quickly, but I was so nervous my voice, which wasn't the deepest at that point, went up a couple of octaves! He said, 'Go on!' I'd been let in! I'd passed for twenty-one! It was probably because I looked right, i.e. I wasn't dressed like a log or a little kid.

When I got in there I thought the music was good, all soul, pretty funky, no reggae, and when I looked over at the deejay booth I heard, 'Norman? What you doing in here?' It was a kid who had been two school years above me, therefore couldn't have been any older than eighteen or nineteen, and *he was the deejay in there*! I never would have believed that if I hadn't seen it. He was an old skinhead, an old suedehead and always a dickhead! Now he's playing the music, good music too, in this London club! All that's going through my mind is how you had to be twenty-one to even get in, he's only two years older than me and he's deejaying! Wow! That's when I realised the key to it all was familiarity and confidence. The next time I went up there I looked at the same bouncer that let me in the week before, strolled up like I ought to be there, he recognised me and gave me a nod as I went in. The others would have noticed this, so I was becoming a 'face'. I got confident enough to go back regularly, seemingly secure that I'd get in, but when you least expect it . . .

Out of the blue one Saturday night I was told 'Not tonight, mate!', and it was still just as crushing! Thankfully it only happened a few times. Once I spent three hours outside the club with Brian Beaton, who was a Grove boy and became the rapper Dizzi Heights, and Danny John-Jules, the dancer who played Cat in *Red Dwarf* and Dwayne in *Death in Paradise*, and they had both been knocked back too. One thing I learned at Hunters was never argue with the bouncers if you don't get in, because then they remember you as the guy they didn't let in, and you'll never get in!

For while, first on a Sunday then a Saturday, Hunters was the cool place to be. The music was good and it was where people met up, little crews and posses from all over London, to find out where the house parties were that night. That's why we would wait outside there if we got knocked back, because of where you'd be going *afterwards*. Every week there'd be two or three parties you'd hear about in Hunters and everybody would pack into cars and go, sometimes you'd go to all three of them, one after the other. In the mid-70s, it changed its name to Beagles and started to turn into a bit of a logs disco, but by then the trendsetters and fashionistas had moved on anyway.

chapter twenty-one: suburban soul clubs/northern soul

The real change in my raving horizons came about in spring and summer of 1976 when a few of us bought our first cars. I didn't get my first wheels, a Mini, until the next year, but as enough of the others did it became a case of 'get in somebody else's car, will travel!' It meant Bournemouth or Brighton on bank holidays and opened up a whole new world of soul music to us, in the suburbs and home counties. I was an avid reader of *Blues & Soul* magazine by then; it was the only place you could get information about American record releases, which I used to buy at the record shop Contempo, owned by the same chap who owned *Blues & Soul*. The magazine was full of adverts for soul nights and clubs out in the sticks, Scamps in Hemel Hempstead ... Scamps in Sutton ... the California Ballroom in Dunstable ... the Bali Hai in Streatham ... Twickenham Bird's Nest ... So off we'd go, sometimes it would be a convoy of cars, other times just me and maybe a couple of others in my Mini, because I went to them all. I was a serial clubber by then and going all over the place – Surrey, Essex, Buckinghamshire, Hertfordshire, with a circuit that took me to a different club each night. The music was usually a bit sanitised, but there were millions of girls at these places and none of the dancing peacocks you'd get in London – they wouldn't get let in because the management thought they didn't buy enough drinks.

It was quite funny when we saw the adverts for the clubs in *Blues & Soul*, or the reports they'd write, as so many of them had pictures of dancefloors crowded with all these afro'd heads bobbing, then when we got there we were often the only black kids there. The Goldmine in Canvey Island in Essex was a real case in point for that – I'd heard so much about it as a top, top soul club, and the deejay Chris Hill was great and had his own page in *Blues & Soul*, but it was nearly all white people. I shouldn't really have been so surprised, as it was deepest Essex! It had taken me ages to persuade my mates to go up there, and although most of them weren't impressed – if I'm honest the music wasn't all that – to me going to that club was another milestone.

I used to go to Northern soul clubs as well, places like Blackpool Mecca and the Wigan Casino; these were places I'd read about for years in *Blues & Soul*, then I saw a BBC documentary about the Wigan Casino and I knew I had to go. A few weeks after I got my car it was the first long distance trip I made. Five of us went up in my little white Mini Cooper: three black guys, a mixed race guy and one white guy, Mark, who shared the driving with me. That was an adventure in itself, but we found the place, arriving at one o'clock in the morning and having to queue outside until the place opened at two – it reminded me of being at a football match, getting there early to queue. There were all these coaches with places like Gloucester or Carlisle or Manchester on the fronts, pulling up and letting people off outside to line up. I'd never seen anything like this at a club before.

I remember us getting really nervous when we came over to the queue because there were no black people in it at all, and we looked so completely different from anybody there. We'd all come up in our West End soulboy gear, probably making a bit of extra effort because it was such a big road trip – I was wearing bottle green Fiorucci cords, my first pair of Fioruccis, which had cost me £29, a small fortune in 1977. I suppose I was showing off, I'd always fancied myself as a bit of a dandy, now up here I was a soulboy, a London soulboy, and we had standards! But what we find is a bunch of guys in cap-sleeved t-shirts, like what we'd moved on from in 1974! It was little wonder one of the girls in the queue went up to one of my mates and told him she'd never seen a gay black person before! I realised we must have looked ridiculously camp, cowboy boots and all of that – so London!

We got in and it was like getting into a different world. This was a time when we were going to clubs like Global Village and Crackers, and on first look this was like a throwback to the very early 1970s. Completely different music, completely different vibe, and I thought '*Wow!*' At first I didn't under-stand it, but that's what intrigued me and I quickly learned to love it. My mates were less convinced and that first time they were really digging me out: 'Norman ... You seriously drive all that way for *this*?' I figured the music wasn't what we were used to, but it was still soul, so let's make the best of it. Then I was watching them trying to fire into the girls and getting knocked back all the time – none of the girls up there would even talk to them because all they were interested in was dancing and swirling their skirts around. My lot wouldn't stop moaning. 'The music's shit, the girls don't want to know, and what the fuck is that smell?' It was the poppers they were doing – it took me ages to work that one out because the only smell I was used to in clubs was weed.

There were two rooms up there, the main room with a younger crowd where all the girls were, and this side room, Mr M's, and it was full of guys with long sideburns and long leather coats, older guys. They were the pill dealers, and doing a roaring trade from what we saw. In fact, we felt a bit intimidated going there, although we had nothing at all to fear. As soon as they heard us speak they were offering to buy us drinks and were amazed that we were there: 'What? You cockneys drove all the way up here?' I just fronted it out and told them we'd been into it for ages, or at least I had.

That was my first time at Wigan and it wasn't always easy for me to persuade my mates to go back there with me. I was happy to go by myself, but if I couldn't get anybody to share the petrol I'd hitch or bunk the train because I was broke all the time. I loved the vibe up there because those Northern soul kids were passionate about their music and I could always relate to that – they weren't there for drinking or pulling, just for the music. The poppers and the pills weren't even to get them off their heads, but to keep them dancing for longer. I got to love the music too. Not all of it was to my taste, but it was a new experience for me and I felt I was learning something. I wasn't worried that there were no black people there. In fact, I always seemed to find myself doing something or getting involved with something where there were no or very few other black people – when I first used to go to football very few black boys used to go there; when I used to ride with the scooter club there was only one other black guy . . . I was never afraid to go outside of my peer group and do something they wouldn't.

I used to go up to the Blackpool Mecca or the all-dayers in Manchester quite a lot, much more than I went to Wigan, and I preferred it because the kids looked much more like me. There were quite a few black kids on that scene and they were wearing what we called London fashions – you'd see kids in carpenter jeans and plastic sandals. They were a younger crowd and the girls were more amenable, which made all the difference as it meant we could get amongst them – my mates were usually happy to go up there! The locals loved that we'd come all the way up from London on a Sunday, get in the queue with them for an all-dayer that began at two in the afternoon and finished at ten, then sometimes stay up with them and go on to another club, bleaching – that is, staying out all night – and going back down Monday morning. I didn't really care because I had no work.

Music-wise I felt we fitted in much better there too, it was a soundtrack much like ours but *slightly* different inasmuch as they had the same albums as we did in London, but their deejays were playing different tracks. The music was new and forward-looking, which I liked, so I found the whole scene up there fresh and exciting. Apparently there was a schism between these 'modernists' in Manchester and the other Northern soul tribes at Wigan and elsewhere.

Often I'd go to the northern clubs after football. There

was a period when I was going to practically every Spurs away game so after the match I'd stay up north and go to a club. The first time I went to Blackpool Mecca I went by myself after a match and then told my mates about it when I came back. It was when Spurs were in the old Second Division and we were playing Blackpool. I'd read all about this place in *Blues & Soul*, so when I went up on the coach for the game I took a change of clothes in my duffel bag. My mate Keith, who organised the coach, asked me what was in it and I told him I was staying up there. I'm not sure he believed me, and after the match I picked up my bag and got off as everybody was getting on to go back to London. 'Why?' ... 'I'm going clubbing, I'm going to Blackpool Mecca.' ... '*What?*'

After I got off the coach I felt I was taking my life in my hands! A couple of hours before I'd been an away football fan and there was a really good chance that something kicked off at the game. Now I had to kill a few hours in the town. Although I would have been on the fringes of whatever it was, my footballing philosophy was always, 'Come five-thirty that's all over, let's get to the record shop or let's get ready to go clubbing!' I didn't drink so I wasn't going to go into a pub and carry on any rivalry, but not everybody thought like me, so I knew to be safe I had to stay away from pubs and the city centre. I found myself a café or an amusement arcade, then as soon as the club opened joined the queue to get in. That was usually how I handled it every time I stayed on after a Spurs game, and through football I went up to Wigan, Manchester, Cleethorpes, Bristol, Lincoln ... all over the place. Once or twice I persuaded a couple of my Spurs mates to stay with me, but usually I was on my own.

part four:
new york

chapter twenty-two: new york arrival

When I walked into Acton travel centre in 1979 and bought my ticket to New York I was *so* excited. It was one of those red and orange multi-layered affairs with the carbon paper in it, and I walked home staring at it, barely believing I was going to New York. 'Book your passage', as my mum and dad would say, I had just booked my flight! The first time I would leave the country, the first time I would go on an aeroplane.

People I knew in London were always travelling to and from the West Indies but as a dedicated soul boy, America was the foundation of so much of my world and New York was the centre of all of that. So much of how I imagined black culture was New York, what I'd seen in films and on TV and as for music . . . it was Mecca. I could always understand why people made pilgrimages to certain places – like Detroit, the home of Motown, or New Orleans for jazz – for me it was New York for the soul and funk I loved, and *then* I'd go to Detroit or Chicago or New Orleans.

This came after a couple of pretty bleak years when I'd been unemployed or just doing little bits and pieces, but I had a young son so more recently was knuckling down with my job at Quaker Oats. I'd opened my first bank account, at the Midland in Southall, I was budgeting – another first – and I was single-minded about saving to go to America. My dad was keen for me to go; at the time he was making louder and louder noises about us emigrating as most of his family were there, but my mum was adamant this wasn't going to happen. They said because I was the oldest boy I should go and see what was what and then come back and report, so I was on a bit of a family mission too. My dad had been talking to my uncles and aunts and cousins over there, most of whom I hadn't seen for years, quite a few I'd never even met, and everyone was excited about me coming over. The only hard thing for me was saying goodbye to Mark, my son, who was just two, and his mum was quite distressed because I'd never been away before, but I was looking forward to how this could help me develop into what I wanted to be when I came back.

When the day arrived and my dad gave me a lift to the airport, the flight went by in a bit of a blur and suddenly I'm through customs at JFK with my Uncle Leo there to meet me on this blisteringly hot day. It was one of those 'if somebody pinches me I'll wake up' moments! Going through my head, on some sort of loop, was that line from Stevie Wonder's 'Living for the City' – 'New York, skyscrapers and *everything*!' I even said it out loud to my uncle! He was completely brilliant, as before we went back home he gave me a tour of the city on these outer roads and the approach to Manhattan made the view of the buildings look absolutely spectacular: this was the first time I'd seen it and it seriously did not disappoint. We drove all the way round the perimeter of Manhattan Island, with him pointing out the different places: 'This is the East Village' ... 'Now we've crossed into Harlem' ... 'Now we're on the West Side ...' Then we crossed one of the bridges into Brooklyn, and he's pointing out places to me that I'd heard about so much that I felt like I knew them. He drove us past Yankee Stadium in the Bronx ... It was a good three hours before we got back to my aunt's house, where all my uncles and aunts and quite a few cousins were waiting for me. It was fantastic.

I met my younger cousin Wayne, he's passed now, who was a real boffin, a technical genius of a sound engineer who could fix or build practically anything to do with a sound system. He was the New York equivalent of Joey, while cousin Terry, who was a couple of years older than me, was my counterpart. He was in the US Coastguard and he'd taken leave to hang out with me and we hit it off immediately. He was a total muso like me, but whereas I was a bit more happy-go-lucky but still culturally aware, Terry was a militant brother and very pro-black. He was a deep thinker and had deep views of the racism that went on, he would try and school me: 'Don't trust these kinds of white people ...' which basically meant, 'Don't trust *any* kind of white people.' It wasn't like I didn't know, but here in New York at that moment I was naive, I was the equivalent of 'fresh off the boat', and I felt like Caribbeans must have felt when they arrived in England for the first time.

Terry gave me some good tips about navigating New York and the area we were in – Brooklyn – which was really fortunate because I wouldn't listen to my aunts, who would try and instil the fear of God into me: 'Don't go here ...

don't do that ... watch out for these people ... don't speak to anybody ... ' I'd just get exasperated: 'Aunt Daphne, I'm not a child! I might look young but I'm twenty-one going on twenty-two – a big man! I can take care of myself in the city!' The truth was I might have thought I was streetwise, but I was assuming it would be like England, where I might have been a bit wary but still essentially accepting of everybody. Terry was close to my age and very cool, so I'd take notice of him. Very early in my stay there I came out of my aunt's house, walking to the subway, and I saw a black panhandler, begging. He literally lived on that corner and it was the first time I'd ever seen a black homeless person. I would come to pass him several times a day, but that first time I gave him some cash and my cousin went mad! 'Don't you ever pull out money in broad daylight and give to people on the street!'

OK, Lesson One learned – my kindness and generosity of spirit will be easily abused in a place like this. And he was right. There were eyes on me that recognised I was a stranger and some people out there are unscrupulous, because all of a sudden I'm surrounded by all sorts of people and it's, 'Hey brother ... Hey man ... ' In the beginning it took real willpower not to revert to my natural English politeness and answer; I had to focus on the ground in front of me and plough on to the station.

Within a week of arriving I had done all the touristy things – I went up the Empire State Building, I went to Grand Central Station, I went to Times Square, I walked down Broadway and 42nd Street, I went and stood outside Studio 54, I was going to go and stand outside CBGB in the Bowery, but I never got there. I walked all over Manhattan, from the Battery to Harlem, loving the wide streets and just looking at buildings and people and things, it was like being in the movies I used to watch. I loved Chelsea, it had a quaintness about it almost like Dickensian England. I remember staring up at the famous Chelsea Hotel, I loved all of that area, especially because the clubs I was interested in were around there. This was exactly my idea of a holiday. I'd never been on one before and every year after that I went back to New York – I never went anywhere else, that was it.

The one place I didn't go through was Central Park. At that time it was *dread*, there were rapes and murders in the middle of the day and I was too scared. I'd seen that film *The Warriors* before I left London, and if the thought of the street gangs wasn't enough, every night *Eyewitness News* carried a story about people getting shot or stabbed or something terrible happening in Central Park. It was the only time I listened to my aunts and uncles, and the closest I got to it was walking *round* it because I wanted to see the brownstones on the posh Upper East Side.

However, I ignored my relatives when they tried to warn me off 42nd Street at night. They were telling me it was a real centre of sleaze and a respectable London boy had no business at all down there. That was like a red rag to a bull. Two o'clock in the morning I'm sneaking out, off to 42nd Street. It was an amazing experience – like Lou Reed's 'Walk on the Wild Side' come to life! I see hustlers of every description (' ... *Come here man, hold this, man* ...'), I see dice games, I see card sharps doing Follow the Lady on packing chests, I see pimps and hookers who all look so exaggerated they're almost cartoonish, I see lady boys and boy ladies!

That Whodini record was so true, the freaks really do come out at night and this was the ultimate freak show. I was fascinated, it was like being in the Rocky Horror Show for a hot summer night, everything I imagined it would be.

One of my biggest thrills was standing in front of the Blue Note jazz club in Greenwich Village and thinking about all the jazz greats who had played in there – I totally understood why so many London tourists stand outside Ronnie Scott's! I was fascinated by the Village itself. With all its little artisan shops and cafes, it seemed worlds removed from the common perception of what Manhattan was. Then at the bottom of Sixth Avenue, Avenue of Americas, there was a basketball court behind a wire fence, where there would be some fantastic games going on, faster and more intense than practically anything you'd see in the NBA. All black boys, really athletic, really skilful and some of the cussing was so funny – from the players and the audience! I found out later that it was a very famous street basketball venue called The Cage, where the standards are really high and the action isn't for the faint-hearted. I'd end up down there most afternoons, just watching, that is, not trying to hustle a game! Of course I'd be keeping an eye on the sneakers they were wearing too, because if I wasn't in a record shop I was in a sneaker shop.

Watching that basketball was the same sort of street culture vibe I used to enjoy when I'd come across body poppers and break dancers, who were putting down the cardboard or pieces of lino all over Manhattan. To me this was fantastic, I've always loved street performers and the ideas of kids hustling their talent to make some money, but this was hip hop culture in the very beginning. I had never seen it before, I had never even read about it and now I was watching it establish itself – I felt privileged to see some of those kids. I was checking out their sneakers too, because I loved shopping for the New York street fashions that hadn't made it to London yet and I would walk for hours searching out shops. I'd be on a mission, with the same single-minded attitude I'd have if I were on a record hunt.

My only regrets about being a New York City Tourist on that first trip was I dropped my camera and broke it, so I had no visual record of the amazing things I saw, and I never went to a Broadway show. I still haven't and I still want to. What I also regretted was eating pizza. I'd never had it before, in fact I think this was the first time I'd ever *seen* a pizza. I didn't like it all and I never went back! I felt vindicated with that decision pretty quickly, as just around the corner from my aunt's was this pizza joint serving pizzas the size of wagon wheels, with this cheese that looked like plastic. I used to watch these enormously fat people scoffing them down in broad daylight and to this day I've never eaten another pizza. Not that it mattered during that trip, as almost immediately I discovered Nathan's Hotdogs, fifty cents, and White Castle Burgers – little mini burgers – and as somebody who'd barely eaten a Wimpy I saw McDonald's for the first time! I was in heaven.

I thought the subway was fantastic – the hubbub, the noise, the heat, the smells, much more exciting than London's tube trains. I'd read about the graffiti on the subway trains and used to wonder why anybody would do that, but once I saw them in real life spray-painted like that it made sense, it was a really powerful statement of who these artists were and where they came from. I remember going down the subway at Utica Avenue thinking '*Wow!*' As well as the sight of the trains, I used to love the smell. I'm not sure it would be to everybody's taste but there's a certain smell of the New York subway, and every time I get a sniff of it I'm taken straight back to that first visit in 1979. What fascinated me was that all the trains were numbered or given letters – the number 2 train . . . the D train! *Wicked!* Suddenly these places made sense to me and then in the early days of hip hop and rap, when all these groups were naming themselves after their precinct or their street or the train they rode on, I understood why and I loved it. This pride in where they came from was something that Americans were really good at, and although it could seem naff it's something we could do with a bit more of in the UK.

I'd always bunk the fares to get into Manhattan – it was only a fifty-cent token, but practically everybody used to jump the barriers so doing it made me feel like a proper New Yorker! What hit me the first time I got on a train was there were no white people at all in the carriage. It's packed, full of brothers and sisters all going to work in the city, and that was when I became very aware of how the different areas of the city were so rigidly divided into ethnic groups. Perhaps it's less so now, but this was forty years ago. Also, they were going to work in Manhattan and the majority were dressed for the office. That was another thing that made an impact on me – so many white-collar and middle-class black people in the same place, it wasn't anything you'd see in London at that time. When the train goes under the tunnel and just as we get to the south end of Manhattan, towards Wall

Street, there's white people and people of other colours getting on the train. Then by the time I get to 42nd Street it's mixed – the first few times I experienced this I thought it was amazing.

About the only bad thing that happened to me in that first couple of weeks was I got a migraine that went on for days, which was entirely my own fault! I was jet-lagged but I couldn't sleep, so I didn't go to bed and went round the clock, which wasn't difficult as there was so much to distract me. I had the radio on all the time – *black radio*! I'd never heard anything like that before. All I'm used to is Tony Blackburn on Radio 1 and the best I can hope for is a couple of hours of Greg Edwards on a Saturday night, but over here there's sensory overload. WBLS with Frankie Crocker, there's mix shows going on, there's reggae here, there's Latin there, there's soca ... *woooahh*!!! Then there's twenty-four-hour TV! Turn on the TV and there's a million channels – I can't go to bed! And I was fascinated by the adverts – they were all about selling medicines! If you'd watched American television in the 1970s you'd think everybody had haemorrhoids! I remember thinking this is either a nation of hypochondriacs or people who are dying – we never had such a thing in England, you were lucky if you got an advert for aspirin! The other thing I noticed was how American adverts were so hard sell. Our adverts were witty and articulate and used to draw you in, but these just got straight to the point, 'How can I separate you from your money? As quickly as possible!' I found it really amusing and used to think, 'You'd never get away with this in England.'

chapter twenty-three: black culture as everyday

I had never been in a black-only environment before, and that blew my mind. My aunt lived in Crown Heights, most of my family members lived around there, and there were hardly any white people. It was a real black melting pot of all different types: there were African Americans, there were black people from all over the Caribbean – it was the first time I'd ever met Haitians – and some Africans. I loved it, everybody with different stories and cultures all living side by side. Although it was virtually an all-black neighbourhood, it wasn't what most people would think of as a ghetto. Yes, there was crime and people had a ridiculous amount of locks on their doors and bars on their windows, but it wasn't run down, it was mostly middle class and skilled working people, which was something else I'd seen so rarely in London – large pockets of middle-class black people who were obviously proud to be black.

I was overwhelmed by the fact that the businesses in the area were nearly all black owned – as well as the barber and the black bookshop, there were the grocery stores, the newsstands and the diners. I really took all of that on board because I'd never been exposed to anything like that – where I had come from white people ran everything, then the Asians ran the corner shops. Here, the professional people in the area were black too, lawyers, doctors, accountants and such like, which left a deep impression, as I'd never seen any black role models who owned and ran businesses. I had always thought we were capable of that, but by that time in London I hadn't seen any evidence of it. This was like discovering New York's black radio – it seemed so far removed from what was on offer in London that I had never really imagined it could be like that. Immersing myself in that for the four months that I was there left me stunned. I absolutely loved it.

What really interested me when I was walking around, especially in the neighbourhood and up in Harlem, were these little black bookshops and little black record shops that were full of black American history and artefacts. I would go into them and look at books and artworks that totally fired up my imagination. Books that you'd never find in England: obscure magazines and stuff from the early 1960s and '70s like Black Panther literature, illegal bootlegs of rare records, or dodgy live recordings or albums of speeches by black leaders. Straight away I'd buy the records, and I still have a sizeable collection.

I was really taken with some of the everyday stuff like figurines and ornaments depicting black people, or the more mundane things like biscuit tins or shopping bags or fridge magnets that were decorated with black scenes. These were general domestic things that represented black life, but you would never see that at home and the fact they were so ordinary was brilliant. It wasn't making a big deal out of celebrating blackness, it just *was*. I was very, very aware of how this almost casual approach to it made you feel properly part of something – like the amount of black faces that were on television or adverts on the subway, or that you could buy Afro Sheen in any drugstore and didn't have to hunt it down. This was all a bit awe-inspiring for an English kid born in Grove and brought up in Acton. I've still got my Malcolm X figurine I bought in a local bookshop. I bought two at the time and lost one, but, thankfully, the other has survived the last forty-odd years.

There was a downside to all this, or at least there was in my mind. Compared to London so much of this was great, but the level of black on black crime and violence was staggering. I'd talk to my cousins about it when they would ask me what I thought of New York. I'd tell them that I couldn't live with the fact that so many people had guns, that there were guards on the school gates and that everything had to be locked down with chains and enormous padlocks. I'd asked my uncle about that last one and he told me, 'In this country people will t'ief anything if you don't lock it down.' The suspicion that black people have of other people there – black and white – was a bit unnerving in the beginning, maybe because I came from a multicultural situation at home.

I loved New York and I realised that New York was not America and America was not New York – but as impressive as so much of it was, I knew I couldn't live there and I certainly wouldn't want to bring my family up out there. That's when it dawned on me that where I lived in London, how I lived and how I was brought up to be accepting of everybody, with a punky open-mindedness, was probably as good as it gets. After my first trip I began to make the comparisons and thought, 'What would I do if I went to America?' I'd end up working for the post office or on the subway, but by then I'm harbouring ambitions of becoming a deejay and after that trip I quickly realised that England would be the only place to do that, once I got past the gatekeepers that are there to keep brothers and sisters out. No doubt I had been inspired by what I'd witnessed in America to do something creative, but equally I was motivated to do it in London.

chapter twenty-four: buying records

The most fantastic aspect of being in New York was something that kept me going back year after year: it was, of course, buying records. Coming from London, where black culture among young people was largely Caribbean, it was fantastic for this soulboy to be in a place where what he loved was the default setting. Sometimes I used to get so excited about music and records that I felt the New Yorkers didn't fully appreciate what they had!

Everything crystallised for me in that moment I arrived. While I was enjoying meeting and greeting my relatives, a big part of me was thinking, 'Right, I've put my bag down, now I want to get out of here, get into Manhattan and buy some records!' When I did get to go out, I didn't even make it as far as the subway because everybody's got records for sale, regardless of what their business was. *Literally.* I go into a barbershop round the corner from my aunt, he's got records for sale! The pizza place across the road, they're selling records! The stall on the sidewalk selling umbrellas and jeans and stuff, *he's got records there*! And of course they're all American releases, some stuff was new, some stuff was old and some stuff I didn't even know, but I knew the labels or the producer or the artist, and they're just being sold out of boxes on their counters! In London I'd have to travel seven miles from Acton up to Contempo to get what I wanted; here are what to me are pre-release singles everywhere, there's albums, in their shrink-wrapped cellophane *everywhere*. It's like I've died and gone to heaven!

I was never just a clubber – musically I was a boffin, a collector, so now I'm like a kid in a sweetshop! Where do I start? *Aaaaarrggh!!* Again, sensorial overload! The end of the 1970s was an absolutely brilliant time for black American music and there was so much of it being made, so there was always such a lot of choice, which was why so many places sold records. I can still vividly remember those moments when I discovered those shops and I was so over-stimulated, I didn't know what I was looking for! But at an exchange rate of two dollars sixty-eight cents to the pound, I could afford to take a few chances! 'Dollar ninety-nine for this album? Yeah. I'll take it!' . . . 'Fifty cents each for these singles? Great, I'll have that and I'll have that.' Then as I had loads of uncles and aunts, and it was my first trip, everybody kept giving me cash! Fifty dollars here, a hundred dollars there, pressing these bills into my hand with, 'Enjoy your trip, nephew!' . . . 'Here, nephew, hold this!' I was loaded and I became a standing joke, because every day I used to come back with bags of records and they used to tease me relentlessly about it.

Some of the big downtown record stores were like musical department stores, with music on several floors and a selection of soul and funk like I'd never seen before. But for me it wasn't all about the stuff that was easily available to everybody. As often as going to those Manhattan temples, I'd spend many a day – all day – in tiny shops, in dingy basements, picking up stuff that might have slipped under the radar or maybe been forgotten about. It was like gold dust for me – literally. This was music that English shops weren't stocking, yet I knew from my experiences people still wanted this relatively obscure stuff and I could sell it for a handy profit back in London. Almost by accident, going to New York turned me into a low level but very specialist independent record dealer. That first trip I hadn't really got wise to that, and for me it was all about plugging the holes in and building up my collection, so although I took back a shedload of records I kept most of them for myself. The next time it's different, I don't need to keep so many, but I'm seeing all these records and I'm thinking, 'I can't leave them there!' In the end I'd buy them all.

Once I'd got them home, because I knew a lot of people who deejayed I'd be straight down to Soho or standing outside Bluebird Records just off the Edgware Road asking, 'So what do you want?' I knew all the titles I had brought back with me, so if I had it I'd say, 'Yeah, I can get that for you by next week', like I had an organisation behind me! If I didn't have it, I'd always say I could get it, although because I only went over once a year, often I'd have to look thoughtful and say 'Yeah, but that might take some time.' Because these were off-the-grid records, not the new releases they could get at Contempo or Bluebird, I knew they'd wait. As I had a memory like a muthafucka, I could remember every title and every album sleeve picture, I could remember where I saw it and I *knew* when I went back there next year it would still be in that dusty, ratty basement. This was pre-internet, so if a deejay or a collector wanted a particular record they had to come to somebody like me, and I started to earn quite a reputation for getting the impossible records that no one could find.

The first time I went to New York, I was there for four months because I had no job to come back to in London, but after that it would be about two months, usually June and July, sometimes into the beginning of August, but always sure to be back for Carnival. What this meant was that when I played Carnival, I was sure of some brand new music *box fresh*, still sealed! Naively I'd play this stuff straight away, with my, 'You ain't heard this one before' mentality, and often it wouldn't go down too well because the records were too new and unfamiliar. Unlike the traditional reggae crowds, who *demanded* new music therefore expected the sound systems to have dub plate after dub plate, the big crowds on the soul scene tended to want what they knew. Sometimes it could take them a year or more to get into records I started playing on my return from New York! However, this worked out well for me in the long run, especially after I got my radio show on Kiss FM.

Because the widespread demand for my new music wasn't immediately there, it meant the importers and the shops wouldn't have picked up on the records either. When I, or other black pirate stations, aired these for the first time there'd be some smart kids out there who'd want to buy them, only to be told in the record shops, 'Nah, mate. We never had that, or if we did we only had a couple of copies.'

I'd overhear conversations like that all the time and say, 'You want one of them?', because the chances were I'd brought home more than one. 'Give me your number, I can get it for you in a couple of weeks, but I'll want X for it.' Then I'd come back and I'd sell them the records.

I started to realise how records I played first would gain street currency on the London soul scene: they would become popular through our house parties, then make their way on to the black pirate radio playlists. Higher up the soul circuit food chain the deejays are white, but in order to maintain their credibility they need these records and put the word out through their black mates, 'Can you get us one of those . . . ? I lost my copy!' That old chestnut used to come out all the time – they'd always already got it but somehow could never find it! I quickly discovered which high profile deejays were doing that because I'd approach their mates with, 'You want a copy of that? I'll sell it to you', then wait and, sure enough, in a couple of weeks the deejay would be playing it. I'd take great delight in thinking, 'I know exactly where you got that!' There were a lot of big name deejays who had to do that in order to save their credibility because we'd been banging those records in our parties and dance-halls for ages. They didn't know these records or even some of these artists, but they'd sit there telling their audience they were playing it a year ago and only just found it again! I used to almost track records I'd sold because I knew where they were going to end up. I'd say to my brother, 'Watch this, in a couple of weeks you'll hear CJ Carlos on the radio playing these particular records', and sure enough we'd listen and I'd be going, 'Yeah, that's one of mine! . . . So's that . . . '

The other aspect of it I used to love was helping my fellow black deejays by making sure they got this music first. I was quite a militant brother around that time and was all about giving back to my peer group because I realised I couldn't do this thing on my own.

chapter twenty-five: clubs & club culture

I was fully aware of the big clubs in New York – Studio 54 was the biggest on that first trip. I would stand outside but never plucked up the courage to try to get in because I was scared of getting knocked back. I looked so young that I always had my passport in my pocket – you had to be twenty-one to get in anywhere and although I was, I looked about fifteen and was always being challenged. I'd stand across the road at three or four in the morning and watch people arrive or get in line – never before had I seen door staff going up and down the queue picking who was going to come in. It was, I thought, such a New York thing to do! While on the one hand I was fascinated by the comings and goings, on the other I found it all a bit naff – which sort of sums up a lot of what I came across on that first trip! While I kind of regret never having been bold enough to try and get in to Studio 54 just to see what it was like, I consoled myself pretty quickly by thinking it was really only the equivalent of the Talk of the Town in Piccadilly on a Saturday night, or Tramp in Jermyn Street on any night – I certainly wouldn't go into those places just to strike something off a list.

Terry was never with me on those occasions and when I told him about it, the first thing he said was 'What do you want to go down there for?' He schooled me about their door policy, how they frowned on young black guys who weren't famous, and told me there was nothing for me down there. *'It's nonsense!'* he'd tell me in no uncertain terms. Terry was so well-connected, he went everywhere and knew everybody – he'd even been to a few of David Mancuso's loft parties. I didn't have a clue who this was and Terry explained to me about this guy just over the bridge on Broadway who ran these exclusive, invite-only parties at his loft apartment. Terry told me I wouldn't have been into that crowd at all, although I would have known a lot of the music, which was always cutting edge. He said he wasn't overwhelmed but the invitations to them were so coveted that if you got one *you went*. I think that would have been enough to put me off and in later years I got to know quite a lot of people who did go, and I'm so not part of that crowd. This very New York In Crowd, completely up its own arse. This was all pretty much confirmed to me by those big name New York deejays like Tony Humphries and David Morales, who became good friends of mine over the years, but they also told me that if you did get an invite the last thing you were going to do was turn it down!

In later years I went to a few parties in loft spaces and big studios, which were fascinating, but I couldn't help thinking they were all a bit sub-Mancuso: pretentious without even the cachet of being the best. I went to most of those big name clubs, too. I went to the Tunnel, I went to Limelight, I went to Nells, and at that time I really thought they were all pretty much of a muchness, although I became a bit of a Paradise Garage regular in later years. I loved the experience of going, but the atmosphere and the people weren't anything too special. What they all had, without exception, were sound systems to die for. That was a lot of what I was going to them for: first to hear what music was being played, and then what equipment it was being played on. It was the sound system operator in me – I'd stand there amazed, 'How are they making this music sound so good?'

I had really mixed feelings about New York club culture – the more mainstream clubs, both black and white. I'm in America and I'm hearing the very latest stuff, in the clubs and parties that are the absolute context of where it came from, which to me was very important to the experience. *Wow!* I'm getting properly excited. Then at the same time I used to think these clubs were a bit naff, or at least they were compared to our clubs. My first problem with them was they weren't mixed, it was as if they'd been racially segregated! The first time I went to black parties out there, they were like funk versions of our reggae blues parties: exclusively black and there was always that edge that something might happen. I came from a mixed music and club culture background: black, white, Asian – everybody – in a kind of fun element. I found the American party thing quite stilted, especially the straight parties – they never really let go. At the time ours was underpinned by the pill culture, so we'd lose all our British reserve and go mad, but while the American parties were great up to a point, they never tipped over. Their parties had a controlled way about them that suppressed any madness – Americans simply don't get, '*Oi Oi! Let's 'ave it!*'

The age thing didn't help either. In America you needed to be twenty-one and everybody was ID'd everywhere, whereas at home it was eighteen to get in most places and kids would just blag it like I used to. This made a huge difference in how the respective club cultures took off. Back then when people could afford to, kids had calmed down at twenty-one, they were getting married and buying a house, they weren't free to go mad in the evenings. London clubbing started when kids were thirteen or fourteen, with no cares or inhibitions – it didn't matter if they couldn't go to school the next day and they bunked off. They'd bring an unrestrained attitude to clubbing that would be unheard of in America.

Terry had a good handle on all of this and would tell me if I really wanted to find some decent clubs I should go over to the Bronx, and he was right because I was definitely more into the underground things. I used to go to Prospect Park in Brooklyn, another place I was initially scared of because my aunts had made a big deal about telling me not to go there. These were the early days of hip hop and rap, and when I eventually ventured into the park I discovered little sound systems or ghetto blasters playing and these freestyle rap battles going on. The sound systems were being powered from lampposts, the kids took the covers off the bases of the poles and tapped into the electricity, which I thought was fantastic, a real two fingers up to the authorities. I'd never seen anything like what was going on down there, I was taking it all in and absolutely loving it. We didn't have anything like this in England, the nearest we had was the reggae sound clash, and pretty quickly I made the connection that this was actually a successor to that. There's a huge Jamaican community in Brooklyn, so many of those kids would have been of Jamaican descent and very aware of the sound system thing that came over with their parents and their grandparents. It all made sense to me: it was a Caribbean thing and all that was different was the soundtrack. The battling, the running down of opponents, the off-the-cuff wit was exactly the same – we called it toasting, they called it rapping.

The real difference between their sound systems and ours was the equipment, they had stuff we had *never even seen*! I remember telling Joey about it, he was all ears as I tried to explain what level they were on compared to his Great Tribulation set-up. I saw Technics turntables for the very first time and was thinking, 'Fuck me! This is what we need!' At home we had these little Garrard belt drive turntables on a Citronic unit, and if we wanted instant control on them we had to take the belt out, cut it and stick it back together again with a slightly smaller circumference. Now there I was looking at these kids in the park who have got these huge Thorens decks – the platters by themselves were really heavy – and even now they're one of the most expensive decks you can get. I'd heard about them but this is the first time I'd actually seen them. They used rotary mixers too, which seemed like something direct from Jamaican sound systems because in England we used slide faders. The only switches they had were for sound effects, everything else like volume or cross-fading between the decks was a rotary knob, which seemed to give them all the control they needed to manipulate the records.

*

This is what really got me: these guys weren't mixing the records *per se*, they were *blending* the records together to create extended breaks or to kind of build new jams out of two or three others. What I was watching, although I didn't realise it, was rudimentary scratching and cutting. They would take a little seven-inch 45 and stick it on top of an old 12 inch record so that they could pull the deck back to where they wanted the tune to cut into the previous one for the blending. Then the other first for me was watching scratching for the first time, only I didn't know what it was called then. They'd mark with a little bit of chalk or something the point they wanted to pull it back to, then let it go and pull it back again to make the scratch noise. I didn't know what I was seeing, and what they were doing in the park wasn't perfect, but I instantly knew it was the future and I was seeing it everywhere on the street scenes in New York. Chic's 'Good Times' was the *big* tune of that summer and the one practically all these deejays, all over the city, were cutting up and pulling back.

Although I'm perfectly *au fait* with all of that now, back then it was kind of intimidating because I wasn't to do it for about another four or five years. Of course I didn't have the equipment to go home and practice, because apart from the big heavy turntables, their rigs were totally set up for this. I'd never seen anybody playing a sound system with a monitor facing them, and remember staring at it thinking, 'What's that speaker doing there?' Our sound systems in England were, essentially, set up for weddings – all the speakers facing the crowd so it's Smashie and Nicie and talkie-talkie. This was set up with the deejay in mind, so what happened was you heard what you were playing on one deck on the headphones, and on the monitor you truly heard what was coming out of the speakers for the crowd, then all you did was match them up in your head to balance what you were trying to blend. Simple really, but at the time that was a whole science for someone like me.

It was seeing this sort of thing going down in the park, combined with some of the larger clubs I went to on subsequent trips, that affected me most during my trips to New York. More than just bringing back records, I brought back ideas and inspiration that would shape my future as a deejay. Something which began close to home, at my Uncle Leo's.

chapter twenty-six: uncle leo and the block party

Uncle Leo was the entrepreneur of the family and he had done really well. He's my dad's second-to-last brother, who was only about ten years older than me, and I really looked up to him. Of all the Josephs he was the most successful, the wealthiest and, in many ways, the smartest. My dad, Luke, was gentle whereas Uncle Leo was far more streetwise and had learned very quickly how to survive and get on in America. Just like my mum and dad's house in Acton, Uncle Leo's house in Brooklyn was the family hub – members of the family walked in and out all day long and most of the time my aunt would feed them. But the similarities between my dad and his brother pretty much stopped there. My dad was upstanding, dependable and law-abiding, he studied hard and had progressed that way, but Uncle Leo was the one who took risks. He was wily, he ran businesses out there, and he owned several properties, one of which was a nightclub called The Flamingo.

I'd known about Uncle Leo's nightclub for a while. He'd told Joey and me about it when he'd come to England a couple of years before and we were totally dismissive! Joe's into roots'n'culture and all he wants to do is build a sound system exactly like they have in Jamaica, while I'm thinking, 'I go to *discos*! Your club will be like one of those horrible old school Caribbean clubs that's trying to be all scampi in the basket!' When I got there, however, I couldn't have been more wrong. The Flamingo was a proper discotheque, with a deejay booth and everything, it was brilliant. It was done up like some Caribbean beach hut inside, but looking really uptown, with everything made of wood because my uncle had trained as a carpenter. He had his own sound system he'd put in there – Dr Wax Roadshow – that my cousin Wayne had built. Wayne was a real hi-fi kid: he bought all the newest kit, there was gear all over his bedroom in different stages of being dismantled or rewired, and he could talk the pants off you about 'spec'!

This sound system they'd built was unbelievable, and Uncle Leo made a lot of money from the club. It was a hub for the Grenadian community around that part of Brooklyn – every wedding party, christening or celebration was held in there – and it was packed three or four nights a week as a disco. I thought it was brilliant!

As hilarious and fantastic as the Flamingo was, Wayne and Leo really blew my mind with one of their block parties, because, once again, I'd never seen anything like it before. They just set it up so casually, they got permission from the police to close the street for their block – this was no problem, in fact they even supplied the 'Police: Do Not Cross' barriers for each end of the block – then rigged their sound system up outside their house, with speaker boxes on each side of the street. Before that they had these little flyers printed at a print place round the corner and began circulating them all over the neighbourhood – this is happening on this date, contribute this or bring that food, we're going to do this and you'll provide the food. Suddenly everybody produced loads of dishes, jerk chicken and all manner of food, mostly Caribbean, which surprised me because I thought it would be American food. Then, early afternoon, as people began to turn up, they started blasting the music.

That's when it hit me. Really hit me. I had never heard a sound system sound that good, and it was out in the street! Especially when they're playing soul and funk! I'd never been part of such a technically excellent black event, open to all, where the music being played wasn't reggae – in fact I'd never been to a big outdoor soul scene. *'Fuck!'* I'm thinking. 'This is unreal!' I was truly blown away by the power and clarity of these tunes, and suddenly – *bing* – a light bulb went off in my head – *this is what I could be doing at the Carnival* . . . No, this is what I *should* be doing at the Carnival. This was the first time I went to New York, so I hadn't done Carnival yet. Earlier I said I'd been leading up to it for four or five years, but I now realise I needed something like this to give me the inspiration I required. This was how I needed my music to sound at Notting Hill. As soon as I got home, Uncle Leo's block party became the template.

This was in 1979, before we'd played the Carnival and before I'd deejayed in public, although the New York side of the family knew about my birthday parties and Joey's sound system. I spent most of my time standing by the rig, fascinated with what was going on, and Wayne said to me, 'You deejay a bit, don't you? Take a turn.' I was so intimidated by those big decks and watching the kids that worked for my uncle using them that I came over all bashful: 'Naaaah ... Not really ...' But inside I was desperate to play! Understandably it didn't take too much for Uncle Leo to talk me into it, and I soon overcame my shyness and realised there was nothing to be scared of – people *wanted* to like what you were doing because they'd come out with the intention of dancing and having a good time. This was it for me. It was like a revelation – the first time I'd ever deejayed in public, I was out on the street, *in New York* and the crowd loved it. It filled me with an unbelievable vigour and a certainty that this was where my destiny lay. I knew this was what I had to be doing.

If I needed further convincing of what this was really all about, the block party gave me another unforgettable experience when, some time in the late afternoon, either Wayne or my uncle played 'Love is the Message' by M.F.S.B. At this point the tune is about five years old, I've known and loved it since it came out, so I'm thinking 'Good choice', then I look around and I'm like '*Fucking hell!*' The whole street is up and doing this funky boogie! Everybody! About three hundred people, all black, cheering, throwing up black power salutes, running out of their houses, if they're eating putting their plate down to get into it, if they're sitting down they aren't any more ... To me this is unreal! This is the response I'd dreamed of getting if I played these records, but we'd never get it in our clubs. Carnival could never be like this, quite apart from it being cloudy or raining so often – this block party had glorious New York summer weather – and the crowd at Carnival would stand there and watch! *Watch* the selector, with the MC shouting at the people standing in front of him. But here they're dancing, and they're all doing the same dance! I'd never seen that before and I'm knocked out! Wow! This is the real deal. *This* is what this level of black music means to us. *This is our music.* This isn't no British suburban Soul Mafia scene, this isn't Chris Hill or Froggy playing at it, this is the real deal. I always knew from my clubbing experiences that what was being served up to us in England wasn't an authentic thing. I tried to imagine what that would be like, but my perception of it, like so many of my peers, was the *Saturday Night Fever* version. I instinctively knew there was a black end to it, but I didn't really know what it would look like until that moment.

What I loved so much about that 'Love is the Message' moment was how the tune wasn't new but it resonated with the entire block party, from the oldest to the youngest. Terry was always using the word 'classic' when he talked about certain songs and I'd never fully grasped what he meant by that. In that instant, though, I understood – it's a tune that never dies because spiritually there's a deepness to it that can resonate forever. Years earlier I'd bought 'Love is the Message' as a single and absolutely loved it, but couldn't put my finger on *why* I loved it. Then half a decade later in New York when that one tune comes on, people are celebrating being black and being out on that street at that time. Immediately I understood that at home we were being spoon-fed our own music but without celebrating the history and meaning behind it. In most cases the music was served up to us disconnected from the culture that created it, and so what I was witnessing at that block party was what happens when that connection is made.

That's what makes a *proper* anthem, and even now, nearly forty years later, it still gets that response at some parties. In my deejay career I've created a few tunes like that – it might be an album track or something old or obscure, but I've known there's something deep going on there, so I play them for other people to experience it with me. They become signature tunes.

It wasn't all completely positive. At about seven or eight o'clock, just as it was getting dark, there was a gunshot at one end of the street. Everybody scattered, a cop car came down the block and basically I'm thinking, 'Oh shit!' I'd never even heard a gunshot before – I'm from England! – and I guess some of my aunt's warnings must have been getting through because I was paranoid about getting shot. My heart was pounding, but because this was so far from normal for someone like me I was really curious to see what was happening. I was really scared but I still wanted to be nosy, to stay on my uncle's stoop to see what was going on. I did, and that was pretty much it – within ten minutes everything had calmed down and people just carried on enjoying themselves like nothing happened. That unnerved me, that this was just a regular thing, but I wasn't going to dwell on that then because the party immediately started jumping again. It wound down by about ten o'clock, but not for too long – it carried on at the Flamingo, which was packed until two or three in the morning. I was loving it, all the more so because I had felt very inspired.

The other big thing I learned from my trips to New York came from the other end of the clubbing scene, the lofts and the studios. Although I found it all a bit up itself, I loved the way they used space brilliantly. They were opening clubs in places that would never be considered in England – not only factories and warehouses, but the 'Tunnel' was actually two old subway tunnels, with the track still down there, it blew my mind! These places were essentially concrete and steel – industrial spaces – which we had in England but weren't exploiting, and because it was all so hard and cold the acoustics were brilliant. It was funny: the music in these clubs was always quite commercial, but because they had the sound systems to deliver it in those spaces I would always accommodate it!

What really made an impression was how music's cultural differences spread into these quite upmarket, pretty main-stream places. Anywhere there's a club culture the high profile deejays are controlling the musical narrative, and in England we had white deejays controlling the tastes of what we heard and how we heard it. In New York however, even in the trendy, upmarket places, the deejays were *black*, the music was *black* and it was coming from the heart. This was the way nature intended it, how people across the board should be hearing the music – in its purest form, in its proper environment. I realised English clubs were taking the records and creating their own Anglocentric environment in which to hear and enjoy them, which was fine up to a point, but as soon as I heard the music played by these deejays it had a far greater meaning and sense of purpose for me. I'd been clocking everything and knew this was how it should be and used what I'd witnessed in New York as my template.

I used to go back to England fired up, thinking I could

never afford to do it this way, *but* I'm going to make sure these same rules still apply: we make our sound system brilliant, I've got all the records – we're halfway there. Over time, Joey built an amazing sound system, so all we had to do was find an empty industrial space and set it up. When it happened, nothing gave me a bigger thrill than setting up and running those illegal warehouse parties. More than the house parties or the clubs, even more than the Carnival in those mid-80s years, although it could get frustrating because it was always fraught with danger. Also, the warehouse parties always took me right back to those days and nights in New York when I was discovering all this stuff from all walks of society, from the Brooklyn block parties to the Manhattan lofts, and working out how to put it all together in London would really set me on my way as a deejay.

part five:
becoming a deejay

chapter twenty-seven: raving III

During the second half of the 1970s, I properly discovered the West End. Up until then the suburban clubs had been an adventure, or at least they had been for us west London kids. Just getting up there had been a big part of it, because we could drive our cars up there – *fast*! We could get to Scamps in Hemel Hempstead in about forty-five minutes, meaning the North Circular and M1 became our racetrack, especially when we were coming back. There were about a dozen of us that had cars: I had my Mini Cooper, my mates had 1600Es, Escorts or Cortinas, a couple had Capris, and we'd thrash them along those roads. My Mini Cooper was fast, but one night coming back from Scamps I pushed it too hard and completely burnt the engine out! It blew up on the roundabout at the bottom of the M1, with black smoke billowing out from under the bonnet and everybody else stopping to laugh at me.

These clubs had been good for dancing too; they were packed and there were always dance-off competitions going on, in which we could show these out of town soulboys how good we were. Or how good we *thought* we were, because when we got to go to Crackers in Soho, we'd just stand and watch! When we went to Scamps, there was only really one dancer up there: a white guy we used to call 'Durex', because he'd wear these latex shirts with his Smiths carpenter jeans. He was a wicked dancer – they had a big mirror by the dancefloor and he'd be in front of it doing these amazing, balletic moves.

There had been quite a crossover period between my clubbing in the West End and in the suburbs, because we kept going to Scamps on a Monday night either out of habit or just for the chance to race up and down the motorway, but I was quickly losing interest. When we first started going out of town, we were going to loads of little out-of-the-way places – as soon as I heard about a new club I'd be, 'Come on! Let's go!' Then, as that scene began growing it was getting sanitised and the music became more commercial. I was still going for the girls, but I wasn't getting the buzz I wanted any more. I felt I'd moved on and I needed more action, more excitement, and then around Christmas 1974 I ventured up to the 100 Club on Oxford Street and straight away I was hooked. By the first few weeks of 1975, I was going to Crackers on a Tuesday, where Mark Roman was playing, and I fell in love with West End nightlife. By the end of that year, my clubbing circuit had shifted from Hertfordshire and Buckinghamshire to Soho, Covent Garden and Charing Cross.

I was discovering places I'd never even knew existed from reading *Blues & Soul*, places like Upstairs at Ronnie Scott's that were *Soho* and they simply didn't think to advertise in those magazines. Clubs were aware those magazines were essentially set up for white suburban audiences – middle

England – and the scene had grown around them. I totally got that, and I won't do *Blues & Soul* down too much because they gave me my first front cover, but I quickly became aware there were two soul scenes in the south east and I became a real Soho Boho.

I was going to any club that would let me in – I still looked younger than I was – Crackers, Studio 21 at 21 Oxford Street, Columbo's on Carnaby Street . . . For a little while there was an after-hours speakeasy in Wardour Mews where if your face fitted you got let in. Upstairs at Ronnie Scott's, Gossips on Meard Street, with the Language Lab in the same venue, another place on Frith Street at the top of the road where they'd play a mash-up of black music and punk . . . I'd go anywhere. Global Village under the arches at Villiers Street by Charing Cross station, when Norman Scott was deejaying – that club would become Heaven, The Duncannon pub on Duncannon Street off the Strand, Chaguaramas in Covent Garden, which would become the Roxy, and I went to a few gay clubs because the music was always so good and there was never any trouble. Quite a few of my mates went to functions at Central Saint Martins, the art school, but my tastes were a bit too black to go there too often . . . We even went to two or three logs discos on Coventry Street, which runs between Piccadilly and Leicester Square, which were exactly the tourist discotheque traps we thought they'd be, but we had to go just to see how crap they were! That's how seriously I took the West End.

I was also fascinated by the grittiness of Soho – because I was completely serious about my music, the fashions and the dancing, I immediately felt the difference between these places and where I had been going because the standards set in there were so high. These clubs had the best music, real cutting-edge soul that often surprised even a nerd like myself; the top London dancers would be there banishing pretenders like myself to the sidelines when they cleared a circle on the floor; and the street fashions were wild and inventive and wouldn't reach the shops for a year or more. The kids at these clubs were never seen in Berkshire or Surrey.

Up until that point I hadn't really been following any dee-jays, other than the Northern ones spoon-fed to me by *Black Echoes* and *Blues & Soul* – Richard Searling or Colin Curtis or Ian Levine. I knew we must have had our own equivalents down here. Mark Roman was the first one I discovered. That was almost by chance, because he used to put his charts in *Blues & Soul* and his choices were so upfront that they would be records I either had or wanted to buy, and then my mate Clive Clarke took me to this out-of-the-way club in Kingsbury where Roman was doing a night. When we got there, there was nobody in the club, nothing going on, but this guy's playing Donald Byrd's 'Change (Makes You Want Hustle)'. The first time I'd heard it, he played 'Let's Do the Latin Hustle' months before it became a hit, and I'm hearing tunes I've never heard before, every one of which is bang on.

Clive told me I had to check this guy out at this base-ment club at the top end of Wardour Street, on a Tuesday night – Crackers. I did, and it was packed! All the faces, all the people in the know, the uber-hip of the London soul scene, they were all there! This was the crowd that knows what time it is, this was the deejay who's playing the most spot-on music, and I was looking around thinking, 'I'm in the West End ... I'm in the in-crowd ... *I've arrived!*' I was seventeen or eighteen, and considered myself to be way out in front when it came to music because I was in Contempo every Friday dinnertime when the American deliveries came in – those records were in the shop a week before they were in the *Blues & Soul* charts and everybody knew about them. Suddenly I was in this club where this white dude's playing all these tunes!

Crackers became my default setting for music, dancing and fashion. Although I went everywhere else in the West End, I was ever-present at Crackers, even after Mark Roman left and it was touch and go for a while because Roman took his white soulboy crowd with him. Then they had a succession of deejays down there, among them was that bald black guy Freddie Mack, who called himself Mr Superbad – I went once and he was awful. Nicky Price played for a bit but he was far too pop. Then they brought George Power in, a north London Greek guy, and after a couple of weeks I knew this guy was right! He was playing stuff I'd bought but never heard out anywhere else, which was just what I wanted because I was being educated and challenged by George's choices of music. It took him a couple of months to truly put his stamp on the place, but when he did it really began to take off – the legendary Friday lunchtime sessions were his idea.

The other brilliant thing about clubbing in the West End was the completely new set of people. They came from all over London into the centre, so I was meeting people from the north, east and south. I loved it because they were people like me: black Londoners, who were as seriously into soul and funk as I was; they were adventurous, whereas some of my west London posse who had jobs opted to play it safe. As I've said before, I made friends easily – I think I just had a face that fitted – and was often going to these new clubs on my own. I felt alright and I believe I got accepted by people *because* I was by myself – if it had been a group of us there was always the risk of looking like a mob. This way I was obviously no threat.

Through Crackers, I started to move with a north London posse from Stroud Green, Arsenal boys, ironically, who seemed to know where all the exciting parties were in north and east London. This was fantastic because after exhausting the possibilities of where I lived, there was nothing fresh any more, no excitement. Now I'm going to parties not knowing anybody and thinking '*This is wicked*'! During the late '70s I used to go to parties along a road off Stroud Green Road, in the big houses that were up by the park, and these were like blues dances – charged on the door, charged for drinks and curry goat – but they played soul music, hardly any reggae. I thought they were brilliant, but for me it would be a nightmare getting home to Acton. The parties would finish about five or six in the morning and I'd just bleach it and stay there all night, or doss in someone's passageway, sitting on the stairs and falling asleep until the buses ran. I loved those parties – the music was well funky, deeper, with more of an edge than anything I'd hear in the suburbs. We'd go to parties in Walthamstow and east London as well, and I'm still friends with a lot of those guys.

I was going to concerts all the time, too. The mid-70s were fantastic for touring American funk bands and I'd go and see anyone who was in England if they played the Hammersmith Odeon – and *everyone* passed through the Hammy Odeon. I only lived a couple of miles away so I was either buying a ticket or bunking in – Hammy couldn't keep me out! I saw everybody there: Brass Construction, P-Funk, the Detroit Spinners, the Trammps, the Chi-Lites, Fatback Band . . . anybody who had a concert advertised in *Blues & Soul*, provided it didn't clash with a football night! Or if I missed them down there, I'd jump in a mate's car and go up to the California Ballroom in Dunstable and catch them the following night or the following week.

I still look back on that summer of 1976 as one of my best years ever: the hottest summer, the best records and the partying was unbelievable. I wasn't working so I was just a stop-out – I wouldn't come home for days, going from club to party to club. I was on the dole or surviving off my mum, and when I really felt the pinch was when I had no money for tunes! I was furiously collecting records all through this period – I was like an addict, somebody who goes into a betting shop and just can't stop betting, that was me in Contempo! Then as soon as I got back in work and I had more money, I went back and bought everything I'd been forced to leave behind.

It was towards the end of that period that my whole attitude to clubbing began to change, and by the time I first went to New York I was much more militant about things and looking for something different from what was on offer. I wasn't going to black dances because they'd become a magnet for the police. Whether there had been any trouble or not, when you'd come out the police would be hovering around outside, then when it was down to two or three of you at a bus stop you'd become a soft target for them. Also, the blues dances were a bit too full of testosterone – if you accidentally stepped on somebody's crocs you'd get attitude – I always felt uncomfortable in all-black crowds, just the same as I did in all-white crowds, and I much preferred places where the crowd was mixed. At the same time, I wanted a black experience, because we were young black kids from inner-city London – although the West End clubs spoke to us far more than those in the suburbs and I *loved* the music and the vibe, I always sensed something was missing.

Looking back I realise it was all the same feelings I'd had about so much of the London or south-east soul clubbing scene, back from when I was younger and went to the early Caister Soul Weekenders and the Purley National Soul Festival thing. I was ever present at these big events, but I can remember thinking 'this is bollocks' without really being able to articulate why. I had lived and breathed the whole '70s clubbing experience, I had a seriously geeky attitude towards it. Then as I got older, 1977 or 1978, I was becoming very aware of the status quo in the club world: how there was a set of self-appointed gatekeepers, deejays, record companies and magazines – almost exclusively white men – who had separated the music from the culture that created it so that there was no lineage or no sense of purpose to it. It had become purely entertainment with no cultural value – if I can make money out of playing this music I'll play it, if not I'll play something else. When a style fell out of fashion or the industry felt they couldn't sell it any more, it was just gone. Dashed away. These so-called guardians stripped out the bits they didn't need or thought of as worthless and soul music in the UK was becoming a strictly commercial enterprise, rather than the cultural experience that so much reggae was. In fact, it was as if the reggae boys had the monopoly on consciousness, which was far from the case – that's why I got so excited by the reaction to 'Love is the Message' at my uncle's block party.

I was reading *Blues & Soul* and *Black Echoes* regularly, but I recognised that I was only really doing so to keep up with the record releases. The magazines themselves, which were the full extent of soul music media in England, didn't reflect the world I was in, the places I went to or the people I went there with. What really brought it home to me was towards the end of the decade when electro was emerging and these custodians of What We Should Like waged war on it. I thought if you don't want to play it, that's fine, but don't go out of your way to keep slagging it off just because you don't happen to like it. Where we young forward-looking black kids go, this is our soundtrack, and if you're not going to respect it as that then just leave it alone and stick to your Japanese jazz and whatever.

I understood what the split between us and them was. We were always looking forward to what was coming *next*; we were well versed in new music trends; and we were very receptive, as opposed to wanting to maintain the status quo or constantly harking back to what had gone before. The only time we ever looked back was the rare groove thing, and that was more a case of plugging in to a bygone age that so many of that generation missed – they were hearing snatches of the songs in hip-hop samples and were fascinated by them. I loved the old records *and* I was right up for anything new. The very first electro records – I was on it; the very first go-go records – I was on it; the very first house records – I was on it . . . I loved the experimentation because I could see the lineage, how it all connected.

By 1978 or 1979 I was a serial clubber in the West End, and although I was very much immersed in that scene, I knew I wasn't getting the music satisfaction I needed. I wasn't hearing what I'd have liked to be hearing, because by then I was an aspiring dancer and wanted to hear the stuff that made me go crazy . . . the *real* floor fillers. Also I felt like the music wasn't adventurous enough, when I was out I wanted to hear the esoteric, the left-field, so there was a mounting frustration. Maybe I hadn't consciously realised I wanted to deejay, but I guess the seeds were being sown more by default than anything else.

chapter twenty-eight: becoming a deejay

Although I was the original vinyl junkie, and was amassing a huge record collection in that second half of the 1970s, I didn't harbour any mindful notions of being a deejay – it just never occurred to me. I'm pretty sure I always thought I could do better than what was on offer at so many of the clubs I went to, but perhaps because there were so few black deejays on that soul circuit, I simply never considered trying to be one. It was a combination of seeing my uncle's set-up and other situations in New York, and my mum and dad letting me have my birthday parties in our house from 1977 onwards, that prompted me to make the jump.

Joey had his sound at that point – it was only really big enough to play houses or church halls, but the quality was unbelievable, it always sounded fantastic. As we got older and Mum and Dad let us all hold our own parties, they ended up being big affairs as often my brothers and sisters used to share their parties. It wasn't all harmonious though. I was a real snob, and felt superior to their reggaefied crowd, I used to think of them as the local oiks, and they used to think of me as being weird – the *soul bwoy*! But I didn't care, when I had my parties it was all going to be about me, so I could invite my friends I saw at Crackers, my friends from 100 Club, or from Global Village . . . They were the dancers, fashionistas . . . they were the *stylers*. And I was rigid about the music – a total fascist! No reggae whatsoever! I'm doing the music, so I want to play Reuben Wilson, I want to play the Tavares, I want to play Ten Per Cent's 'Double Exposure', I want to play Roy Ayers's 'Running Away', I want to play 'Wicky Wacky' . . . I just wanted to play my record collection!

When I look back at those birthday parties, I realise they were prototypes for the house parties we did as Good Times in the 1980s – that was what awakened a latent aspiration in me. It was like it was something I always knew – that the records I wanted to hear in clubs would work and there was no need for the deejays to be so conservative. Imagine how I felt: there I was playing all the records I wanted to hear in a club, going pretty leftfield with some of them, and the party is really swinging. I've got this crowd in front of me, who are mostly a cool West End crowd, and they are loving it the same way as I'm loving it. I felt more than just triumphant, I felt vindicated.

Then the next week I go back to the clubs and start being critical and disappointed again, thinking, 'This is shit! Why am I still going to these places when I'm really not enjoying it?' That was what eventually manifested itself in me persuading my brother we needed to do Carnival – realistically that was the only option open to a frustrated young wannabe deejay, because I soon found out I wasn't going to get a squeeze on the club circuit as it stood.

*

I didn't do any other deejaying in between my birthday parties in 1977 and 1978. I'd go out with the sound system to support my brother, especially when he did sound clashes. These were mostly local things, I didn't really enjoy them and there was no way he was letting me play any of my records! His operation wasn't just reggae, it was strictly roots reggae, with maybe a bit of lovers rock thrown in to keep the girls interested. I was far too disco! But those couple of trial runs at my parents' house had given me confidence – the second one convinced me the first wasn't a fluke. Now I'm a serial West End clubber, so I've got to know quite a few of the deejays on the scene, so I thought I'd try and blag something. For a long time this was soul destroying – I'd badger deejays asking to do warm-up for them, get told 'Yes', turn up with my records and get fobbed off with, 'Not just yet . . . not just yet' for hours, until they'd say, 'Not tonight, mate!' To them I was just this annoying anorak kid, but an annoying anorak kid with a bag full of records they would have died for! Then I tried George Power and I thought I'd turned a corner.

I'd known George for about four years, and always admired the music he played, so I felt most positive about badgering him and went to work. I told him I had all sorts of experience because we had a sound system, a soul sound system, so he asked me where did we play. I said, 'The Carnival . . . every year at the Carnival.' At this time we hadn't done it once. I told him we had a load of house parties under our belt, although I didn't tell him they were family birthday parties at my mum and dad's house. Essentially, whether I'd played two parties or two hundred parties, I'd seen enough around

Soho and the suburbs to be sure I could hold my own in any club in London.

George relented, told me he was doing a gig in Ealing the next week, and asked me if I wanted to do warm-up. *Fuck do I!?!* What an opportunity. It was in a little piano bar opposite Ealing Broadway station, a far cry from the West End, but so what? This was me, an Acton boy, warming up for George Power, practically on my own doorstep. That week I went out and I bought practically every American soul and funk single released! I borrowed money off my mum and dad, I begged or borrowed off practically everybody I knew, and it all went over the counter in Contempo! I traded records, and as I'd not long got back from that first trip to New York, I was so ahead it hurt! I hadn't even broken the cellophane on a lot of these tunes, so I was ready to go. I was playing out with George Power and thinking, 'Yeah! I can do this deejay thing!'

All my brothers and sisters came to support me and because it was local to me, my Grove posse came, my Acton posse came and this little place is packed. Naturally I got there early, but so did George! He showed up before I'd even put a record on and said, 'I'm playing now.' The disappointment was crushing. Not simply because I was just left sitting there, but because George himself had misread this crowd and I would have done much better. He played all the obvious party tunes as he thought that was what the people there would want to hear, but I don't think he'd properly looked at them and seen most of them were like me and wanted to hear the *newest*, the *up front*! They didn't want regular floor fillers, they wanted what I had in my bag. In spite of how I felt, though, because it was George Power and I was so in awe of him I let it run.

Then at about two o'clock he wants to go and says to me, 'Come and play!' By that time the place is more than half empty – so many of my lot have gone because I didn't know if I was going to get any time at all – and I've got an hour to play. I think that hurt worse than all the knockbacks I'd been getting and I was livid – George Power or not, this was one more white bloke fucking us over. It hardened my attitude and it's at that point I started thinking I needed my own sound system. Because I'd experienced Uncle Leo's, I knew a *proper* dedicated soul sound system could work. If I had my own sound system I could do what I wanted when I wanted, with a bottom line that no white bloke was ever again going to tell me to warm up or do this or do that.

I was still a regular at Crackers, so of course I thanked George for giving me the break, and even though I was still a big fan I started looking at things a bit more realistically. One of the things that stood out was George's treatment of the black club deejay Paul 'Trouble' Anderson. Paul passed while I was writing this book. I miss him as he was a really good friend and one of London's most talented deejays – through funk, hip-hop, house and garage, hardly anybody could match his record collection or his knowledge of music. He could dance a bit too, so he intuitively knew what the dancers in a club wanted to hear. Paul was a regular at Crackers, where everybody knew what a top selector he was, but the only break George would give him was when he went on two weeks' holiday. As soon as he came back George took over again and it looked like Paul had been relegated – he was known as 'George Power's Box Boy', because he was reduced to carrying George's record boxes and stuff while he waited for another chance. It wasn't right.

It wasn't only the white guys that weren't giving me a break either. Towards the end of the 1970s, I got word there was a really good funk night going on at 21 Oxford Street. It was Trevor Shakes deejaying, and he was one of the best dancers in the West End soul clubs, so although it wasn't very busy, all the London circuit dancers were there so it had real atmosphere. The music Trevor played that night blew my mind – *all new* and I'm standing there making a mental list of what I'm going to get next week! I was feeling fantastic, because I'm in a black West End club, cool funky bouncers, top of the range music played by a black deejay, in a little space on a Sunday night ... At last! Home! I felt so relaxed that out of the blue I said to Trevor, 'Listen, I'd love to play here with you one night.' He just looked at me and said, 'Bring your records.' *What!?!?!* 'Bring your records down next week.' That week I bought everything. Those were expensive times, but my record box was the freshest out there – I'm sure I turned up with more new records than Trevor! I got down the club, he kind of ignored me and I was too proud to go and ask, 'When am I coming on?' So I didn't. I came back for two or three weeks with my records, and he never let me play. He probably forgot all about what was, to him, just a throwaway comment. I thought had a better chance there, so from then on whatever I did had to be on my own terms, on my own sound system. No more of these humiliations.

That's when I put the notions of club deejaying out of my head. Joey had a fantastic sound system and I would make an arrangement with him, but I didn't want to do the church halls and community centres he was doing. They were strictly local affairs. I had ideas and ambitions for what I wanted to do and knew I wouldn't get the crowd I needed to do those sorts of things. It was then I figured the only place to get the opportunity to do it exactly how I felt it should be done would be at the Notting Hill Carnival.

chapter twenty-nine: clothes II

For the time when Soho was the centre of my world, it wasn't just for the music – the same went for style or fashion or anything creative. When I was hanging out up there, it was a meeting place for likeminded people who came from the suburbs or the inner city to share that space and their ideas. I was meeting kids of different mindsets, different aspirations from what I'd been used to. I knew it was for me, I always considered myself a styler kid – but because of my limited resources I loved youth style or street style, not what was known as *fashion*. I loved the soulboy look but couldn't afford most of it, so I was limited to a few bits or market copies and knock offs. Crackers was always interesting. It was always very upfront when it came to how the kids dressed, but because it was the beginning of that crossover with the punk look it was never too expensive – the first time I saw kids wearing plastic sandals was in Crackers.

I didn't start off as a styler when I first started going up the West End in the mid-70s. Back then I'd see the way the kids would look at certain places and think, 'Wow! That guy looks fantastic. I wanna look like that!' This was when *The Great Gatsby* film had just come out so it was all 1920s suits, high-waisted trousers, silk scarves, baker boy caps ... I called it the polished golfer look! But, brilliantly, it was mixed with American ghetto, a big afro and a kind of Donny Hathaway look. That's how I'd see the older cats in the West End look-ing – *the dudes*! I loved all of it, but couldn't afford it so I just aspired to it, like with the mod look or the black skinhead look a few years earlier. I loved the Biba look too and I spent many hours wandering around Biba, where the girls' clothes looked even more fantastic – I fancied any girl who had the Biba look! It was all about aspiration, though, and I was never going to be able to afford that kind of thing. The trouble with street fashion was it moved so fast that by the time you'd saved up for something it had moved on.

There was such a difference between the suburban soul clubs and the West End. Out in the sticks in 1974 or 1975 it was that sort of Northern soul-ey look with Oxford bags, tunnel belt loops, double or triple belts, zips up the sides and all the pocket flaps – the sort of thing you'd get a tailor in Shepherd's Bush market to knock up for you in forty-eight hours. I went to Crackers looking like that and I was seeing kids in workwear gear! Sanfordised jeans, with the loop for your hammer, painters' trousers, carpenter jeans, dungarees by Lee ... And they're wearing plastic sandals or canvas shoes, while I've got footwear from Derber's or Ravel's! It was at that time in Crackers I first saw anybody wearing bondage trousers – this was way before the punks were wearing them. I looked down and saw this guy had a strap and a buckle that joined his trousers together! I didn't know they were called bondage trousers, but I knew what they were because I was always up and down the King's Road and had seen them in that shop Sex, which I later found out was owned by Malcolm McLaren.

I didn't think that was strange, I thought it was fantastic because I never saw any black people at the time looking like that – this was a time of what I called William DeVaughn suits, that kind of ghetto high roller look. I loved this kind of punky, almost DIY fashion that was going on at Crackers or Chaguaramas or the 100 Club, because the other way that black club fashion was going was upmarket, like Browns in South Molton Street or Stanley Adams, that sort of thing. One of those Browns canvas bags was a real prize: they were the right shape and size to put a few albums in and they proved you shopped at Browns! Of the people I knew, it was only the older ones who had finished their apprenticeships and were on full wages who could afford to shop up there. While I liked that look on occasion, those clothes weren't convivial for dancing in and the guys that wore that stuff normally liked the wall – they'd stand in the darker recesses of a club, probably with one or two girls, chirping and looking fantastic. I was a dancefloor kid and it wasn't right to be in one of those jackets and an expensive shirt, getting sweaty. So when American bowling shirts and Smiths dungarees were in, with plastic sandals, they were perfect for the dancefloor.

Even better than that, they were affordable. You could go to Flip in Covent Garden or Antiquarius Market in Kensington and buy good second-hand clothes in those places that were really, really cheap. Laurence Corner was another place, the army surplus store on Hampstead Road by Warren Street station, because the army look was big for us. Jungle greens, genuine US Army Jungle greens for fifty pence! I've still got my jungle greens from back then, when I was a twenty-eight-inch waist! We wore the air force ones as well, in khaki canvas, but I think they were £1.50! When those peg trousers came in, that kind of 1940s revival swing look that all my black mates were into, Laurence Corner was the place for them. It was the best place to get those canvas shoes for just a couple of pounds too. Laurence Corner was big for us and because I thought of myself as a styler, this cheap, inventive fashion always meant more to me than just buying something in a regular High Street shop.

I always thought of myself as ahead of the curve and because so much of this was pretty cheap, I could change stuff quickly without too much worry. I might have had to work a bit harder though, like when I got my first pair of Levi's with selvedge, and I bought them cheap in Portobello Market after seeing a couple of guys with the little red line down their jeans and thinking it looked fantastic. I didn't know what it was but I was too shy to ask. Of course it meant I spent weeks trying to work out where to go for them, but that was part of the fun of that fashion subculture, going into shops *looking* – checking out unlikely places to *look* for these jeans or to *look* for this shirt, because so much of the time you'd stumble across something else, so the look was constantly evolving.

I used to spend ages in Flip, on Long Acre in Covent Garden; you never really knew what you might find in there. The garments I remember most are an orange bowling shirt – a genuine American bowling shirt – and a 1950s overcoat, again second hand from America. That coat was massive, proper tweed, and used to see me through every winter, it was brilliant – in fact it still is because I've still got it. I wore

Smiths carpenter jeans, but I didn't like their dungarees so I wore Lee dungarees with a jumper underneath or a bowling shirt over the top in 1976. Prior to that at Crackers – 1974 and 1975 – the black boys were all in FU jeans from Jean Junction in Oxford Street, with cap sleeve t-shirts, and boxing boots began to come in as the American boxing brand Everlast found some favour. Because I took dancing seriously, I took my shoes seriously, so I didn't buy the horrible jelly plastic sandals, but the Solatio lattice ones they did in red, black and brown looked better and gave much better support.

I didn't do the bondage trousers fashion, even though I admired it and a lot of my white mates did. They were really big on Lurex too, and gossamer this and gossamer that – a few of them even did the safety pin thing! I just thought all of that was a step too far, especially where I lived, and all those chains and straps and things would have got in the way while dancing.

How I dressed was something that brought me into conflict with so many of the black guys round where I lived, as the reggae styling was the complete opposite of what I wanted to look like. They were into that Italian knitwear, suede-fronted Gabiccis, Farah slacks, Bally shoes and a beaver hat with a feather in it. I hated it in the beginning because I hated the world it represented, but later I've realised how much I must have appreciated the sense of style and swagger involved, as nowadays a lot of my styling is based on that look.

At the time though, subconscious appreciation wasn't much help when I'd step out of my house wearing red Smiths carpenter jeans, a white fluffy mohair jumper, which was the only thing I could ever afford from Seditionaries in the King's

Road, brown plastic sandals, and I always had a pick in my afro. Straight away it was all 'Batty bwoy!' ... 'Soul bwoy!' Then, as the bus stop was right by the bookies, I'd have to wait there, and all I'd hear from these guys outside it was 'Marmer man!' ... 'Batty bwoy!' until my bus came along. It didn't bother me, in fact I liked getting stared at because it meant I was looking the way I wanted to look, so I'd just walk on thinking, 'Fuck you! Dickheads!' More than a few times I'd get on a train or go to the bus stop and I'd get looks from black people of my mum and dad's age, people who you might see in church. I'd hear little bits of patois from under their breath, making insinuations that I was funny, or I was weird. I had to look straight through that and never met their eyes, because I didn't want any confrontation with people like that.

Sometimes, if I simply didn't fancy going through all of that, I used to dress in a normal pair of cords and a top, these leather moccasins that were really cheap and easy to wear – although not for dancing or running for a bus – and put all my clubbing gear in my duffel bag. When I got to Tottenham Court Road on the tube I'd wander down to the end of the platform, get changed and walk out. It was a transformation, like Clark Kent coming out of the phone box as Superman! When I walked out of the station I'd see black kids and white kids dressed like me and I'd walk tall! I was a West Ender. I was *Soulboy*!

By the end of 1977 Fiorucci was the next step, as Smiths had become too common, they were practically *de rigueur* in every logs disco. I distinctly remember one Saturday night at Global Village, when my mates and I were standing outside under the railway arches chatting, cooling off from dancing, and I saw this guy come out wearing these amazing black jeans.

Suddenly my Smiths looked so old school and totally tired. It was always brightly lit down there so I could see the label – Fiorucci – but had no idea how to say it, so I went over and said, 'I'm not being funny, mate, but how do you pronounce the name of those jeans?' He told me 'fer-oo-chee' and it was just burned into my brain – I needed a pair of those jeans! But he told me they were really expensive and you had to go to the Fiorucci shop that had just opened in Knightsbridge, a little way up the road from Harrods.

As soon as Monday came I was there and was knocked out by all these really bright, bold colours in this huge shop, then I saw the price on the jeans! Twenty-nine quid!! I think I was unemployed then, but even if I'd been working that would have been way more than I would have earned in a week. I thought it would be ages before I could get a pair, but my mate Ceophus's girlfriend got a Saturday job in there and she got me a pair of jeans – blue corduroy – for about fifteen quid and put a mohair jumper in the bag that she didn't ring up. She sorted Ceophus out, too, and it was such a great hustle we were shopping in there every week! We looked the bollocks, everything was Fiorucci, and it all fitted me because I was small and back then I was skinny – the cuts were really good if you were an average size, anything above that and you'd have problems.

*

Into the 1980s and for me it was high-end sportswear, what the style mags came to call 'football casual', but this would have been a good couple of years before any of the media picked up on it. At that time the terraces were the catwalk and I'd see kids wearing certain stuff and think, 'Wow! He's rocking them well!', and make a mental note. The whole trainer obsession that dominates street style today grew out of those football casual days. I was properly brand aware, because I was working in the print shop by then and could afford it. Benetton ... Lacoste ... Tacchini ... Fila ... Adidas ... Diadora ... Tracksuits and trainers were coming in big. Bjorn Borg Elites – even though I had no interest in tennis, I'd watch him at Wimbledon just to see what he was wearing! Seeing him in that Fila tracksuit was another of those '*God!* I want to look like that!' moments, and I can remember desperately trying to see what shoes he had on.

There was a shop in Shepherd's Bush called Stuarts, right by the market on the Uxbridge Road. He was like the old style gentleman's outfitter that used to be on every high street, and I'd say he was the original London casuals shop. He was always the first with gear from Europe when we didn't even know what trainers they had in Germany or in Spain. He get it weeks or sometimes months before anybody else, just a couple of pairs of each, and put them in the window. If you were too slow they'd go, but then in two weeks' time he'd be stocking another trainer you'd never seen before. I was quick enough to get a pair of Adidas Trimm Trabs from Stuarts very early on, when I'm sure he was the first to get them in. Kids from all over England used to make the journey down to Stuarts, and it was why away fans used to love coming to QPR, because they'd go shopping in there first. Not that that wasn't without its difficulties, as none of this stuff was cheap and the local black boys used to tax kids if they saw them with Stuarts bags, especially the out-of-towners. They'd wait for them on the tube station platform and it was all 'Let me hold that bag!' and it would be full of Fila or Chevignon or Tacchini.

This sort of taxing used to go on in Soho too, especially on Saturday as there were hardly any coppers about because they'd all be on duty at football matches. These kids would go to in Nick-Nack on Carnaby Street, another shop that was on the casual gear really early, then they'd get bushwhacked before they made it to any Tube station because the sticks-men virtually had the place to themselves. When they saw the Nick-Nack bags it would be 'I'm having that!' and whatever had just been bought would be gone. When I worked in Denham Street, and I wasn't at football myself, I used to wander up in my lunch hour and watch it all unfold, and I'd laugh when the northern football firms were in town because it got so much worse – these guys doing the taxing used to terrorise Liverpool or the Mancs when they came down.

I never got a curly perm – I hated them! Come the early 1980s, all my black mates were Michael Jackson clones, but I couldn't deal with any of that processed hair and preferred to look like a Jackson 5 Michael Jackson, although as we came out of the 1970s I trimmed my afro down a bit.

When I used to go over to New York I would try and buy the same gear for my kids, because I wanted Mark, and later Russell, to wear what I was wearing – Mini Me! I wasn't going to put them in market clothes, but I'd searched all over London, where the only place I found anything like that was a tiny shop at the back of High Street Kensington station, and even then they never had that much choice. In New York, though, there were kids' versions of everything – I'd find kids' versions of the Adidas trainers I was wearing, I'd find little Lacoste shirts, little Pumas . . . These days we take the availability of kids' sizes for granted – Weeboks – but in the 1980s you couldn't get anything small. One year, just after Michael Jordan had done his deal with Nike, they were premiering Air Jordans and I knew it would be ages before they sold them in child sizes in England, but I found a shop that had them in New York. My son was made up when I got home with them and I loved it when people would say to me, 'Where did you get that?', and I'd smile and say, 'I got it in New York!' Later on, the boys used to tease me about the lengths I'd go to get shoes and clothes for them, but they're also really glad I did because it instilled my sense of style and fashion into them.

I never got into the mod revival fashion. I think I must have been too old because I thought it was too close to what I actually remembered in the original skinhead days – a lot of my mates from ten years previously had been suited and booted mods. I felt like I couldn't go there because I'd already done all that. I liked the whole Two Tone thing, and dress-wise, although there was a load of kids in silly pork pie hats, a few of them had the real thing and looked great when they pulled it off. It wasn't my look, but I always admired kids, male or female, who carried off their look whatever music or style trend they were into. I've always admired the street fashions and given special respect to the black boys and black girls who dared to be different.

We take dressing how we want for granted now, but it wasn't always that way. Whether it was because of our finances, or lack of them, within our community we tended to be very straight. Most kids in their teens were going to church and they couldn't take risks, it was all very conservative, very regular. Because I was never forced to do anything, I liked to play around and experiment as far as my meagre finances would allow me. Also, I had no problem with people on the margins who looked different. In fact I absolutely loved that and I had no problem with the punk thing when it came around, although a lot of my mates did – or they simply just didn't get it. I totally got it, it was pure rebelliousness, which to me as a young man was what so much fashion was about.

These days I'm far more relaxed about fashion, because I think I've arrived at a look and I'm confident enough to stick with it. Because I'm not constantly counting the pennies when I go clothes shopping now, I can pretty much indulge myself and have arrived at a look that's a combination of so much of what I've loved in the past. I'll mix and match, with the only constant being hats – I love hats and am very rarely seen in public without one.

Stuarts is still there on the Uxbridge Road, he's expanded into a double-fronted shop and he caters for blokes of my age who still aspire to that football casual – you can still get a lovely Fila tracksuit top there. John Simons, who had the Ivy shop in Richmond, has a shop in Marylebone now, so that look is still available and still as stylish. I'm really pleased I came up when I did, because I had all the advantages of the adventurousness and rebelliousness of fashion in the 1970s and '80s, but didn't get caught up in what came next when the big corporations turned it all into McDonald's versions of clothes. Of course it helped that I had the eye as well as the ear.

part six:
deejaying

chapter thirty: sound system

I wanted to share Joey's sound system with him, but there were a couple of things I wouldn't share, the first being the name 'Great Tribulation'. I wanted to create my own separate identity for what I wanted to do, so nobody would think it was part of the reggae sound that was reasonably well known locally. Also, it was far too roots reggae a name for me. That said, Joey had a perfectly good reason behind it – the actual building of the sound system had been a tribulation because he physically built it over that winter of 1974/1975, and at the time he was outside in knee-deep snow soldering, screwing, sawing with no help from me. However, I thought it was a miserable name and it didn't express the kind of Saturday night party vibe I wanted to put out.

He had finished the speaker boxes with 'GT' on all of them, so I figured when I was doing my thing on it I'd just call my operation that, GT. Then I had a flash of inspiration, a real light bulb moment. During my first trip to New York in the summer of 1979, the year before we first played Carnival, Chic's single 'Good Times' had been massive out there – all I was hearing everywhere I went was, *'These are the good times / Leave your cares behind . . .'* I was at a gig Joe was doing and just staring at the boxes and it hit me – I'm going to call this sound system Good Times, that way we've still got the GT. When I'm using it it's going to be Good Times, when Joey uses it it's going to be Great Tribulation. My one proviso was that when we went to Carnival we'd go as Good Times, because it was me that wanted to go there, and Joey never did. So it was agreed. I even kept the red, green and gold colours in all my branding – logos, flyers, posters and so on – it's subtle and not at all in your face, but it was in keeping with how the sound system looked and a nod to the whole sound system heritage.

The other thing I insisted on was having double decks, because I wanted continuous music and I'd seen how well they were used on Uncle Leo's sound system. Back then, all reggae sound systems used only one deck – it was like a tradition thing maybe, because that was how the first rigs did it in Jamaica in the 1950s! So double decks were like an anathema to my brother, and although he was totally in charge of all the technical and physical aspects of the sound, he basically told me if that was what I wanted I was going to have to go and get them myself! I went out and bought second-hand Disco Dave decks, set them up in my mum's front room and Joey was actually pretty impressed. Within hours he'd taken the whole thing apart and rewired them to work with his pre-amp and amplifiers. Although he still wanted to use the single deck as Great Tribulation, he supported me with what I needed.

The sound system wasn't very big, it was house party size, but Joey built extra boxes before we went to Carnival because he was looking to move Great Tribulation up a level in order to play church halls and community centres. I loved the way he built it, his attention to detail and quality of sound were second to none. Quality-wise he was easily as good as the bigger, more powerful sound systems.

After the first Carnival I didn't do any deejaying anywhere, but Joey was working hard to build up his sound system's reputation and I'd often go with him to support it. Sound systems are real collectives, so although I didn't much like the gigs they were doing I was very much part of it and when it was Good Times I never considered myself a deejay on my own, like I am today. Back then it was, 'You want me? You book the sound ... Deejay? What's that?' I did get offered one or two bookings, but that meant the whole sound system: me, playing the music as the selector; my brother, the sound operator; my MC/hype man; and all the crew, so we get paid and the money goes to six men equally after expenses. Sound systems of that size rarely make any money – it's more like a hobby, the guys 'in the sound' have jobs and put money in each week to maintain the equipment and buy records. I can't remember making a penny out of it in those days.

This approach could be a bit limiting if we wanted to move out of the church halls, because there weren't many clubs and purpose-built venues that were going to invite us to wheel in the sound and stick speaker cables all over the place with gaffer tape. A few places did, but then they tell you your music's too loud and to turn it down. There was a whole circuit of Caribbean clubs around London, and also other cities with big West Indian populations, but they were kind of jacket-and-tie, chicken-in-the-basket places aiming for an older, more 'respectable' black clientele – really they saw themselves as cut-price versions of Baileys or Top Rank suites. This one in Willesden, the Apollo, let us put the sound in there so we played it every Friday, and it was a million miles from the world I inhabited and the things I wanted to be doing. It always smelled musty, the clientele weren't there for us, and getting paid was like getting blood out of a stone.

Although I used to think, 'Who's going to go to the fucking Apollo club in Willesden?', I wasn't wasting my time because I was constantly learning by observing what *not* to do. Most of it had to do with ambition and marketing and creative nous – I was a creative, I understood marketing, I understood PR and I knew there had to be a way to move the whole sound system thing forward. I realised it was essentially a generational thing, as the first generation of sound systems that had set up in this country were very traditional and would only do things in the original Jamaican way – like the single decks thing. Now, the reggae industry in England was keeping it that way because all concerned felt comfortable with it. These clubs like the Apollo were very traditional, which is why they wanted a sound system in there. I was part of a new generation that recognised the sound system as having the potential to be the perfect creative and commercial business model, if managed properly, but saw it as having potential far beyond reggae dances, which hadn't evolved in thirty years. Even soul guys only ten years older than me were so set in their ways that it never occurred to them that a sound system could play funk, to them sound systems were reggae and that was that. My generation were asking, 'Why can't we use the same methods and play James Brown instead of Dennis Brown?', and starting to do something about it.

If I hadn't seen all this I might have ended up stuck in that old-school world, professionally, but what I wanted out of that life was completely different and I was learning what I needed to do because I knew it was time for me to make a move.

This would have been the very early 1980s, when I'd immersed myself in how sound systems worked, and my soul club scene really wasn't doing it for me any more. Soho was in decline, Upstairs at Ronnie's had stopped, Crackers was past its heyday, and the West End opinion formers and cultural leaders seemed to have disappeared. I have no idea where they went, because it was always a loose network where you'd just nod and smile at people you saw, not like today where everybody exchanges numbers. The soul scene had gone completely suburban, and although keeping up with music was a constant with me, I was going to football more and more. Also, I had a young family at the time, and knew I had to knuckle down, so moving away from clubbing every night wasn't such a bad thing. Not that any of the above stifled my ambition.

When I first went to New York, I had watched hip-hop and electro culture emerging; now it was reaching England and shifting black music's focus, as the existing soul establishment didn't know how to handle it. I loved this, because early hip-hop was completely anarchic – there was something so punky about it – and it was putting the music back into the hands of the people who were making it, reconnecting it with the culture. This was very important to me, and made more so by one new booking I did get, not for the sound system but for me as deejay in a club.

A friend of mine, Paul, who used to rave with us and was the first black guy I knew to go to university, was quite connected and a definite wannabe manager/promoter. He got me a gig at that disco in Denham, Buckinghamshire, straight down the M40 from where I lived. He'd spun them a story about how I'd played in loads of London clubs, and as this is out in the sticks the manager takes a chance – twenty-five quid and Paul took his percentage. The club wasn't very busy at all, after two or three records there's about twenty people in there, girls at one end of the dancefloor, blokes at the bar – logs. I'm playing all the latest stuff, nobody's dancing and I'm rapidly losing interest. The manager comes over and tells me he's taking me off, 'I think you're good', he said. I'm thinking, 'No you don't!' Then he tells me, 'They don't like the music, your music's too black.' I put on one more record, packed up and let this log deejay come on, but I never forgot that! While it taught me that tastes are different the further you go from London, I also vowed that nobody would ever tell me my music was too black again. It was one more thing pushing me into doing my own thing on the sound system.

That night did have a happy ending, because over twenty years later I was working for a promoter who actually booked me into the same club, which this time was rammed because I was playing there. I was banging out all the Ibiza and acid house tunes, the crowd are going crazy, dancing on tables, dancing on the bar and the manager's loving it! 'Norman, can you play for another hour?' He's locked us all in there! And

I'm saying yes, but really I'm thinking, 'Fuckers! Tell me my music's too black now!' He even tried to book me as a resident and I just told him, 'Nah, mate, I don't do residencies.' That gave me the most satisfaction.

By the time I'd got two or three Carnivals under my belt, I was ready to start deejaying for real. The desire was burning a hole in me because by the time we got to 1984, people were turning up just because I was there. I'd seen the potential of Good Times at the Carnival and developed it as a music evangelist; I'd allowed us to do our thing and we'd ended up with a huge crowd around us. As I said earlier, a crowd that were there for *us*. By then I was sitting on fifteen years' worth of black music that had never been heard, plus I had everything that had been on the Crackers playlists in my record box; I had all the 100 Club playlists; I had all the B&S playlists . . . plus I had all the stuff I would have loved to have played but couldn't because the crowds weren't ready for it yet. Nobody could touch me for music.

I had what I'd learned from going out on the sound with Joey, and I knew I had deejay skills now because in 1983 and '84 I was ripping it up at our spot. Through that I'd learned to trust my instincts when playing the music and what I thought was right. I'd check out the music at clubs and think, 'Yeah! I could do better than this . . . he isn't reading the crowd.' Or I could feel when a place was ready to go *off* – I could sense it on the dancefloor – but the deejay didn't play the tune that would be driving it. By then I knew that because my instincts were so upfront I could come with literally any music.

It was all amounting to a general sense of frustration, and I had to find an outlet other than Carnival once a year, because we all knew the Good Times sound system was armed and dangerous and ready to go.

chapter thirty-one: house parties

Round about 1983, when we were looking for the best way to move Good Times up a level, I stumbled on this house party up on that big and infamous estate by Queen's Park, just north of the Harrow Road. Freshbeat was playing, one of the soul sound systems from the Carnival who were run by an old Crackers boy, so I thought I'd hear some decent music. We'd been up the West End, heard there was a party going on in that part of West Kilburn, and as it wasn't too much of a detour on the way home we thought we'd pass by. When we got there, we couldn't get up the road because there were so many cars parked outside – the place was *rammed*! So crowded down there at first we thought it was a reggae blues dance, but if it was Freshbeat it couldn't be.

Eventually we found somewhere to park, walked up the road and couldn't get near the front door! It was a big three-storey house and coming out of the first-floor windows I can hear something soulful, something funky. And I want to get in, but I can't see how! Then one of the guys taking money on the door recognised me from Carnival – he didn't know my name, he just knew my sound system, so he's calling out, 'Good Times ... Good Times ... Come in, man!' They squeezed me in and I made it up to the first floor – they really couldn't have got another person in there – and the deejay's playing in the back room. He's playing Reuben Wilson and quite a lot of 1970s stuff, which is, if I'm honest, boring the crowd, but I'm still fascinated by what's going on in there. Then another guy comes on with a new head and starts playing new, upfront stuff and suddenly the crowd is bubbling away nicely. I'm taking all of this in, and thinking, 'Yup! This is how to do it!' We got there at about one in the morning and I only intended to stay for about twenty minutes, but I didn't leave until eight o'clock in the morning. I was one of the last in there.

This party was so good, and I saw how they organised everything, how many people on the door, how the sound was set up, where the deejays could work, where the bar was and how it operated ... I was clocking *everything*. This was what we should be doing, so as soon as I got back home I started talking to my brother.

To me, this was proof that the soul blues could work – the same late night, pay-on-the-door, drinks-for-sale house party model, but playing soul and funk instead of reggae. It wasn't just the local herberts at this party, because the Freshbeat guys were faces on the scene. I was seeing all the West End club faces in there, and I'm thinking, 'How did you get the Crackers crowd, the Global Village lot to come up here?' It wasn't just a black party either, it was a well-mixed crowd with plenty of white people and a very chilled-out atmosphere. I was watching those guys closely: they were totally in charge of the whole thing, they could approach the music exactly how they knew it should be played, and they had a crowd that completely appreciated it. It was like what I aspired to do at Carnival, but this was in a local house and could happen more than once a year. All I could think was, 'Wow! This is what I need to be doing, this is the crowd I need to be reaching!' I knew if I could use our sound system and create a platform like that for myself, I could really grow as a deejay.

It didn't take too much to convince Joey we should try to do our own. Freshbeat did another one a couple weeks later, so we went and checked that out, then put on our first one a few weeks after that, in my sister's flat. She lived above shops in Harlesden High Street, at the end of the terrace down by Hawkeye Records. Her flat was on a corner so it was massive, and we put on the Good Times Soul Blues! This was before I was on the radio and there was no social media then, so I did flyers myself and handed them out anywhere I thought the crowd I wanted would be – clubs, other parties, record shops, clothes shops and so on. I spread it by word of mouth as well as I could, got some drinks in to run a bar and waited to see how it would go.

We were really looking on this as a trial run. It wasn't going to be huge and we were fully expecting it to be OK but not brilliant, more a learning curve than anything else. It was *mobbed*! The locals didn't have a clue what was going on, but I'd managed to pull in a load of the old Crackers people and because this was strictly my thing I could play what I liked. It was brilliant, in some ways better than Carnival because there were no people just wandering past or not really committed, this crowd was up here for no other reason than to hear soul music, the more upfront the better. I was probably showing off a bit, but they loved it. I knew we had found what I had been looking for. That's what kick-started us into doing house parties.

I wasn't playing in clubs yet, so that was all we did for quite a while. I was rapidly building a reputation as a deejay, and our parties were getting known as something people could rely on for a good safe event, so they became bigger and bigger. We were putting them on in these massive old houses around West Hampstead, Kensal Green, Kensal Rise, Grove ... I don't know how many parties we did, but it was loads, and we were making some serious money because this was something we controlled. We set it up the way we wanted to set it up, we could put as much or as little of the sound as we wanted in there, we ran the door, we ran the bar, with no overhead for the premises or money to split with a promoter or club owner. The procedure was always the same: scout a place, get in somehow and have a good look around, work out where to put things, where to run the bar and how to get power in. Then we'd print off the flyers and pass them out during the week before; we'd come back on the day to clean up, secure the back or other entrances; get the gear in, set up and we were away. Take the sound out as soon as the last record finished and that was that. Most importantly we could set the music agenda however we wanted, we didn't have to follow any pattern, no rules, no template ... all we had to do was get good people in, not just any people, but get that kind of West End/Soho party crowd that I was part of, and we were away.

The timing of this was perfect for me, because being a

conscious brother I had become so bored with that suburban soulboy/funk mafia, and used to sit there in these long
reasoning sessions with Joey saying, 'Why don't we get anywhere? As blacks, why isn't it happening for us? Why are we
letting them just take our music and our culture?' We used
to have serious debates on this level, talking about how we
can create this stuff but after that we don't control it – look
at our acts, with record companies that don't understand
them and radio and clubs that, essentially, do what the record
companies tell them and we have no say! I had a desire to be
independent that was really driving me – hence my sets at
Carnival. I was going through a phase when I saw an 'us and
them' situation and my aim was to do it without any help
from them. Or, as so often was the case, any permission from
them. My attitude was: I can't bring my sound in to your
club? That's OK, I don't want to go into your club anyway. I
didn't want anybody else's rules keeping me down. We were
from the street.

That's why this house party thing made so much sense to
me, because it was what sound systems were made for – that
whole blues dance subculture that sprang up when black
people were refused entry to clubs and dancehalls in London
in the 1950s. We understood it and weren't scared to go the
DIY route when it came to our music. Doing it like this felt
rebellious and made me feel like I was in control.

It was all working out brilliantly for us, Joey was there as
a cool brother and loving it because *it was working*. Whatever
he might have thought of our music or our crowds, why rock
the boat? In his view, Norman's making decisions that are to
our mutual benefit, the sound's playing out every week, the

sound's making money, the sound's getting popular – what's the problem? He was making wages out of it, which never would have happened if he was still just doing his reggae things; also, he was having his cake and eating it because he was still out there as Great Tribulation doing his christenings, and still doing his sound clashes in community centres on a Sunday.

There were so many places to choose from back then; we were never short of big places to play. I did a really big one in a disused girls' school on Hampstead Heath – which turned out to be pretty notorious; I did one in one of those enormous posh mansions on The Bishops Avenue, it was being squatted at the time; I did a massive one right next door to Richard Branson's house at number 11 Holland Park. Another one was on Chiswick High Road, and we did it to raise funds for Erin Pizzey's refuge for battered women – Chiswick Women's Aid, which was only half a mile from the party. I shared it with a sound system called Menassah and we called it Hammetyville – Hammersmith/Amityville! – it was huge and it was the closest I ever came to getting arrested and having our gear confiscated when the police tried to close us down.

It was in this big Victorian house next to Gunnersbury station and it was dangerously overcrowded. Hundreds of people trying to get in blocked Chiswick High Road and Old Bill couldn't get anywhere near it. Because this party was nearly all white kids, students, middle-class kids, they just put a couple of cars across the way and watched – had this been a black rave every copper in London would have been there closing it down by any means necessary! That was great, but then I started to get worried, thinking that when this lot had gone they'd be going to collar us. I was really concerned about how we were going to get the equipment out, and thinking on my feet I came up with a plan. When we were stringing down at about six in the morning, I went on the mic and asked everyone left in the room to help us string down, and then for everyone to carry a piece of kit outside. What I didn't want was for the place to be empty of punters, Old Bill rushes in, sees only us and all our gear and nicks us. We took down the tweeters, we took down the boxes and when everybody's got something, I said, 'Right, on my signal all walk out at the same time round to the van.' I knew all these white kids – there was a couple of dozen of them – wouldn't get nicked!

Meanwhile I put on the overalls I'd been wearing when we cleaned the place out, grabbed a broom and stood by the front door. Everybody's walking out with stuff, Old Bill is clearly baffled and finally gets brave enough to come over. I'd started sweeping and they asked me who the organiser was and where could they find him. I just acted really cross: '*Organiser?* I'd like to find the organiser – I haven't been paid! You find him, let him know I haven't been paid yet.' They were just standing there as kids streamed out with bits of kit, loading it up in the van around the corner and pretty soon the house is empty. One thing I could always guarantee with white people at a rave was that once you'd packed up, there'd be a few of them asleep on the floor somewhere, drunk or off their heads. Counting on that, I told the coppers, 'Try the top of the house, I haven't been up there yet.' This would be four floors up, and as soon as they went up the stairs I slipped out and closed the door. I've got no idea what happened after that – we'd got all our kit out safely and we were away. It was close but we'd pulled it off! What I did find out later was when I'd asked people to carry everything out, they'd taken me literally and taken *everything*! This house had a fully fitted kitchen and they'd stripped it bare, stolen the microwave, the oven, *everything*!

By the middle of that decade the house party scene was really blowing up across a whole spectrum of black music, with some of the smaller sound systems being particularly inventive about getting premises. A soundman would pay off somebody in an estate agent to give them the keys to an empty house for the weekend; or decorating parties weren't uncommon – if a sound system knew somebody who was about to move into a flat, they'd say let us have a party in there and we'll decorate it for you after! Then there were really big events like this one that used to happen practically every Saturday in Tottenham, different house each time, with Rapattack playing. They were in those huge houses up by Tottenham Green and they were always rammed, late night, yet the police never did anything about them. The pro-moter who put them on was real old school and kept trying to get me to work with him – every time he saw me it was all, 'Good Times! Mister Good Times! Come, mek we talk! Let's mek a dance!' I always tried to swerve him, because I knew my crowd and that Tottenham crowd wouldn't have worked together. He used to make me laugh because he'd offer me a sound clash with Rapattack, thinking that would sway me!

We stayed away from that black ghetto scene, where there

were plenty of sounds like Rapattack doing the reggae cross-over scene. We kept our crowd select and it was always just below the mainstream radar. I was paranoid about attracting the ragga posse, the same posses that used to distress me at Carnival. I didn't want any of them there, so the consequence of that was we hardly played any reggae, we only played rare groove, soul, funk and early house.

Our parties were becoming so big and so successful that the risk of us getting busted was rising rapidly. Old Bill had properly caught on to the house party scene, and quite a few – notably the black parties – were getting raided. Although we were making our reputation and a fair amount of money, the last thing I wanted was to get arrested for doing them. Also, as you get better known you attract attention from the wrong crowd. We'd heard about a few house parties that were getting robbed by these two south London gangs that were travelling across the city and using CS gas, like the gangs that had been at Carnival. Two or three of them would steam in, gas the house by spraying it everywhere, then as the people ran out they'd snatch watches, bag and chains, throwing them into bin bags, then they'd get out of there. Because our reputation was spreading, I knew we'd soon be on their radar, if we weren't already – we always looked like easy pickings because it was such a relaxed atmosphere, with so many girls. With all this in the background, I knew we had to get out of the house party scene.

chapter thirty-two: kiss fm

There were other reasons for wanting to move on from the house parties too. I won't say I got bored with them, but I believed we as a sound system were in danger of stagnating. Everything goes in cycles and that scene had got as big as it was ever likely to get – and the police attention wasn't helping. Being as naturally restless as I was, I was looking for a new challenge and once again was turning my attention to how London's black deejays, who had created and controlled the house party scene, could advance themselves to the recognition they deserved. What prompted me into action at this point was that I had just met a young deejay, Derek Boland, or Derek B as he was known, who also pushed me into thinking harder about what I was doing.

There was very little on the London soul club scene that didn't come across my radar, and two or three times I'd heard about this mixed race kid who was doing warm-up for Froggy, an Essex deejay who was part of that Soul Mafia crowd. How he was *really* good – better than the guy he was opening for. They'd just started on a Sunday at Bentley's, the old Bridge House in Canning Town, and I went down on my own to discreetly check him out. I didn't even know his name at this point. It wasn't very busy, but I paid to get in, bought a drink and stood at the back to watch him warm the place up. As it got busy so did he: he played brilliantly, cutting, mixing, scratching, the crowd was absolutely loving it. Then he played a couple of Leroy Burgess tunes, and I was like, '*What!?!?!* Nobody plays this!' I had to go and talk to him.

When he'd finished his set I went up to him, told him his set was brilliant and asked who he was. He was really friendly and affable, just said, 'My name's Derek', and I just introduced myself as Norman – I didn't say Good Times, because he would have known about the sound system. I told him that was the first time I'd heard anybody play Leroy Burgess outside the West End, he was amazed I even knew who Leroy Burgess was, and asked me if I knew other stuff by him. I told him I've got everything he's ever done, and I'll bring some up for you next week, and that was it – two music nerds bonding over Leroy Burgess!

I took Derek's number and as soon as I got home it was another reasoning session with my brother. I told him about this kid who was unbelievably good, but he was never going to get a squeeze, he's going to warm up for Froggy forever. I told Joey that Derek was actually pulling his own crowd at Bentley's because he was so much better than the headline deejay. Boland reminded me of me from a few years back, and the root of what Joe and I were talking about was how I wanted to take it upon myself to help all the black deejays I knew who weren't getting the breaks they should be. I had the music; I knew how to play it; I had the knowledge of how the club and sound system business worked; we had the sound system . . . These days, this would be called mentoring, because what I wanted to be able to do was tell these young, talented deejays, 'If you need advice or you need stuff, if it's to help you move up in what you're doing, it's yours. You just tell me what you need.' I felt like a bit of a drug dealer – tell me what you need and I can get it for you!

The next time I went up to Bentley's I stayed around for Froggy's set – which was okay in that suburban soulboy kind of way – but Derek wanted to talk to me afterwards. He gave me a lift back to his house in South Woodford and we reasoned until about six in the morning, talking about music, obviously, but also how the business worked and the whole politics of the London club scene. That's when I really knew that what Joey and I had discussed was the right way to go. I told Derek whatever music he needed that he didn't have, I would sort him out.

A couple of weeks later he came round my house and he was brilliant – he *charmed* my mum and dad, to the degree that he only came for a couple of hours on a Friday and I actually got him out of the house on the Monday! I thought they were going to adopt him! He was the first person I let in my record library, and he said he'd never seen so many albums and singles in his life. As well as playing tunes virtually non-stop, we got into a couple of deep reasoning sessions in which he told me I was doing myself a disservice. He was telling me that with all this music I should be deejaying on a much larger scale, that myself and Good Times should be sharing this music on a national level. He convinced me that I should be taking this more seriously, because up until then the Carnival and the house parties had been more like a hobby – we were well known locally, but nowhere near what you could call famous. Derek argued we needed to be bigger than that, or what's it all for?

This was 1983 or 1984, and Derek made me think about the future – how if I wasn't going to do this deejay thing forever, then he and his generation were the future and it was up to us to help them all we could. I'd got to know Paul Anderson by this time and I remember talking to him about the same thing, and that made me realise that none of us black deejays or sound systems really knew each other. And if we did, we were probably in competition. The Soul Mafia thing dominated because they all knew each other, went to school with each other, stitched up the circuit and the business between them. There we were, north, south, east and west, all the big soul and funk sound systems in London, and although we could probably all find each other if we had to, we didn't even have each other's phone numbers. Why haven't I got Skanky from Funkadelic's phone number? Why haven't I got Paul Anderson's phone number? Why haven't I got Jazzie B's phone number? . . . The only way we were going to move forward was to organise ourselves. For ourselves.

We needed to network, we needed to know each other, but – and this isn't just among the black sound systems – there was all the ego and self-interest getting in the way. We never got along for long, we got along for a few minutes when it was in our interests and when it wasn't we reverted to dog-eat-dog. We had to understand that working as a collective, even if something may not benefit an individual at a certain time, is always going to be stronger. I was well aware of the

realities and knew that one of my biggest tasks was to over-
come that perception that black people can't work together
for the common good, so I called a meeting.

I managed to get hold of virtually every black soul sound
system or deejay in London and invited them all to come
to my mum's house in Acton. It turned out to be quite a
historic meeting, as it was really all representatives of the
sound systems. There were very few independent black
deejays at that time, and I didn't invite any of the white
deejays – no Westwood, no Steve Walsh or the like. Paul
Anderson of Troublefunk was there; Derek Boland came –
sadly Derek has passed now; Tosca Jackson came; Jazzie B
was there; Bobby and Steve from Zoo came; Rappattack's
Allister; Tony Freshbeat was there; George and Skanky from
Funkadelic in south London turned up; Chris of Winner
Roadshow ... there were about twenty of us in my record
room, where more than a few of us were enjoying a spliff!
It was the first time many of us had met. We'd all heard of
each other by reputation for months or maybe years, but
there'd never been anything like this. I wish I had a photograph of the assembly, but nobody took photos back then.

What I was aiming for was a forum where we all shook
hands, exchanged numbers, realised who was actually in
charge – us – and kept in touch to work together. It was
an introduction more than anything else. Derek, however,
wanted to talk about starting a radio station, and so did Tosca
Jackson, but they had two very different ideas about what
the station should be. Unfortunately that summed up the
way the meeting had gone. Derek pitched his idea for a station, based on the talent that was in that room at that time,

but there were so many disparate voices, all driven by self-interest, all wanting to have their say on his concept, that I knew it was never going to happen. I remember saying to my brother, just before the meeting broke up, 'This is no good, there's too many fucking egos in here. This is a complete waste of time.' It disappointed me hugely that those white boys had the pirate radio thing locked down with stations like JFM, Invicta and Horizon, and we couldn't even get on in this room. The meeting wasn't a complete bust, however. Now people had met, and whether they worked together or not after that, at least they had the means to now they'd exchanged numbers.

As everybody was leaving, Tosca held back, asking for a quiet word with me. He said he didn't want to talk about this in front of the others, but he and Gordon Mac, a former JFM soul deejay, were a long way down the road to starting their own new radio station, and they wanted me and my brother to be part of it. He said the fact I'd managed to organise something like this made us all the more impressive, at which point I said, 'If it's going to turn out anything like this I don't want to know!' I didn't really know Tosca, but I knew he had a reputation for being quite shrewd; I knew Gordon Mac vaguely and I trusted him, but when Tosca told me George Power from Crackers had invested in this new station, my ears really pricked up. Also, I liked his attitude over the name of the station, which I think came about because the three of them all deejayed at Kisses nightclub in Peckham – when Peckham was black. I said, 'Why call it Kiss FM when there's a famous American radio station with the same name?', and he said, 'Let them sue us! They're so far away, they won't come to England!'

Three or four days later Joey and I rang him and he told us they'd already done a couple of very discreet trials. It was stuff that Joey and I had often thought about but had figured was pie in the sky, yet they'd already tried and tested it. I was learning very quickly that Tosca didn't say much because he was a doer, not a talker, and I came to admire that in him. I also realised that they were all a good few years younger than me – this generation knew what time it was and they weren't going to get screwed over like we did. It was up to me to contribute all I could as they were definitely going to move things forward. I couldn't say no, but I didn't hear anything back from him for so long that I pretty much forgot about it. Then out of the blue the phone rings at my mum's – this is pre-mobile days, remember. When Mum told me it was a guy called Tosca I had to think for a second about who that was! 'Tosca, what's going on?' ... 'Remember that radio station I told you about, we've already started it, you've got a show on it, so we'll see you at the studio on Wednesday.' That was so weird, because I hadn't spoken to him since that phone call, so I'd had no chance to turn down or accept this thing. I found his number, rang him back and he couldn't stop laughing! Essentially he told me, 'Here's the studio address, it's south-east London by Greenwich Park, you're on air from seven until nine. That's your show. Bye!' *Click.* I said he was a man of few words.

I was more than a bit intrigued, so Joey and I drove down there in the Ford Escort van from the print shop – our only form of transport – and arrived at this really decrepit tower block. I had no idea what to expect. I go in, Gordon's in there because he's just done his show, and I'm nervous as hell as I've never done any broadcasting before. I told him this and he just said, 'There's nothing to worry about – it's a very basic set-up, just cue up the next record after the one you're playing, and you don't need to talk much.' I didn't, either, in fact I don't think I said a single word for the first twenty minutes! But in spite of the sweaty palms, I was comfortable behind the decks, my brother had come down to give me a bit of support, and I got right into it.

It gave me an amazing buzz, far beyond what I normally got out of deejaying on the sound system. The fact that we were reaching more and more people as they tuned in, far more than any gig I'd ever done, got me thinking about how powerful a medium radio is. I could understand why the government controlled it so rigidly, and could see what an opportunity this pirate radio was in our grasp – we didn't get a look in on television, but now we had a look in on the radio, where they couldn't stamp us out. It was also a big nod to the power of networking, as this came about out of that meeting at my mum's house, with Tosca getting the chance to see what I could do and talk to me face to face.

It was all going so well for a few months, then I get a panicked call from Gordon telling me the station's going to close down in a couple of days' time if we don't get some advertisers or investors. We'd been losing aerials through raids at a much quicker rate than anticipated, and George had been the only one fronting up the money for replacements. Him and Gordon had been doing gigs to raise cash, but now he was about to pull out. Gordon said he didn't want to ask but he knew that Good Times was making money – did we want to put money into Kiss? Straight away I said no, we didn't want to get involved at all, the money we were making was for improving the sound system, not to build a radio station we didn't even own. Then Gordon asked whether we wanted to take George's place as an *investor*. That was different. We would have some ownership. These were exciting times, so I jumped in and Gordon told me it would cost Joe and I £1,200 – £600 each, a king's ransom back in those days. They were so close to closing that we had twenty-four hours to think it over and come up with the money. Gordon said any longer and Kiss would go off the air, never to come back.

Another all-night reasoning session took place, during which we discussed how much London needed a black-owned and -run soul music station – the only other black pirates were DBC (Dread Broadcast Corporation) and LWR, who were both a bit reggaefied. We also looked at it on a purely self-interested level – just think of all the gigs we could promote, given those white stations advertised clubs and gigs all over the place. We could see so many advantages, so I rang Gordon back and told him we were in and to just give us a day to raise the money. Of course we didn't have it, but my dad was very cool and after we told him all about it he lent us half and we scraped together the rest. I told Gordon to come round my parents' house – they wanted to meet him – and we'll do the deal. A few months ago I'd never so much as broadcast, now Joey and I, as Good Times, were part-owners of a functioning radio station.

And, whatever way you want to look at it, we'd saved it,

so I felt entirely justified in taking it upon myself to recruit some new deejays, or at least strongly recommend them. What I didn't want happening was for Gordon and Tosca to turn it into another LWR, because we were far cooler than that. LWR was right for their listenership – if you've ever been to Lewisham or Peckham – but I was a west-end kid, and those other stations never surprised you. The whole point about being a pirate was you were breaking the *actual* law, so why not break the supposed laws of broadcasting and shake it up a bit? When they started LWR, one of the two brothers who owned it, Zak Dee, wanted me on it, it was all, 'Good Times . . . Come in!' but I was always, 'No thanks, if I do any pirate radio it has to be from a cooler standpoint than that.' Jazzie B had the same mindset – he was never going to join LWR or anything like that, and he understood the importance of rebranding when he changed the name of his sound system from Jah Rico to Soul II Soul.

Or worse still, I didn't want Kiss to become a ghetto clone of white pirate radio stations from North Kent or Surrey or Berkshire, which were, essentially, *Blues & Soul* on the air. They all got their tunes from record companies and all the deejays wanted to be Robbie Vincent or Chris Hill, but my perspective was that we ought to be Soho cool with an artistic edge. I wanted us to be a democratic mix of black and white deejays, male and female deejays, who were doing cool parties, a world away from that suburban disco thing. I wanted no part of either the black or white suburban thing, but because Gordon came from that end I had to be on him all the time to dissuade him from hiring all of those sorts of deejay.

By the time Kiss launched in 1985, I had clearly defined what I was doing with the sound system: when I was playing to a black suburban crowd, such as in Grove, it was Good Times; then I was also doing a series of underground parties under my trendy alter ego Shake and Fingerpop, parties inspired by the whole punk anarchic thing. That's what I wanted to bring to Kiss, and I knew from the diversity of the crowd I was getting that the audience was out there for it – I was getting all kinds at Shake and Fingerpop parties, from rockabillies to new romantics, to goths, punks, soul boys, jazzers, mods . . . even clued-up Rasta men who, through my brother, wanted to see what the underground was like. Plus I'd make it my mission to go and check out other places, to see who was pulling the people we wanted, so just as I'd go to Derek Boland at Bentley's, where he was playing good groove and boogie, I'd go to Flim Flam at Goldsmith's College in Deptford on a Monday night. That's where I met Jonathan More, who went on to become half of Coldcut, but back then he was an art teacher there and ran that night, which would get a thousand funky, punky, arty kids in there. He'd play a mash-up of black music, go-go and rockabilly and I loved it.

I went back to Gordon, telling him the guy was brilliant, that he's getting a thousand kids, that this wasn't the Chris Hill soulboy thing, these were cool kids, the next generation. I was raving about Jonathan, saying we need to get him on the station if we want to move forward. Gordon agreed to give him a couple of weeks on a trial basis, an afternoon show, before they made a decision.

When Jonathan did his first show, like me he was really nervous because he'd never done radio before, and at the

With my brother Joey and sister Carol, Ladbroke Grove 1961-62

Acton 1976

At my son Mark's christening, Acton 1977
Left to right: Mark O'Brien, Me, Elvis Thomas and Adrian Browne

Outside Manchester Piccadilly station, 1978
Left to right: Mark O'Brien, Cifas Charles, Justus Cox and myself. On the way to the Ritz Jazz Funk all dayer

Liverpool St station, 1978. On the way to Petticoat Lane market

With my sons. Left to right: Russell and Mark in the late 1980s

Doing my thing at pirate Kiss 100 FM in the late 1980s

Raregroove 1986/7. Left to right: Joey and me

Outside Bagley's nightclub, King's Cross, in late 1990s. This is from my personal collection of Raleigh choppers

Soul II Soul at Brixton Academy with Jazzy B, Russell and Mark

Miss Moneypenny's in the 2000s. Lee Garrick in the foreground in T-shirt

MBE – Buckingham Palace, November 2002

The MBE after party, with Jazzy B

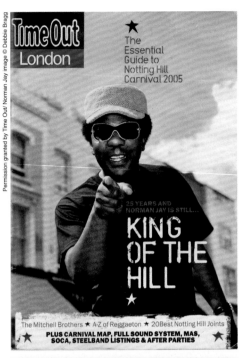

Time Out article 2005

With the Godfather of Soul,
Mr James Brown, 2005

Island of Jersey, Channel Isles in the 2000s. Left to right: Jazzy B (Soul to Soul) and Grant Marshall a.k.a DJ Daddy G from Massive Attack

White Hart Lane, Tottenham, 2006/7

With Paul Weller at Latitude Festival, 2012

Carl Cox, Ibiza 2012

Sunsplash 2009 – Antalya, Turkey with Jane, my wife

Aboard the Good Times bus, 2012

Notting Hill Carnival 2012 with DJ Marky (centre), MC Stamina (far left), bystander in the back

With my best pal Bryan Webb – HMS Good Times party, August 2015

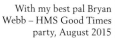

Good Times family 2013. Left to right: Sister Patsy and DJ Rudy Ranx

Mum, Dad and Russell with me, 2013

I did a line of clothing for Gabicci in 2013 in association with '40 years of soul'

Promo shots for for House of Common festival 2016

Christchurch, New Zealand 2017

Kiss inner circle's weekly deejay briefing, they were unani-
mous: 'He's shit, get rid of him! Don't bother with his second
show!' I went nuts! I really fought Jonathan's corner. 'Fuck
you lot! You just don't get it!' I told them he was more than
your Peckham or your Notting Hill or your Hackney, that
no other black music pirate was doing anything like this.
With our so-called rivals it was all either sunny-side Surrey
or Streatham 'n' cammies, nothing that reflected the cooler
London, what was happening in Camden or on the King's
Road. I laid it out because back then current black music
radio was either *Blues & Soul* or *Black Echoes*, but there was
no Face Radio, no iD radio, no City Limits radio: the existing
stations weren't in those magazines and neither would we be
if we didn't shift our approach. I told them there were pockets of cool all over London that I knew about because I went
to those events, but they had no black representation and we
could be that. Which was why we needed to keep Jonathan
on the air, because those kids didn't know who we were and
we had no way of accessing them, but he had schooled them
into this left-field mash-up music and that talent ought to be
reflected on the station. To give Gordon his due, he listened
to me – maybe as he was a little bit older, a bit more worldly,
he could see the importance of it.

We recruited Jonathan, and when he came he turned the
heat up on the other deejays on the station and definitely
helped to establish the Kiss FM that everybody remembers –
the cult Kiss that wasn't like the others and was much bolder
with its programming. Saturdays with my *Original Rare
Groove* show, followed straight after by Jonathan More's

Meltdown, established us as uber-hip and the new generation of style magazines loved us. With no disrespect to the
other deejays, everybody contributed to what Kiss became,
but trendy Camden wouldn't be listening to Trevor Nelson
or Paul Anderson or Colin Dale if they were on any other
station. We attracted all these cool characters who went on
to become massive: Jazzie B ... David Rodigan ... Judge
Jules ... We became the new media darlings, which ultimately helped us when we came to make our application to
become a legal station.

chapter thirty-three: warehouses I

Warehouses were the next logical step for me. There had been a couple of times when I had almost got my collar felt doing the house parties, so I knew I needed to move off that scene. I knew about warehouse parties in theory, because a few years before I'd read about one that happened in Sydney, Australia, where Grace Jones was headlining and twenty thousand people turned up. It wasn't licensed, therefore pretty much illegal, and the event is legendary among older Australian clubbers. Back then I couldn't quite imagine playing to that amount of people at a rave, but the image always stayed with me at the back of my mind. The house parties were great, we were blessed with all those big Victorian houses out in west London, but I knew that if we were going to get any bigger, we needed to come out of the houses. We needed to find something like a factory space.

The first warehouse party I went to was while I was still doing the houses. It was off Rosebery Avenue in Clerkenwell, very hush-hush, but I got a whisper about it from somebody at the Wag club in Soho. Yes, I hated the Wag's blatantly racist door policy (and I should say that it didn't come from the promoters, who were never racist to anyone and are friends of mine to this day), but they used to let me in – maybe, to them, I didn't look threatening. The warehouse notion had appealed to me since I read about the Grace Jones thing, and when I got there it was Phil Dirtbox on the door, who was something of an icon on the 1980s London club scene – well over six feet tall and always wore a bowler hat. I knew it was going to be interesting. There must have been 100 to 150 people in there. The music was absolute crap, the sound system kept breaking down, but I loved it. I loved the crowd! It was full of real post-punk party types, creatures of the night, ne'er do wells, punks, the homeless . . . I loved the dark-side mix of people. There were even a few Rastas in there . . . a few gays in there . . . to me, this was my utopia crowd! Within seconds I'd realised I needed to be doing one of these things – these were the sorts of people I ought to be playing my music to on the sound system.

These were West End stylers, fashionistas, creatives, and I very much saw myself as part of that kind of thing because I had such big ideas for Good Times. We'd already broken all the rules of sound systems, and now I wanted to go further and basically drag Good Times into the twenty-first century, demonstrating that this was how things should run now. If I could make this jump – and I didn't see why I couldn't – I could be successful, I could make a name for myself, I could make some money and I could be playing at all the coolest parties. My brother was as amenable as ever, because if it was a Good Times thing he trusted me and I had his full backing.

I wanted to check out a couple more before I made my

move, so I put myself about, asking the faces I recognised from that party, 'Where's the next one? Where's it gonna be?' It was in Battle Bridge Road behind King's Cross station, on the old Peabody Estate, which was about to be knocked down for the Eurostar terminal, so it was derelict. You had to really be in the know to have been able to find this party! There were these two white guys playing, Noel and Maurice Watson, who were young kids from Northern Ireland, and they were scratching and mixing brilliantly, they were hip-hop kids and doing it like I'd seen no black guy doing it. It's not something I'd ever think about, but they were so good I made a note of who they were and went up to them to tell them, 'That was badass, man, you were wicked!' I'm still in touch with Noel, but Maurice passed a few years ago.

They also did music reviews for *The Face* and *Arena*, so that crowd was there and it was when I bucked up with all those media people who went on to run those magazines. People like Dylan Jones and Sheryl Garratt, but at that time I didn't know what they did. I found myself rubbing shoulders with all sorts of people, there were a few cool black dudes in there – I did see Jazzie B in there. It wasn't the music or the people that really knocked me out, though, the whole event was incredible. It was a big space and it was as if there was a circus going on in there – fire eaters, jugglers, acrobats! I was just standing there thinking, '*Wow!* I have to do this for myself.'

I talked to a few people, got a few phone numbers, and I was constantly clocking the runnings – how everything worked – and asking loads of questions. 'How did you find this place?' ... 'Somebody tipped us off.' 'How did you get access?' ... 'It was empty, we just broke in!' 'How come there's no police here?' I think they thought they'd just been lucky with that, but I understood it was because they were never going to raid an all-white affair – I saw some of these parties where they'd turn up, talk to a couple of white girls at the door, it's all smiles, they'd go and the party would crack on. This was a huge consideration.

Away from it, when I was thinking it through properly, I knew I couldn't do anything like that as Good Times. By that time Good Times was massive, we had a brilliant reputation and we were attracting huge crowds, but although those crowds were mixed it was essentially a black thing, so we had a large black following. These warehouse parties were a different scene entirely; the Good Times crowd would never take to this sort of people and never take to this sort of music, because they were essentially conservative. This was a brand new, alternative culture that appealed to my sensibilities. After being in New York and going to counterculture things, hanging out with my punk mates and watching the rise of the mod revival, Two Tone and so on, all of this sat comfortably with me. Conversely, my black mates who were just out of reggae were so conservative that Good Times, which pushed it further than any other house party sound system, was as far as they would go.

My head was into playing music for this funky London elite art crowd, which I saw as something of a challenge. By the time I'd been to three or four of those parties, I was hearing Northern soul, go-go, a little bit of reggae, some hip-hop, they're playing rockabilly, some new wave tracks, and it was all underpinned by a black music soundtrack. Even if I didn't like all of the music – I've never particularly cared for rockabilly – I loved that anarchic mix. It left me thinking, 'I *know* I could do this. I've got all these records. And I'd do it properly.'

I needed to reinvent the sound system and create an alter ego that could attract this warehouse crowd and pass below the radar of the Good Times following. That's when I came up with Shake and Fingerpop as a separate entity, named after a '60s Motown tune by Junior Walker and a Northern soul dance. It seemed perfect. Same sound system, different moniker for the parties, and apart from deejaying I'd keep a very low profile. When I got into actually doing warehouses, I was partnered up with Judge Jules and his Family Funktion outfit, and he was smart enough to understand how it had to work. He was the front man, and he dealt with the police if they turned up. He was under no illusion that this couldn't happen if Old Bill thought I was behind it and that it was a black thing.

It was meeting Judge Jules and his crew that tipped me into doing warehouses, although in many ways we appear to be complete opposites. He was a very intelligent second-year law student at the London School of Economics, a middle-class white Jewish boy from Kentish Town via Hampstead, who I suppose by running the Family Funktion thing was rebelling in his own way. There was a whole posse of them who were pretty much from the same backgrounds, and what they had was a deep love and affection for black music. In a different way from that suburban Funk Mafia lot, who were basically running it as a business for their own ends, these guys were fans, they were no different to us – they loved the music and they loved the parties. That's how I connected with them so quickly and I loved working with them.

I learned an awful lot from Jules and his guys: they showed me how to organise, how to market what we were doing, how to network . . . Much of it was stuff I *thought* I knew, but this was taking it to another level. I was taking Good Times completely out of that black ghetto situation, as I realised what a big market there was out there, which if I was smart enough I could reach. There's a saying in the Caribbean that luck happens when preparation meets opportunity, which was exactly how I got together with Jules, another example of me being in the right place at exactly the right time.

I was by myself, driving back from some boogie rave in Wanstead or Leytonstone, one of Derek B's functions, and for weeks I'd been hearing whispers about this big, illegal party going off in King's Cross. It was about two in the morning and I was going to go home round the North Circular, but had a last-minute change of mind and thought I'd detour to see if I could find this party – I had no details of it. At the bottom of Pentonville Road, I saw loads of people walking away from the station. At that time there was nothing down in that area, maybe a few people left over from a late night at the Scala Cinema, but no nightclubs, so no reasons for crowds like this to be there. I parked round the back of St Pancras Town Hall, crossed over Euston Road and asked a couple of passing flat-top rockabilly types where the party was. 'Just up there, mate, under the arches at the side of the station.' I turned the corner and suddenly there's a crowd like a football crowd, but it's nearly three in the morning and these are real arty-looking Soho Boho types. There's about three hundred people in a six-deep queue, and I'm thinking, 'This is brilliant!'

I walked to the door just to suss it out and I heard, 'Norman! That you? Norman Jay! Good Times!' It was Jazzie B's older brother on the door, and he's ushering me through this little doorway entrance. This in itself was brilliant, because at that time we were used to getting knocked back from clubs with a mostly white clientele – you couldn't even walk to the front of the queue, let alone be taken in! Inside it was huge, there was easily a couple of thousand people in there, with more waiting outside as it wasn't full. It was two tunnel-like long spaces running the whole width of St Pancras station; one had a light on, the other didn't, which was funny, because it made it two raves in one, as the white kids had gone where the light was while all the black kids were in the dark.

I heard a soul selection being played, so I walked over to the black side where I recognised the Soul II Soul speaker boxes. Jazzie's deejaying and when I saw him all I could think was, 'How on earth did you pull this off . . . ? Where did you find all these people?' And at the same time I was gutted because I'd planned to do something like this and they'd pulled it off before me – I saw it as stealing my thunder! To make matters worse, Jazzie's sound system didn't sound good at all – like a reggae sound struggling to play soul – and I remember wandering around in there, taking in the sheer scale of it, and thinking, '*Fuck!* This should have been me.'

I walked into the other room, where there were lights

but no music, just a load of white kids standing about in the light, and I bumped into Femi from Young Disciples, who was one of my mates from Ealing. Femi was one of the cool kids, always on radar, always on point, and always knew what was going on before anybody else, so seeing him down there gave this party extra kudos. He told me there was another sound system supposed to be playing in there, but it had broken down about two o'clock, then he said there were some people he wanted me to meet. He took me over to these two frustrated-looking white kids, one tall and one short, who were the guys that had put this on. It was Jules and his business partner Mark Rayner, and as soon as Femi introduced me with, 'This is Norman Jay, he runs Good Times', before I'd shaken anybody's hand I said, 'If this was my sound system this would not have happened!'

My mind was working in overdrive. It was Mark who had done the party with Jazzie, but he and Jules were very close, and Jules was really exasperated by the situation but didn't have the bottle to go and front up Jazzie about the sound systems. I knew what was going down, and made sure I told him I run Good Times but when I do bigger parties I go under the name of Shake and Fingerpop – I hadn't done any bigger parties but I wanted to establish the division from the very beginning. I told him we ought to do a party together, and if we did I could give him a sound system that sounded ten times better than this and was guaranteed not to break down. Then Femi made sure we all swapped numbers – the only phone number I could give him was my mum's house! I left after about an hour, but I'd been clocking all that was going on – where the bar was, where people were going in and out, how much security there was ... and thought it could have been so good if the sound system hadn't let them down. My head was rocking and reeling. I got home at about five and woke my brother up, telling him I'd just come back from this amazing party that Soul II Soul had done, a couple of thousand middle-class white kids, and I'd got the number of the guy who was running the other part of it. I couldn't wait to take this further.

I have to give Femi props for this one, because he didn't let it slide and within a week he had hooked up a meeting with Jules, Mark Rayner and their third guy Dan Benedict up in Kentish Town, where Jules was living at his mum's – we had the meeting in his bedroom. This meeting was an eye-opener, because these were the guys running Family Funktion, calling themselves a sound system but they weren't, they were just a name, a brand. I was thinking, if you want to be a sound system you have to have equipment – an actual sound system. I've got a sound, Jazzie's got a sound, Paul 'Trouble' Anderson had a sound – Trouble Funk – even Madhatter Trevor had a little sound. How are you white guys doing this? How are you operating without a sound? Mark told me it was easy, they just hired stuff, that he and Jazzie were close and they hired equipment from him. That immediately explained what went wrong at the party in King's Cross, why Soul II Soul was firing in one part, while the sound had broken down in the other – Jazzie was never going to hire out equipment to rival his!

On the one hand, I thought this lot were the biggest chancers for trying to operate like this, but on the other I was both envious and respectful because they'd pulled it off. I told Jules and Mark that if we did an event together I'd bring a proper sound system, and although they didn't know me, Mark, who was very on the ball, knew all about Good Times and knew I wasn't lying. Then Jules says OK, he's going to give us a shot, he's got another venue lined up but he doesn't want to do it with Soul II Soul, am I interested?

What!!!

chapter thirty-four: warehouses II

The first thing I want to know is where the venue is and when I could go and have a look at it. It was somewhere in Southwark and in a couple of days' time I met up with Jules and we went down to look it over in his Land Rover. That made me laugh, this middle-class white kid running round London in an old Land Rover while I'm driving an Escort van! We went right to the back of beyond, proper Southwark, near Shakespeare's Globe, and down a little lane to the south side of Southwark Bridge, then we pulled up in front of this big five or six-storey building that's totally derelict, all boarded up. This was 1986, before any of those sites down there were developed – there's a pizza place and a hotel there now, but back then it was just old warehouses and industrial buildings. It turned out that Jules hadn't been in there yet, he'd just scouted the outside. When he told me that, me being street I kicked the door in. Put my foot right through it. It *stank*, and quite obviously nobody had been in there for years, but I could instantly see the potential. My thoughts were whirring, I could see us setting up the sound here, putting the bar there . . . and straight away I was telling Jules, 'This is it! This is where we're doing it! No question!'

I told Joey what we were doing, he was cool with it, and it turned out we had just over two weeks to get the venue ready physically – it was World Cup year and I can remember being there in my Brazil top sweeping it out! Then we had to sell the event, which is where I really learned the difference between how Family Funktion approached an event and how I'd been doing it. The first thing I found out was when you got to 'uni' you make these friends and you make these connections that stay with you for ages. Mark, I think, had been Entertainment Officer at University College London, and the others had worked in ENTS offices and had experience in putting on gigs for one or two thousand people, so it didn't faze them at all. I asked him where he got all the people that came to his parties from and he said, 'The student union – they're all from UCL!' When I had been standing outside clubs giving out flyers to regular clubbers, who I thought were who would be interested, I wasn't realising there was a whole student market out there desperate for somewhere to rave. Then, because so many of them were from out of town, first time away from home, safety was their big concern and they trusted anything run by Mark and Jules because they had this ENTS background. If they tell these students they're doing a party under the arches at King's Cross they're all going to come.

On a Saturday I went over to Jules's flat, where the three of them and Dan's girlfriend, Savonne, were getting ready to do a mail-out, something else I'd never experienced before. What they'd done was what would now be called 'data capture', as they'd taken the names and addresses of most of the people who'd come to their previous parties, and now they

had a great big Family Funktion mailing list and were send-
ing out invites – flyers – for the upcoming event. Sabine was
designing the flyer, with my background in print I knocked
up the artwork, then I took it to this place I knew on the
Euston Road that was the only place open on Saturday. I
knew the guy in there and got several thousand printed in
twenty-four hours, then back at the flat they're surrounded
by piles of brown envelopes, systematically addressing them
by hand and stuffing the flyers in, and they had sheets of
stamps they were licking and sticking – it was like a production line! I just joined in, thinking how brilliant an idea this
was: it never occurred to me that you could use something
as establishment as the Post Office to reach people about
an illegal party! But why not? Their organisation was clear
when Jules told me, 'Make sure you address one to yourself.'
Why? To test how long the post takes. Simple but brilliant.

This took a few days, as there were a good few hundred of
these envelopes – two sacks full – then, in the Land Rover,
we took them to the post office by Rathbone Place, just
off Oxford Street, which was open until nine o'clock and
because it was a main post office they would go straight away.
We got them there on Thursday and, sure enough, second
post on Friday lunchtime the envelope comes through my
mum's letterbox, I open it up. 'Family Funktion & Shake
and Fingerpop Presents . . .' Up until that point I thought I
understood the marketing of these parties and dances, but I
was there looking at how white people run t'ings and realised
how far behind we had been. They were organised on a scale
we hadn't even considered, but I was taking it all in and was
intelligent enough to understand that this was how you got

to grow. The moment that envelope arrived I knew this was going to be a success, I just hadn't realised how big a success.

On the day of the party, the following weekend, my crew and I went down with the sound system and Jules had hired all these film lights and props, and there's video cabling running up the walls. It looked like there's a video shoot about to take place. Our arrangement was to split the take from the door and the bar fifty-fifty *after expenses*, now all I can see is them spending money on all this stuff when we don't know who's coming and we haven't made a penny. I honestly thought we were just going to turn up, kick off the door, set up and get on with it! Once again it was a learning curve. There were some flats just down the road and if anybody down there was nosy and called the police, we'd have to have some sort of cover. The story was to be that we'd been there all week setting up for a video shoot that was happening that night.

Sure enough, in the afternoon we're unloading the sound so we can string up and the police come down the road. Straight away I'm thinking, 'God! We've had it!', and waiting for them to start on me. Because I'm so used to doing these things as just us, Good Times, I'd forgotten I was with a bunch of middle-class white boys. This time Old Bill's looking for who's in charge, ignored us and went straight over to Jules. In his bordering-on-posh accent he said, 'We're filming a video, it's a thing for our university student union and we'll be shooting through the night.' Old Bill took a look around, and got back into the car and drove off, good as gold.

Hats off to Jules: he was prepared for it, in spite of him telling me he was crapping himself because it was the first time he'd ever actually been challenged like that. All that was going through my head afterwards was all those years of black guys' house parties where Old Bill were parked at the end of the road all night, in numbers, then when they want to come they rush the place. Hooking up with Family Funktion was going to be a very different experience.

We'd put some blood, sweat and tears into cleaning the gaff up, all three floors, and it had come up really well. Because my old man worked on London Transport engineering, he used to go out to site visits and he had loads of these disposable overalls at home – strong white paper with a zip up the front – and I took a bunch of them. Then I recruited a load of the kids from round our way and told them, 'Come on, help us clean up this old warehouse and you can earn some money.' I put about half a dozen of them in the back of our van, drove them up there, everyone got a broom or a mop, disinfectant and an overall and they got on with it – it was like an adventure for them! We had the building ready by six o'clock and the sound system and the bar ready to go before nine. That was funny because our MC, Briggie, had been telling me this wouldn't be like a black house party because white people always turned up on time. I was sceptical, but when we opened the door at nine there was an orderly queue waiting outside and we hadn't even started playing music yet.

We'd tried to make the whole party as much like an *experience* as possible – we were on the first floor, on the floor above us was Family Funktion, playing off equipment we'd supplied, and on the third floor we had a live band and had set up an exhibition space and got in these guys called Cooltown.

They were an art collective who were quite big in the 1980s and early '90s: they used to take over warehouse spaces and hold exhibitions in Camden before it was developed. Jules knew one of the Cooltown people and it was exactly what I wanted – the more people in there doing stuff the better.

When we kicked off my heart was pumping, because I knew this was going to be unreal. Within a couple of hours there's *hundreds* of people in there, I'm playing on the first floor with the big warehouse doors open looking out right on the river, Southwark Bridge is on my right, and all I can see is dozens of kids walking down towards us. This is an area that's practically derelict and on Saturdays there's usually nobody around, but now I can see dozens of kids walking around looking for this party. They cross the bridge and can hear the music, then they come down the steps and into the lane where we were and it's chaos!

My cousin Terry, the native New Yorker, was on the door with Briggie, and Briggie's being quite aggressive with these white kids because that's how he is, and Terry has to tell him to calm down, these kids are no threat to him. And they weren't – they came, they queued, they paid and they went in – the only problem was there were so many of them! Terry sent word up to me that they were overwhelmed, 'What shall we do, Norman? There's too many of them, we can't cope!' It was like a message from the front during the war! I said just let them all in. By this time we've got 1,500, 2,000 people in there, we'd made the money, so don't worry about it. Also, the more we fill up the dance, the less likely the police will be able to stop it. It ran for over twelve hours, until about ten o'clock the next morning, and it was full before midnight – our estimates were that, at its peak, there were between 2,000 and 2,500 people in there. I'd never been involved in anything remotely like this, it was absolutely off the scale.

I was determined to use it as the basis for Shake and Fingerpop – so as far as my involvement was concerned, that was all that was on the flyer, and I was quite happy that nobody knew who Shake and Fingerpop was. A few people sussed it out when I spoke on the mic, because I had my Kiss FM radio show by then, but I completely denied it. 'Aren't you Norman Jay? Aren't you on Kiss?' ... 'Never heard of him! And this is nothing to do with Kiss!' Then because anybody could quite clearly see the GT on our boxes, they'd ask if this was Good Times. Again I'd deny it, saying we just hired the equipment off them. It was important to me from a musical point of view that I established this alter ego, because I wanted to be able to play anything I liked rather than what would be expected of me as Norman Jay of Good Times. I wanted the music to be such that the crowd didn't know where it was going to go, but they trusted me enough to know it would be a good place. Anything could get played at any time, which meant moving as far as possible away from those rigid rules you got on the jazz/funk/soul, Chris Hill/ Robbie Vincent circuit, but still keeping a core of black music. I wanted to be the punk rock of black music! To carry on this anarchic vibe I got Jonathan More to guest deejay because I liked his punky attitude and his left-field approach to music. No deejay names and no musical genres on the flyer, I wanted to build Shake and Fingerpop as a properly underground thing – if you were there you'd know; if you didn't know then you'd never know.

We pulled off that party, and even my brother Joey, the usually conservative Rastaman, was impressed – in fact he thought it was brilliant. We made a pile of money – the door made a pile of money, the bar made a pile of money, even the black chancers who had come up from south London to sell puff made a pile of money, because they couldn't believe how much the white kids smoked. But I wasn't overly interested in that, to me it was all about the fact we'd pulled it off. We'd done it. And that it was such a terrific night.

chapter thirty-five: warehouses III

After that party I was on cloud nine. I was hooked on putting on this kind of party for this kind of crowd, and if I wasn't excited enough the next week I discovered we'd achieved notoriety! The newspaper *South London Press* did a big whole page feature on all-night drinking, sex and drugs at that illegal warehouse rave in Southwark. I didn't even know such a paper existed, but Jules got a copy from somewhere. The reporter claimed he saw people openly having sex on the stairs and people openly taking drugs, he made it sound like the orgy to end all orgies and I was incensed! 'You fucking liar!' was my first thought. If you saw how filthy that place was when everybody was in there, you'd know there was no way anybody was having sex there; and just about everybody smokes spliffs just about everywhere anyway, so why the outrage about that? Then I realised what great publicity it was for us. First of all it alerted so many people to the concept of illegal warehouse parties, so they'd know to look out for them, and even if there were no sex orgies or drug fiends, it let kids know it was all outside of the boundaries of normal clubbing. That they could let themselves go a bit at one of them. As a result the next two or three we did were even bigger.

I could hardly wait to do the next one, because what we'd done made sense on so many levels, and although money wasn't my prime motivation it couldn't be ignored, especially by my brother, because it would allow him to build the sound system into what he'd always hoped it could be. The difference between the house parties we'd been doing and the warehouses was massive. We were considered a success at the former level because we weren't actually losing money, we could expect to walk away from one with fifty quid each, one hundred if we were lucky. Now it was simply scaled up ten times with hardly any increase in overhead – the 150 people who would come to a house party became 1,500 in a warehouse, and most of the time we'd be running the bar too.

I became such a keenie beanie, I'd drive all over London looking for potential venues, plus people I knew would give me tip-offs about places. This was Thatcher's Britain, before development had really got a hold on London, and there were big derelict buildings all over the place: Shoreditch, come Saturday there's nobody there; down by the river, particularly on the south side, abandoned industrial buildings everywhere; in King's Cross they hadn't started knocking buildings down for Eurostar yet, but so many had been emptied.

I'd scout a building by driving past it a few times, break in – sorry, *effect entry*! – and look around then. Sometimes I'd have Femi with me, and if I thought it had prospects I'd talk to Mark and Jules about it at one of our regular update meetings. Or sometimes I'd take the decision myself and just tell them, 'I've found this gaff, this is where we're going in

for the next one.' What I was looking for first were exits –
in case anything happened, we wanted to know everybody
could get out, and, most importantly, so could we. Then
somewhere to put the generator, which had to be ground
floor because they were so heavy. The only times we could
consider going upstairs with it was if there was a load of us
who could lift it together. Funnily enough, a lot of the more
recently vacated premises still had electricity running to the
big industrial lifts, because they'd had to get equipment out
and had never turned it off. Running water was a bonus, so
sometimes we'd have those big communal factory toilets
still working but usually it was all pretty rudimentary. The
truth was people didn't expect a great deal – it was a derelict
warehouse, it was cheap and it fitted in with the whole hard
times, punk rebellion vibe of the decade. The people that
came liked the idea that the whole scene was the antithesis
of how the mainstream clubs were getting more and more
up their own arses, telling you where you can dance and
keeping you waiting outside and then the music wasn't all
that. We had the counterculture edge – come in here and do
what you want – and do it to music unrivalled by anything
you'd hear elsewhere.

We'd do our best to make the place fit for use beforehand,
but one thing we could never do anything about were the
smells. Some of these places had been derelict for years and
there would be horrible decaying smells, and much as we'd
leave doors and windows open in the run-up, we then had to
secure the building in order to run a door. Once we did one at
Bear Wharf in Southwark and we hadn't shut the windows –
there were so many people at the door that we couldn't get

them in quick enough and they just started climbing in! And when new arrivals saw other people getting in like that, they joined in. It was like we were being invaded, as I was watching people swarming all over the building – they had found a load of those long scaffolding planks and had put them up to the windows to bunk in! We might have lost some money through that but I loved it, it was like anarchy, adding chaos to the excitement of the whole event.

Of course the police were always sniffing about, but as long as they thought it was Jules's event we'd get away with it. He was a law student and not only knew how to talk to Old Bill, but what to say – legal language! Or I'd have my mate Adam out front, he was a Cambridge graduate, very tall and very posh, and once they heard his accent the police never questioned him. What was really funny was that he was really nervous doing it, and I had to literally write a script for him and coach him through how to deliver it! 'Look 'em right in the eye, use your accent and don't break the stare. Just tell them that you've got every right to be in here, and don't waver.' It was almost too predictable, Old Bill fell for it every time and with either of those two out front we never had a party busted in all the years we did it.

The following day or the following week after an event, we'd meet round Jules's flat in Kentish Town for a debrief. Jules, Mark, Dan, me, my brother, Femi, sometimes my dad would be there. Mostly it was the same as we used to do with Good Times – how can we improve? – but these warehouse parties had one specific problem: how do we get the money out? We were always conscious of this because there was so much involved and it was all big bags of cash, from the door and the bar. We'd heard plenty of rumours about a gang from Brixton or Peckham who had cottoned on to this scene as a way to make money, and were coming in and not bothering with the kids because they'd hold up the organisers and rob the takings at gunpoint or knifepoint.

They were hitting more and more warehouse parties, but so far we had been untouched and we always tried to minimise what we could lose by having my dad make regular 'money runs' up to Jules's flat in Kentish Town or our house in Acton. An old black man driving an old Cortina across London at that time of night wasn't likely to attract too much attention, especially from the police, because they were as much of a threat as the gangs. At one big party, my dad had taken the money out of the building and was on his way to Jules's, but people were still coming in so we had another bag with over five hundred quid in it, when Linden who was on the door came running in and shouting that we were being raided. Jules and I were in this room where we kept all the booze, which doubled as a sort of cloakroom, and we could hear them coming along the corridor opening every door. What we could also hear was that this wasn't a usual raid, they weren't clearing people out and shutting us down, I figured out they were here to rob us – what could we do, it was an illegal party! I told Jules to lie down on the floor on some coats and pretend to be dead drunk and asleep or passed out. We both did and Jules kept the bag of money underneath him. Old Bill kicked our door in and I can hear them searching, so I knew straight away I'd been right, they were looking for the take. They were as crooked as the crooks, they'd seen how many people were in there and that we were running a bar, and thought they'd have some of that. We were pretending to be out of it, snoring and everything, but I could still hear them picking up bags and shaking them, opening boxes, putting their hands into coat pockets, but ignoring these two drunks on the floor! I didn't dare open my eyes, and after about five minutes they left the room. They basically ransacked every room in the building, didn't find anything and cleared off. I was just thinking, 'Bastards! Good job we took the money out and lay on the rest of it!' That was when it really hit home for Jules and Adam that Old Bill was so bent, as this was the first time these middle-class white kids had been exposed to the reality of our police force – what we have to live with every day.

At the earliest parties, because people soon got word that Shake and Fingerpop was run by the same guys as Good Times, we were almost doing two parties in one – double dipping! The first wave, the student types, would be waiting there when we opened the door and they'd get so into it so quickly that come one o'clock or two o'clock in the morning, they're pissed up or drugged up and staggering off home. Then we'd get what we'd call the red-eye posse, who had heard on the vine about this dance – they always called it a dance – with the guys from Good Times and they'd roll up. You'd see the crowd would get visibly blacker and blacker, the ganja smoke, as opposed to hash, would get heavier and heavier, so of course I slowed down the music to fit. We thought this was brilliant, and I could do it because I had the music for both crowds. I could offer the best of both worlds – in the beginning the music was frantic, then as it got later it got slower and more soulful. Then by the time the sun came up at seven in the morning, the late night posse, the bleachers, would be going on to somewhere else and they'd leave us totally happy! We just loved it.

Once we properly got going with these parties, it got easier and we would be doing one every couple of months and in the summer that would go up to about one every six weeks. We didn't want to do them too often, because we'd spawned a lot of imitators and it was starting to become a crowded market, with people getting put off by badly run events or events that got shut down even before they'd started. Too many people were trying to put on warehouse parties because everybody was thinking it was an easy way to make money. The wrong kinds of people were putting on the sort of events that attracted a bad crowd – drugs, violence, trouble in the surrounding area – and they were getting properly busted, as Old Bill would rush in there with their truncheons.

Our team was always on point though. We knew how to organise quickly, we paid attention to detail and we wanted to make sure that everybody had an amazing time, not simply that they paid to get in. I have to say those guys were fantastic and we barely put a foot wrong. Jules was brilliant, but after a while his deejaying had started to take off, so Family Funktion was taking a bit of a back seat. This meant that it was Dan who I'd deal with the most, and I'm still firm friends with him – we used to have Tottenham season tickets next to one another. Mark had always been very tight with Jazzie, and they would do things together, but none of this was a problem as I could still do stuff with Jules and/or the others – we were phenomenally successful – or I could do things on my own as Shake and Fingerpop, and I'd hooked up with the reggae sound system Menassah Sound.

This was three middle-class white kids – Nick, Ed and Bill – who'd been to Westminster public school, and had a love of reggae I just couldn't get my head around! It wasn't simply reggae either, it was *dub* reggae and they had a tiny little sound system they called Menassah. I got wind of a party they were playing in south London and went down to check them out, and although I'm not a particular fan of reggae, I have to give them their props for the way they were playing it and mixing up their dub versions, it was brilliant. They had a huge following, too, as all their public school mates and that crowd would come and support them. I was impressed because they were playing reggae in a different way to a completely different crowd and, culturally, winning over a whole new audience that they could bring to our warehouse and house parties.

This was what I appreciated most about doing the warehouses; I could play the best black music but I was getting to a completely new crowd. These were not working-class suburban soulboys, who mostly looked on it as a fad, but middle-class kids who were hooked for life once you got them into it. They would always support you, and, most importantly, they would always pay money to come and support you because they valued it. They didn't think it was their right and therefore treat it like an affront if you expected them to pay to get into your dance.

Femi's brother Tunji was another entry point into that world, because he knew *everybody*. He was something of an enigma himself, a real face around town who could either be found in the Spice of Life, a pub on Cambridge Circus in Soho, or at all the trendiest events with a stunning girl on his arm. He was Jamiroquai's first manager and he had fingers in many pies. I'd make sure I'd give him a load of flyers and he'd take them to his other hangout, Crazy Larry's in King's Road, Chelsea, where he was well in with the Sloaney set. He was a great networker and had a really persuasive way about him: through Tunji, Michael Heseltine's daughters used to come to our early parties, along with Emma Ridley and her set, that first generation of Chelsea 'wild child'. It opened us up to a whole different world, and a lot of those people used to come to Good Times at Carnival right up until we stopped.

I used to try and cast my net as wide as possible when publicising the parties, to open it up to as many people as possible, and I'd put very little on the flyer. I'd avoid the pyramid of deejay names like the jazz/funk or the acid rave flyers, and just put 'party' because who doesn't like a party? Even at my tender age I'd worked out that every time you put a description of what you think your event actually is, you're instantly alienating far more people than you're attracting. I'd just go with, 'All night Saturday night party! Music by Shake and Fingerpop!', and then the details. Maybe add a few little arty flourishes, but keep it as cool and as understated as possible. Then I'd pass them out at universities, fashion colleges, art schools, hairdressers, up and down the King's Road, Camden High Street, in Soho or in Hampstead ... anywhere I thought the people I wanted at the parties would be. I'd give them to people and tell them, 'Bring ten friends and I'll put you on the guest list, here's my number.' I've always had a strong work ethic and I knew I'd have to put plenty of effort into this, but could quickly see the results.

What particularly pleased me about the people we were attracting was that it included the cooler black crowd, which I always had an inkling was out there but I never knew how to reach them. It was a new generation of much funkier, more imaginative black guys and girls, who were in the creative industries, or were students, or just weren't as restricted in their outlook as their parents or even their older siblings. I was getting to them through the marketing to colleges and universities and the Soho creative networks. Once they found out how a black sound system was presenting black music, they loved it and wholeheartedly supported us.

I loved doing those warehouses as Shake and Fingerpop. It was every bit as exciting as when I started playing Carnival as Good Times, because then I could play soul music exactly how I wanted, now my horizons had expanded and I could play anything! All the Northern soul records I liked ... all the jazz records I liked ... I had a blank canvas and nobody was going to complain. Those parties became bigger and bigger and we played a major part in creating that whole warehouse image, which by the summer of 1986 was attracting thousands of kids every weekend and subsequently became bigger than all the London clubs.

chapter thirty-six: actually doing radio

When I started on Kiss with Norman Jay's *Original Rare Groove* show, it was before 'rare groove' became a thing or a handy catchphrase, and I was playing my old record collection. I called the show that because I wanted to show the deejays who had recently jumped on the soul music bandwagon as a career move that this was where it all came from, that it had a heritage and that it meant something. These were the *original* rare grooves, not the ones you read about last week.

There was a point to this, because I was quite politically minded and very anti the white music business establishment. I suppose I was bitter and I thought this was my opportunity because it was a pirate station, therefore we had freedoms the BBC or Capital didn't. I could make my statements with the records I played, so that was driving my music choice. I knew I had the records, I knew I had the knowledge, but I also knew if I wanted to get my points across, I would have to be as good as any presenter on the BBC. We may have been illegal but the listeners didn't care, the only way they were going to listen was if we were any good. Which meant more than just playing the right records. Practically anyone can be a deejay – although not necessarily a good one – but I had to learn to be a 'presenter', which was very different from just getting on the mic on the sound system.

I was aware I had to do this, so I was very self-critical and used to analyse my early show in detail – looking back at those days I cringe now! My biggest problem was speaking too fast, so I concentrated on slowing down; then there was diction, which I understood because I always did well speaking in English at school. Essentially I had to speak slower and more clearly so that people understood me. More than trying to sound hip or ragga, like so many of the other pirate deejays at the time, I wanted to get my music across to as many listeners as possible and so many of them wouldn't understand street talk and would just switch off.

What surprised me was that it wasn't that difficult to learn the basics of presenting and once it allowed me to relax I thoroughly enjoyed it, although it was a bit unnerving in the beginning because I had no way of monitoring the impact I was having out there, if any. After about six months I began to realise the extent of it, as after the show I'd walk through Camden Market or down to Portobello and as I went in to the record shops people would hear my voice and say, 'Weren't you just on the radio just now?' ... 'You're Norman Jay, I listen to all you every week!' And passing clothes shops or stalls I'd hear radios blasting Jonathan's show, which was on right after mine. This was brilliant because we had become the soundtrack for young London at that time; all the trendy, creative spaces had our shows on during Saturday afternoon. For a long time in the station's early days my *Original Rare*

Groove show and Jonathan More's *Meltdown* were the defining sound.

I met Joe Strummer of the Clash through being recognised from the radio, as I used to have breakfast in this cafe on Portobello on a weekend where this guy would be sitting reading. I had no idea who he was, I just knew of the Clash as a name. One Sunday I was talking to the bloke behind the counter about my show and this other guy pipes up, 'Yeah, I'm a big fan as well, I love that stuff you're playing.' I looked over and I didn't speak to him more than, 'Cheers, mate', but I couldn't stop thinking I knew that face. All week it bugged me, and the next weekend he's there again so I said, 'Excuse me, but I'm sure I know you.' He just smiled and said, 'My name's Joe.' I worked out the rest and I could barely believe it, Joe Strummer! I started gushing like a fan, when he cut me off and said, '*I'm* a fan, I listen to you on the radio every week, you're giving me a proper education in that side of black music.' I met him for breakfast quite a few times after that and we would talk about black music, politics, the state of the country . . . he was a lovely guy and a fascinating character, and right up to the time he passed away he was true to the punk ideals that the system is inherently wrong.

It was my show on Kiss that kick-started the rare groove thing, as I was playing of all this rare, unreleased – or unplayed – stuff by James Brown and the like from the 1960s and '70s. Stuff that was on long-forgotten albums or swiftly deleted singles. It gained momentum very quickly because the new magazines championed us – me in particular, because a few of their staff writers came to our warehouse parties, and they loved the old soul and funk. Although getting all this support was invaluable, I was always thinking a bit deeper about this music, I was trying to give a black narrative about how this music was made, how we as black people in England heard this music and danced to it. I believed so much of that '60s and '70s soul period had been airbrushed out of history because the writers and BBC people and TV filmmakers weren't there, so to them it wasn't important. I was determined to use my status, my knowledge, my records to make sure all of those white deejays and media people out there *knew* about it. Up until that point, the accepted order of things was they knew everything, they controlled everything, but here was a chance for *us* to step out from under that. I was contemptuous! My view on it was that while they were reading about these records, buying them and stacking them up in their bedroom so they'd have a lovely rack of albums, we were playing them at our youth clubs, at our weddings, at our christenings, at our dances! Living them!

The interest in rare groove also boosted my record hustling business enormously, because I had a stock of these obscure 1970s soul records at home that I'd built up when I was a kid, and I often found myself in the basement of the Record & Tape Exchange, a second-hand record shop in Goldhawk Road, Shepherd's Bush. All the record company people used to sell their promo stuff there, and because the shop's rock-snob staff didn't care about black music they used to dump it all in the basement. This was like Christmas for me! It's when I started buying albums – nothing down there was more than fifty pence so I could afford them – I got my entire James Brown collection in there, everything he had done up to that point.

I'd go in there after Sunday morning football, stuff my football bag full of records and pay a quid for two or three on my way out – if the guy on the till knew what I was doing, he didn't care. I'd buy albums that had I already had a couple of singles from, I'd buy stuff I remembered but hadn't been able to afford and I'd buy multiple copies of things, or I'd buy one and nick the others. I got so much stuff in there that my record collection went from a few hundred to several thousand, and the promos and rare stuff I found in there were unreal. Then I started going up to Soho and it was the same up there – nobody cared about the soul music so I caned these shops.

I sat on a lot of that stuff for a long time and started selling it off in the '80s, and the rare groove craze was a godsend for me because I had this huge archive to play on the radio or simply to sell alongside the records I was bringing back from America.

What I wanted to say with my show was, 'Just when you thought you knew this much about black music, we're raising the bar. Here's another level of our history.' I knew from my own experiences these records had never been played on UK radio before, by anybody, black or white, so here was a chance for us to bring black club consciousness to the masses. And what I was finding out with Kiss was that people of all backgrounds were more than ready to hear it. They were *eager* for it – young British people, especially Londoners, are far more robust than the powers that be like to think they are. They want the real deal, not little bits diluted and served out to them because you're trying to protect them. Also, particularly gratifyingly, I had plenty of the deeper thinking brothers and sisters pulling me up on the street and saying, 'Let me shake your hand. Because I can see what you're doing.'

What I wouldn't do was be overtly political on the air, as this was one thing I'd learned quickly: if you start spouting your own personal political views on radio, you'll get shut down. However, if you heard the records I played, in the order that I played them and the context in which I'd describe them, you'd be left in no doubt that this was a committed black brother. I can remember playing the full-length version of 'Mighty Mighty (Spade and Whitey)' by Curtis Mayfield a week after I'd played the edited single version because I'd lost my bottle! During the week I regretted it and ended up thinking, 'Fuck it! We're pirates, they could pull us off next week just for that', so I played the full-length cut. I had this massive collection of politically aware black records, so I played them. Partly because there was a message and partly because we used to dance to them. I'd play the seventeen-minute full-length version of 'Say it Loud, I'm Black and I'm Proud', as James Brown made these records to be played in their entirety, the least I could do was go along with it. This used to cause massive consternation with Gordon, our station manager, who used to ask me why I played certain records. My reply was always: 'Because I had to, because I own them.'

My mindset in the early days on Kiss was very sound system, very punk – if the establishment didn't let us in, fuck 'em, we'll do it for ourselves and do it our own way, but Gordon and George never really got that. I think they were afraid of offending the mainstream white media, but I couldn't be clearer – we didn't need them to legitimise what we were doing. From the sound system days onwards I would tell people that we couldn't let the mainstream start influencing our thinking, or they're going to end up running our show. I'd say that everything they did was built on what we created, so whatever we did now, eventually they'd come over to see what it is and we had to be ready for them – not to lock them out but to make sure they knew who owned this, who's in charge. And the only way we could do that was to keep doing things our own way. My crowd trusted me to do that, and given my history and the music I've played, it added a level of integrity to it – you're enjoying it, but you're subtly being educated.

One of the reasons Kiss blew up like it did was because we were championed by the new media: we were the first pirate station to be continually listed in *Time Out*, in *City Limits*, in *The Face*, in *iD*. At that time this was *really important* and I used to go to great lengths to explain to Gordon about reaching a whole new demographic, some of whom may not be into it, but also others who were just waiting for what we were doing.

Back in the early days of those black music pirates, everything was about being in *B&S* or being in *Echoes*, but by that time that I was so over that! Those stations were all around Kent or Surrey and were extensions of those very conservative suburban soul clubs – logs discos on the air.

We were about London and how it had changed post-punk. I just saw myself as quite a left-wing activist, a progressive, always looking to move things on in a creative way, and for a few years Kiss was part of that whole movement, even driving it in many ways, staying ahead of the game by daring to be different and taking risks. I loved those days on Kiss, my pirate tapes ended up all over the world, and I've always figured my deejay career would have been set back ten years if I hadn't been part of it when it blew up.

We would put warehouse parties on anywhere that was practical, that ticked all the boxes I talked about earlier, and some of the places we put them on were incredible, not just because they were a snapshot of a London that was about to disappear – like the King's Cross warehouses or the Wood Lane factories – but just for their apparent randomness. Old factory estates were normally good places to find somewhere, or sometimes we'd find an old school – there was even an old gasworks in Wandsworth that I scouted and really wanted to use mostly *because* it was an old gasworks! In the end I never did because it was at a time when I had a feeling Old Bill was on to me.

I first met Jazzie B at one of these parties. I'd gone to get something from the van and this dreadlocked guy pulls up and tells me he runs a sound called Jah Rico, Joey knew of it and invited him in. I'd never heard of it but figured we should let him in because he'd come all the way from north London to check us out. We got talking, realised we had very much the same view of what we wanted to do and have been friends ever since.

An audacious one – or two, actually – we pulled off was

at the end of 1985 at an empty carpet store right in the old Acton shopping precinct! It was a big empty unit called Steve's Carpet Warehouse, and we sold it out for a Christmas party, eight hundred people, and it went so well, with no attention from Old Bill or anybody else, that we decided to do another one on New Year's Eve and sold that out as well.

We did one in Paddington station, which was actually on the platform of the old British Road Services (BRS) parcel depot, which was underground at the very end of all the tube line platforms. The depot itself was no longer used, the Underground people didn't seem to want anything to do with it, and you could drive down to it by going around this little roundabout where Paddington Basin is now, then following this kind of spiral roadway down from the Paddington station goods yard, which was also disused. I did several gigs there and it always felt like such a liberty as it was right next to the live Tube platforms. We'd get about a thousand people in there and every time a tube train would come in, we'd see all these people look over at it with their mouths open, because we got a full-scale rave going on just a few yards away! I can't imagine what I would have thought if I'd been on one of those trains – I'd probably be gutted because I didn't know about it, get off and say, 'Let me get to this t'ing!' I'm sure quite a few people did. I was actually a bit disappointed going there because Jazzie had beaten me to it and put one on before me, when I'd been scouting it for months and really wanted to be the first!

There was another old factory in what is now Paddington Basin, down by the canal, and we'd get to it the same way as to the BRS platform. We did quite a few parties there – so did Jazzie. It used to make me laugh that this old factory was about two hundred yards from Paddington Green police station, which was the most secure nick in Britain because they used to keep the terrorist suspects there, and we were running illegal raves there on a regular basis. However, it was our mistake that we thought they didn't know what was going on!

We were just about to open the doors for a party down there one Christmas when Old Bill turned up: three or four helmets and one with a flat hat and a lot of stripes – more than just a sergeant. We went into the regular routine: Adam was on the door and fronted up, Jules was hovering about and because I'd only just finished setting up I was still wearing overalls, so I grabbed a broom and started sweeping, in janitor mode. I swept over close to them so I could hear what was being said, and this head copper was a serious one. Adam was telling him that they were running the show, they were students and it was their Christmas party, no problem. This copper just said to him, quite calmly, 'This is your last one!' and he was looking at me when he said it! I refused to meet his eye and kept on sweeping. Suddenly it's '*You!* Come here!' I walked over with my broom, trying my best to look like hired help. He poked me in the chest and said, '*This* is your last party.' All I could say was a confused sounding, 'Er, what do you mean?', and Jules is attempting to keep up the pretence that it's his event. Old Bill took no notice, he looked at me totally stone faced and said, 'I know who you are, I know what you're about, now read my lips – this is your last party!'

I was gobsmacked, we had been well and truly rumbled, but then it occurred to me that he was just looking for some sort of pay-off, if they knew so much about our operation then why hadn't they shut us down before? Another big mistake on my part!

As they came in we had been just stocking up the bar, so there were crates of champagne and beer all over the place. I whispered to Adam, 'He's obviously looking for a touch, give him a crate of something.' Adam wanted to give him cash, but I told him under no circumstances give them money because then we'd never get them off our backs – I loved the naivety of that lot! I picked up a crate of champagne and asked him, 'Do you want this? Share it with everybody back at the station for Christmas?' Not a flicker. Then he said, 'Is this a bribe?' I was thinking on my feet by now, because I've obviously played this all wrong, and told him, 'No, of course it's not a bribe, we're having our Christmas party and we're all students . . . ' He simply cut me off with, 'Are you bribing me?' By now I'm sounding a bit pathetic, but still said, 'No, it's a gift.' To which he replied, 'And *this* is your last party!' Then turned round and they all walked out.

I was crapping myself, and totally unnerved by the fact that Old Bill had me on their radar. I immediately realised that as good a venue as this had been, we *definitely* weren't doing another one there, although I consoled myself with the fact we'd already done a few and got away with them, and actually laughed at the idea we were going to get away with this one too.

Once we did a massive party somewhere over in west London, and at about five o'clock the whole sound system went down. A big shout went up, 'What's happening?' and we started checking things. Has an amp blown? Has some cabling come out? We knew it couldn't be the generator running out of diesel, because we had wired the sound up to the street lamps . . . then we realised that was it! It was high summer, broad daylight outside and because the street lamps were on timers they'd switched off! It was a good thing it was an all-white crowd, because they'd been there since ten o'clock and by then most of them had gone.

One place I didn't get to use was over in Wood Lane, Shepherd's Bush, where Westfield is now. It was the old huge engineering works at the London Transport goods yard, which was behind White City station opposite where the BBC used to be. It was a great space. I knew about it because my old man worked on the railway and when they closed it down they just left this vast building standing empty. I went to an event there, thinking how I really needed to do something there, but when I got inside I realised how impractical it was. The place was too big, which really showed up that they didn't have enough people in there – they looked like they were rattling around. And because it was so big it couldn't be secured properly so loads of people were bunking in. Then it got raided, Old Bill got in really easily and then they were chasing people around in there, it was almost comical! Mutoid Waste Company, an avant-garde performance art group who would squat industrial buildings, used to do a fair amount of stuff over there, often with Jazzie's crew, but with their performances and big art installations they could make it work. It was too big for me.

The warehouses were really good to me, Joey and the sound system. In the time we were doing them and the houses, about 1983 to 1988, we've gone from this boogie sound system playing the Leroy Burgess, the SOS Band, the Luther and so on to this big operation playing all manner of music to mixed crowds of a thousand or more. I was meeting so many creative and multimedia types, who went on to run t'ings in their particular fields, and I learned from them while they were learning about the best music and the best raves from me. And so many of these characters never forget – they remember coming to my parties or when I came out to their university to play. I'm perpetually meeting older generations who come up and start a conversation with, 'You won't remember, but once you played at Warwick or St Martin's or wherever, and I was there ...' And it was all underpinned by my one continuum, Carnival: many of them would turn up at that every August, and it was creatively driving everything else.

chapter thirty-eight: james brown's funky people

In 1986, the rare groove thing was flying. It had grown into this state of affairs like the Northern scene, where impossible-to-get records were changing hands for hundreds of pounds. This was before the music industry got wise to it and started putting out compilations of 1970s funk, and through doing the parties and the radio and hanging out in record shops I knew exactly what people were after. So Femi, Marco and myself – the Ealing posse – bootlegged a tune, a double A-side of Maceo's 'Cross the Tracks' and the Jackson Sisters' 'I Believe in Miracles'. The demand for our bootleg was so enormous that it actually got into the lower reaches of the chart, and left us sitting on a pile of money. That hadn't been our motivation at all, so we thought hard about doing something that would give something back to benefit the music and the scene in general. I can honestly say what we did was the pinnacle of my career up to that point, and probably the thing that's given me the greatest level of satisfaction and achievement. What we did resulted in James Brown's The JBs reforming and touring Europe.

It began one Sunday, after I'd done a Shake and Fingerpop

party somewhere and we were doing a debrief in my record room at my mum's house, very chilled out, the music and the spliffs rolling. I was playing Bobby Byrd's 'I Need Help', and Marco said, 'Wouldn't it be great if we could get them to reform and tour again?' Their group the Young Disciples was so named because they were disciples of James Brown, so I knew he was serious, and at that moment, after we'd all been on a gig and now we were smoking, I couldn't see why we couldn't. Plus it would be the perfect thing to do with the money we'd made from the Maceo bootleg, so we decided to go for it.

Of course, being young kids with no experience of the regular music business, the only place we had to start was with this guy Cliff White, who worked at PolyGram Records. He was a friend of James Brown's and the go-to guy in England for all things JB-related. We didn't really know Cliff, but we knew he was supportive of us. Marco came up with his number, called him and about a week later he came round my house with a number for Vicki Anderson in Cincinnati – she and Bobby Byrd are husband and wife. We rang it and we were crapping ourselves! We didn't have a speakerphone, so we were sitting in my mum's house, cheek to cheek so we can both hear what's being said. When she answered I immediately recognised her drawling Southern accent, then Marco asked 'Is that Vicki Anderson?' but as he was literally trembling I took over.

I introduced myself as a deejay from England on a little community station – I didn't say 'pirate' – told her I was a big fan, and that we'd love to bring her and Bobby over to London to do a show as they hadn't played here in years. She hadn't heard of us, of course, but she listened politely when I told her there was a massive demand for her and Bobby's music and we'd been championing it in clubs and parties and on the radio. I even named a few tracks she'd long since forgotten about. I could hear her talking to Bobby in the background, and it was the mention of radio that really got her interest, as that's what's so important in the American music business. Then she passed the phone to Bobby, who was really friendly, really affable – Vicki was always the shrewd businesswoman, you wouldn't pull the wool over her eyes, but Bobby was really cool. 'Yeah, we'd love to come . . . when's the gig?' Marco and I can't believe it! This might actually happen! All I could manage to say was, 'Brilliant! We'll call you back in a week's time, when it's all set up.'

I knew I could get the old Town & Country Club in Kentish Town to put it on, so on that wing and a promise from Vicki and Bobby, we booked it with them. We went to see Cliff White at PolyGram, who had a lot of their back catalogue, and he was glad to do anything he could to help us. This was absolutely perfect timing because rare groove was peaking, and Eric B & Rakim had sampled Bobby's tune 'I Know You Got Soul' and they were in the pop charts with it. We talked to Vicki and Bobby again and I asked if they could bring any of the others, like Lyn Collins of Maceo. Vicki said she tried but James Brown wouldn't allow them to tour or do anything together without him. Not that it mattered, just announcing Vicki and Bobby by themselves sold out the 2,200 tickets in a week, and they added another date, which sold out almost as quickly. James Brown's people heard about it and threatened to sue me in the week building up to the concert, and I told them to do their worst! I didn't give a fuck, I was young and fearless, my show was going on – the only concession I made was to call it Bobby Byrd & Vicki Anderson: The Funky People, instead of James Brown's Funky People.

It would just be them, performing to a backing track. We sent them plane tickets, were astonished they never asked for any money upfront, and the day came around when we went to meet them at the airport. I could see something of a shock on Vicki's face when she came through and saw five kids standing there – *kids*. I'm sure she was thinking, 'What have I done?', although she said to me later that she was a very spiritual person and could tell we were good people. She trusted us. Then it got really surreal for us: Joey and I put Vicki Anderson and Bobby Byrd in my dad's Cortina and drove them to their hotel!

It was on that drive into town that Eric B & Rakim's 'I Know You Got Soul' came on the radio and Bobby wasn't really listening, but we turned it up and we're going, 'That's you! That's you!' They'd never heard it before, and while Bobby was just quite amused by it, Vicki was absolutely on it and as soon as they got back she went to work on Eric B & Rakim's record company. The album the track was on was one of hip-hop's biggest at that point, and there was so much of Bobby's voice on the song that they ended up with a huge out-of-court settlement for performance royalties. To this day Bobby says they were eternally grateful to us for bringing that to their attention.

The club was *mobbed*! I was running the night, I deejayed it, I emceed it and when I brought them onstage, I've never heard anything like it – there was so much love in that room it was deafening. I wanted to cry. They hadn't been to London since the early 1970s, and even then James Brown had never allowed them to have their own moment in the spotlight, but now people were going crazy for them. When Vicki did 'Message From a Soul Sister' the whole thing went up yet another level, then when Bobby sang 'I Know You Got Soul' I genuinely thought the roof was going to come off. Not that I had much time to think about it, because while Vicki had her own reel-to-reel for backing, Bobby didn't, so I recorded the instrumental versions of his songs on quarter-inch tape and spliced them together *with Sellotape*, so when he was performing I was getting cold sweats thinking, 'What if the tape snaps?' I brought them back for three or four curtain calls, and to this day I've never experienced anything like it. I was losing my mind up there, I was like a starstruck fan just thinking, 'Have we done this? Are we responsible for this?'

The next day Vicky and Bobby came round my mum and dad's house, sat with them in their parlour and ate our food. It was simply incredible. Bobby was a bit of a spliffhead, so he came up into our room and we smoked and talked for ages, I showed him all my old records and he signed my whole collection. They phoned their daughter Carleen and told her about these guys Norman, Femi and Marco who had really looked after them. I could barely believe this was happening. They couldn't stop thanking us for doing this for them, and as soon as they got back to the US they were talking about coming back the next year. A German promoter who had been at the show got in touch and put together a European tour for them with the whole gang – Maceo, Fred, Peewee,

Lyn Collins and Carleen. We stayed in touch with them, and later Carleen joined Femi and Marco in the Young Disciples and they never forgot that it all came off the back of what we did. Basically, we restarted their careers.

We made no money out of that show, in fact it cost us more than we made from that bootleg record, but the point was about bringing those wonderful people over. I told Bobby that if it wasn't for James Brown's and his music, I, Norman Jay, wouldn't have a career. I believed I was picking up their mantle when I was playing all their records back when it was deeply unfashionable – like that guy all those years ago who had told me my music was too black. When I was standing on that stage with Bobby and Vicki, I felt everything I'd done up until that point led to that moment, and I believed I was completely vindicated.

But I also knew it was the end of something: for me rare groove was over, I couldn't top that, and by now my head was turning towards house and the next new thing.

chapter thirty-nine: the last warehouse

By the end of the summer of 1987, I was thinking it was time to stop the warehouses. Essentially we'd been getting away with it for quite a few years, we'd never had our collars felt, never had a party shut down, so we figured the law of averages meant it would only be a matter of time. Especially as Old Bill was far more savvy by that point, as the developers were taking hold and wanted to protect their investments. Also, rare groove was over, dead, and we could see acid house coming over the horizon – by Easter 1988 it was all acid house in fields. Our reputations were sky high, so we thought one last party, New Year's Eve, make it a real killer, and we'll go out on top.

Some time in November, Jules had found a place on the north side of Southwark Bridge, a huge theatre that used to put on Shakespearean pieces but had long been standing empty – it was on the left if you were crossing from the north, low down and practically on the river. I don't know how I'd been missing it with all my driving around looking for potential venues, and it was absolutely fantastic. Part of it was like a stable block, then as I walked around I saw it had this huge glass wall – too big to merely be a window – that overlooked the Thames.

By now we'd adopted a new procedure with some of the venues we used. It involved squatters' rights and had been explained to us by the Mutoid Waste Company, who squatted big buildings all over London. As Jules was doing his law degree, he had a handle on the law as it applied to squatting. From what I can remember it went something like this: in order to get squatters' rights you had to write out notices that you were occupying the space, stick them up around the building for several weeks – an incubation period – then if that went unchallenged you could legally squat it. I don't think anybody else putting on warehouse parties knew about this.

We put the notices up for the required time and we'd been going in and out of there for quite a while, getting it ready for New Year's Eve, with no problems at all. Come the day, we were all there by lunchtime: myself, my brother, Jules, his girlfriend Savonne, Adam and Dan. Savonne had put up and decorated a lovely Christmas tree, which I was standing admiring when my heart nearly stopped. Three coppers are coming down the walk to the building, one with a flat cap and plenty of silver braid, and two pointy-heads. And they're City of London police, which had a taller height requirement than the Met so they look enormous! Because we so rarely saw police *before* a party, they usually came down during or after, I'm crapping myself, all I can think is, 'We've got a party going on tonight . . . our last one . . . we've never had one stopped . . . please don't . . .'

'Who's in charge here?'

*

Savonne quickly took control of the situation and told him she was a student at the LSE and that they were holding their Christmas party in the theatre, that it was all sorted out ages ago. He was very cool and said 'Oh yeah?' then walked over to the bar where he saw the squatters' notice – I'm pretty sure he'd been in there before and sussed all of this out. That's when we started thinking we'd cracked it, because even if he doesn't believe Savonne we've done the squatting thing. He made out he was reading the notice and took it down, which was when Jules took over. He remembered all my training – look Old Bill straight in the eye, never look away and talk in your poshest accent. But this copper was very clever, he said nothing and just waved the notice in Jules's face. As if this was all some sort of formality, Jules went into his spiel: 'We've been here a few weeks, we're squatting the place which is why we put the notices up, and now we're holding our student party.'

Old Bill let Jules say his piece, then replied, 'I've got to congratulate you kids, I know you're setting up for your New Year's Eve party, which is now only a few hours away, and you almost pulled it off ... ' He didn't say why not, he just left us hanging, and all I can think is, 'What, what, *what*? Why not?' He wouldn't tell us, he just sort of grinned and repeated, 'And you almost got away with it!' By now Jules is becoming indignant: 'We're students, some of our friends have been living here ... ' The copper just cut him off with, 'No, they haven't.' Then he asked Jules if he was at the LSE too and what was he studying. When Jules said he was doing a law degree, the copper almost laughed and said, 'Well, with this particular piece of legislation you're failing, aren't you?' This really took Jules down a peg or two, he was visibly deflating while Old Bill was just as clearly enjoying his moment and seemed to relax a bit. Then he got onto the squatting notice. 'I'll tell you about this piece of paper and why there was never any chance of you doing your party here – the one fatal flaw in your plan was that this is on *this* side of the bridge. It's the City of London, and if you really knew your squatters' rights you'd know that in London it only applies to the Metropolitan area. The City of London is crown property and nobody can legally squat crown property.'

And the first we hear about that is four or five hours before we're due to kick off?! Jules went bright red, but what could we do? The game was up.

Then Old Bill himself saved us, and became pretty much human in the process. He said: 'I don't want to come off as a spoilsport, this is New Year's Eve, I know you've got your party planned and I'm the last person in the world that wants to ruin it for you.' Then he looked up and out over the river. 'This is crown property, because we're in the City of London. Over there it's the Metropolitan Police, and while you can't do your party on crown property, I'm not responsible for what goes on in the Met.' I picked up on it straight away, because I knew there was a rivalry between the City and the Metropolitan police forces, but Jules wanted to argue the case. I gave Jules a look that seriously said, 'Let it go! Let it go!', and got in between him and the copper to ask, innocently, 'So if we go over there, everything will be alright?' He said, 'You just can't do it here. What goes on in the Met is none of my concern.' Once I told him we wouldn't do it there, he was fine with us, wished us good luck with it and a happy new year.

*

By then my head was working overtime, concentrating on a back-up venue and I soon had an idea. I ran to the nearest phone box – nobody had a mobile then – and phoned my sister, CJ, who used to work for British Telecom, and she'd told me that they'd moved out of their main offices and the building was lying empty somewhere round there on the south side of the river. She told me it was right next to Southwark Bridge and it was still unused, which was all I needed to hear. I looked over and sure enough, practically opposite where we were was a huge unloved-looking office block! It's a hotel now, but on that New Year's Eve it was *empty*! I grabbed some tools and ran all the way across the bridge, with Jules behind me asking where was I going! I got down to the ground-floor window furthest from the street and scraped out the putty, carefully removed the glass and within twenty minutes I'm inside the gaff. Looked around and knew straight away this was it – we had our back-up venue! But the clock's ticking.

Once I got out I called my old man, who was brilliant and backed us all the way, and he drove down with fresh putty, a big padlock and chain and a broom. The idea was to put the glass back in the window with the putty and clear up all that I'd scraped out; then we'd hacksaw the lock off the doors and sweep up the filings. My understanding was that if there were no visible signs, you couldn't be done for breaking and entering because they couldn't prove you did. I wasn't a burglar, I wasn't a criminal, but I was desperate! Then as soon as we put our own lock on the door, we could turn a key as we came and went so it looked like we should be there. We called a bunch of our mates to come down and help us move the gear over and set up in the new place. As we're going in for the first time, all I'm thinking is please don't let the police come round here now!

We wheeled the generator in, and ideally I wanted us to go up to the fifth or sixth floor, because the noise and activity of a big party on the ground floor attracts too much attention. I thought I'd try the lift and it worked! It was still switched on, and that point I knew we were going to pull this off. We could get everything up to sixth floor – speaker boxes, amps, everything – and everybody's working overtime to get the place looking presentable and set up ready to kick off about nine o'clock. We did it. Savonne even got the Christmas tree back up.

We did it, we could open the doors on time – all we had left to do was station a couple of people on the other side of the bridge, along the walk down to the old theatre, to tell those arriving that we'd moved and point out where the new place was. We got a good crowd in there, just under a thousand, with people really into it – maybe because I told them to make sure they enjoyed it because it was the last party of this type we were ever going to do! I really enjoyed it, and had mixed emotions about it being the last one. On the one hand, I could look out at the crowd and see all these happy people really going for it, or I could turn around to look out over the river and the City buildings and think this is exactly what I want to be doing and where I want to be doing it. But on the other hand, I thought about how close it had come to this not happening and realised I didn't want that sort of stress in my life – I was thirty years old! Also maybe I was getting a bit bored with the scene, because, as I said earlier, I knew it was time to move on.

part seven:
end game

chapter forty: after rare groove

In 1988, I really needed something to change my direction from rare groove and give me a focus on the new music that was coming out of New York and New Jersey. I'd been to New York that summer, as usual, and hooked up with Tony Humphries, the New Jersey deejay and mixer who was an important figure in the 1980s garage house scene at the Zanzibar club in Newark. Tony took me to the finals of the Jersey Jams Talent Contest over there, which was brilliant, so intense, with these then-unknown local acts Blaze and Adeva performing. It was unreal! Across the river from the glitz and big-time clubs in Manhattan was this wicked scene that encapsulated the black house sound away from Detroit and Chicago. It was raw and urgent, straight off the ghetto streets of New Jersey and New York, and as I stood in the crowd that night I had another of those light bulb moments – I knew this was what I needed to be doing, bringing a version of this to London.

When I got back, my promoting partner Patrick Lilley and I started High On Hope at Dingwalls in Camden Town, playing the new dance garage that was coming over from east coast of America. For the first couple of months it was a disaster – barely half a dozen people in there and we were losing money hand over fist. At one point we were thinking this was never going to work, but I had this unshakeable faith that this kind of New York garage vibe was the next step as far as black clubs were going in London. In the parallel white world, it had gone all smiley smiley and ravey davey, but I knew we needed to stay true to the original house sounds and present an alternative black side of the coin. This was the new disco.

We kept at it, no publicity or anything, this was strictly word of mouth because we wanted it to feel like an underground scene, then the word got round and suddenly the club took off. My god did it *take off*! By the eighth or ninth week we had 650 people packed in there, with another 250 locked out. It was like that every Thursday until well into the next year and it totally got rare groove out of my system.

One of the amazing things about High On Hope was that I met Paul Weller there. Unbeknownst to me he'd been there practically from the beginning, and I can vaguely remember a couple of white guys – him and his Style Council partner Mick Talbot – standing at the bar at the back, but it was too far and too dark to see properly. They were fans of the music I played, which is what had prompted Paul to do a cover of the Joe Smooth tune 'Promised Land'. When through mutual friends I heard they were in the house, we were introduced and they were both really warm and welcoming.

Paul and I became good friends. He had an amazing knowledge of black music and an even more amazing record collection – we went through a phase a few years ago where if there was a tune that he loved or he thought I didn't know, he'd text me. 'Norman do you know this?' Nine times out of ten I knew them, but occasionally he'd get one over on me, and because it was Paul I always checked it out. Before that, though, one day out of the blue his dad John Weller, who was his manager, phoned me to ask if I would come over and do a remix of a Style Council song, at the behest of Paul. I panicked! I was never a remixer. I *hated* studios – still do – but how do I say no to Paul Weller? I gathered myself and said, 'John, let me be totally upfront – even though I play loads of music, I'm not a remixer, I'm not a producer and I've never done a remix in my life.' That didn't seem to make a difference and John got me to come down to the studio Paul owned in Marble Arch, Solid Bond, where Paul and Mick greeted me like old mates and we sat around. Totally relaxed, three old musos talking about music and smoking.

When I saw Paul's record collection in the studio, it was immediately clear he knew his onions when it came to black music, and when I saw the tapes of all of my Kiss shows I was totally in awe – if I was white I would have gone red! We got down to business, the tune was called 'Everybody's on the Run', and I did my first ever remix, not a brilliant mix but not bad either. Then the old man gave me a brown envelope full of cash! I tried to tell him I was a fan and I didn't want money for it – I had a brilliant time just hanging out – and John Weller looked at me and said, 'You'll get paid, and here's your fee.' OK! Fine! Although he was always very nice to me, I subsequently learned that Paul's dad, who's passed now, had a deadly reputation in the music business and a lot of people were wary of him. That might have been a factor a couple of years later when I was at Talkin' Loud records. Paul was out of a contract, I wanted to sign him, but my head of A&R was unequivocal, 'Absolutely not! You are not signing Paul Weller.' It baffled me, because I was young and naive and convinced we could have made a brilliant record, but I had a lot to learn about the music business, as we'll see in the next chapter.

chapter forty-one: talkin' loud

Just over a year after I'd done the last warehouse party I went legit, or about as legit as I was going to get! I joined the music business as the A&R man on Talkin' Loud, a label set up by PolyGram with Gilles Peterson. Not that this was an easy decision to make, as in my world the record companies were the enemy – my job as a deejay was to introduce music to people, to make them dance and enjoy themselves or to enrich their lives; their job was to take as much money as they could from the public and drain the creativity out of the artists. I didn't see how those two paths could converge. I was entirely negative about the idea of working within the industry in the UK, because there were no black people in it, and, as far as I could see, no career path for any that might get in. It was working for me as a deejay – I was in complete charge, I put on my gigs, I earned a good screw and, most importantly, I was a success or failure on my own efforts. What I didn't want was to be was hired by somebody, then when it wasn't working or they didn't like it, for whatever reason, I'd be pulled in front of a manager and told, 'You're sacked!' When I was made redundant from my print job five years previously, I'd said that nobody would do that to me again and I was sticking by that resolution.

But there were two things tipping the balance here: having a proper contract with a proper company would enable me to get a mortgage; and Gilles Peterson was involved, and he and I were close friends. Gilles and I existed in parallel universes, I was running Shake and Fingerpop while he was doing the acid jazz thing, but we had huge crossovers with audiences and the music we liked, from James Brown to jazz. He had been approached by the then-head of PolyGram to start a new label, which the old rock dinosaur company hoped would plug them into a piece of this new funky London action. With all that was happening culturally in London, and the record companies able to read about it in the new style magazines, the company execs were determined not to miss out: they were going to give him a proper budget and creative freedom. Gilles had very successful club nights and radio shows and somebody at PolyGram got a flea in their ear, 'Get Peterson in!'

Gilles is a very smart bloke, smart enough to say he didn't want to do this on his own because he knew he'd need an ally in there, and smart enough to know the ideal confederate would be a credible black guy. One that would recognise things he might not and, maybe I'm being cynical here, bring credence to what he was doing. Whatever the reason, it was a big deal, as up until then at all major record companies, even on the black music divisions, it had been white blokes bringing in white blokes bringing in white blokes. Even so, when Gilles asked me quietly off the record I still said no.

I went to New York that autumn for Thanksgiving and got a call there from Gilles, who'd tracked me down to my aunt's house and is telling me, 'Norman, name your price.

They desperately want you to come and do this thing with me.' He said they needed a decision quickly, but I really didn't care – I didn't need a job, I was happy with my lot, I was in New York, one of my favourite places, so they were going to have to wait until I got back. I did, however, have the foresight not to let this become an ego-driven thing, and for counsel sought out Jazzie, Danny D, and a few of the black people I knew who worked in the record industry. They all told me I needed to look on the positive side, that I needed to go and do this because it would make me the single most powerful black guy in there, and you can only affect change from the inside.

This really gave me something to wrestle with: part of me wanted to do it because of what these guys had said, the other part didn't want to do it because I would lose my independence. As I thought it over, I realised black guys don't get given these opportunities and they shouldn't be wasted, which made me think maybe I was just scared of the challenge, scared of failure. I'd never even thought about anything like this before, so I could only see all the negatives and the positives just weren't coming into my head. This would be a chance to avenge all of those wrongs that I'd rebelled against, railed against and called out, this was my chance to get in there and change it. Patrick Lilley told me I was in such a strong position I could negotiate everything I wanted, so I got a good music business lawyer and went for it. As well as the usual things like a car, an expense account, my own office, freedom to sign artists, and more money than I'd ever seen, I negotiated to be able to keep all my deejay work and only come in a couple of days a week. I signed on the dotted line and I was an A&R man at a major record company.

I'd been there about three months, barely got my feet under the desk, and there's a major reshuffle above us, the guy who had brought us in was out the door. He was the Dutch MD – back then PolyGram was Dutch-owned – and he liked us and genuinely trusted us to do big things, but now we both knew the goalposts would be moved. A week later the new guy calls us into his office, and he's trying to pit Gilles and myself against each other, adversaries instead of partners – I'll be running my own little label and Gilles will be running Talkin' Loud. I knew that if, down the line, I was having to compete with Gilles for money, resources or even legitimacy, I was going to lose every time. I went to Gilles and said, 'This is nonsense, I don't want to be running my own tiny label, I want to come in with you on one big successful label, like the original plan.' To give him his due, he'd sussed what was going on and wasn't happy either.

In the weekly updates with press and promotions, they weren't really able to cope with two black music labels at the same time – they'd get super excited about Gilles's stuff and just went through the motions with mine – and our head of A&R, another old rockhead, was taking neither of us seriously. It didn't matter how many of us were in a meeting, I was always the only black person, and because major record companies had set ideas about black music, they had set ideas about black people too, even those that worked for them. I was severely frustrated, and was figuring that this was why our music never worked – because of meetings like this where hopes and dreams go to die. After two or three of those, I went to Gilles and suggested that the only way to get any leverage to do what we wanted was if we worked together. His thoughts entirely, so I let my label quietly fade away and came over to Talkin' Loud as A&R.

This was exactly the right decision to make, as that first year we put out Omar's record, we put out Incognito and we won an award for Label Of The Year, but success came a bit too early for us because suddenly we're taking massive pressure from above to have more pop hits. This meant making records they thought sounded like pop records, as the management totally didn't get it – the hits we had were hits because they *didn't* sound like pop hits. Then our bands are coming to us telling us, 'Norman, Gilles, we didn't sign with you for this! We're not pop artists!' From midway through the second year there, I'm constantly thinking 'What am I doing here?' This was exactly why I didn't want to join the record business. For a while I had believed in it really passionately, but with the way a major like PolyGram was set up, I was always going to be at odds with them. To them Radio 1 was everything, if a record wasn't getting on that station *immediately* you might as well forget it, and that wasn't how the sort of records we were putting out worked. There was no acknowledgement of the whole world of clubs out there. There are thousands of little clubs around England where if your record gets played a couple of times on a Saturday night, so many people will go and buy it on Monday you've actually got a chart record before Radio 1's even heard it. I knew that it didn't matter how well crafted these records were – they would fall down because I was only the A&R

man and the other departments couldn't get them on to the radio or into the press.

Then by the third year, they actually had me questioning my own judgement, because I'd do things instinctively and they'd get knocked back if I hadn't run them by Gilles first, who would always say, 'If you think it's good . . . ' I began to worry that I was adapting my opinions on things in order to get them past my Head of A&R, picking things because he'd like them not because I knew the kids would go nuts for them. That's when I started thinking I'd been there too long. I was *born* into this music and now I'm not sure? What I didn't want was records I had a hand in ending up in the basement of the Record & Tape Exchange for five for a quid – just like if I come out of a gig and see my flyers on the floor, I start picking them up. I wanted people to be fighting over my records: 'Gimme dat! I'll give you fifty quid for it!'

Also, this was the time when, outside the record industry, deejays were the new kings. House deejays were superstars in this new wave of British youth culture built around clubbing and dance. I was one of the original house deejays, so now everything I loved was going stratospheric, there was no way I was missing out on that for some record company job. We'd signed some good artists, including Young Disciples, but I was really pleased when PolyGram told me they weren't renewing my contract and I could get out of the record business.

chapter forty-two: big time deejay

It was in the 1990s that I realised I'd made it to be a Big Time Deejay. Of course I knew I'd been successful, because deejaying or the direct results of deejaying had provided me with a living for over half of the previous decade, but the deejay ascendancy during the 1990s was unbelievable. Suddenly in the UK youth culture was dance culture, and what seemed like an entire generation was switched on to it through the clubs and the parties and magazines like *Mixmag*. In this environment the deejays ruled – if you wanted your club or your party to work, you *had* to have certain deejays and I was fortunate enough to be one of them. Most Saturdays in the 1990s I did three or four events, most in-demand deejays did, it was quite funny because we'd all be criss-crossing the country at three or four in the morning bumping into each other at motorway service stations. 'Where you going?' . . . 'Cream in Liverpool, six 'til eight.' . . . 'Newcastle, Shindig, I'm on at five.' This period was special, but it could get pretty surreal.

Apart from Ministry of Sound, this whole deejay revolution went on outside London too: up north and in the Midlands, there was this network of massive clubs that were *packed* with literally thousands of kids two or three nights a week. This was before the 'Superclub' era – the club as a brand – and it was a genuine youth culture boom that had grown out of the whole Acid House Summer of Love in 1988. It was a bit like the warehouse scene but most of these were legal – they took place in big disused spaces like theatres or old town halls turned into permanent clubs – and it caught London sleeping. We'd be playing somewhere like Widnes on a Thursday night, pull up and there's a thousand people queuing five hundred yards down the road to get in an old cinema; you go down the West End, you're standing outside the Wag and there's a hundred and fifty people and they're telling you that you can't come in. And they're still paying their deejays £250!

Some of these clubs really were just big logs discos. Dance music was the new pop music and some of it could be atrocious – some of the tunes I played there would never be played at my Shake and Fingerpop parties! Carl Cox and I, the only black deejays on that circuit's A-list, used to moan about it as two black purists together. I used to say to him he had to relearn what he did because this wasn't about the music – it was communal, it was cultural, it was an experience. It was a challenge for me to learn to love that stuff but I did. It was house, but house made by white northern bedroom deejays, which was where the music had evolved to since I started playing it. For me, being a bit older, it was a voyage of discovery, this was new music creating a new soundtrack for a new generation – it didn't matter if I liked it or not as long as I understood the whole thing.

It was a cash cow too. For the big clubs to work, they had

to have the big names on their flyers, and the promoters were like sheep. If someone else's night was packed they had to get those deejays for theirs – Jeremy Healy, Paul Oakenfold, Norman Jay, Judge Jules, Carl Cox ... And the best way to do that was to offer them fistfuls of money. Literally. On a typical Saturday night, a big-time deejay could do a gig, and it's five large in a sock, or in the record box. Walk away, go to another place for another set, three large. Round the night off with one more and it's three more. This is more lucrative than selling drugs, and it's legal. Why would I not want to be plugged into that, regardless of the music?

We were paid in cash for a few years into the noughties, until Inland Revenue got wise to it, jumped all over it and made examples of a few deejays. That was when I realised I had to get proper management and stop the cash gigs. I was paranoid about getting stopped by the police late at night with ten grand in cash on me, because Old Bill's natural assumption would be that I was a drug dealer, they'd never pin that on a white guy. Then if they didn't nick me they'd just take the money. There were a lot of drugs about on that scene – some of the deejays used to get paid in coke and deal it on the side, some of them used to wash it straight into property. I knew I didn't get paid as much as some of the other deejays, even though I was the same A-list, but as I've never been money-oriented, I didn't really care. There was a shitload of money being made in and by those big out-of-town clubs, and I was making a far better living than I could have dreamed about a few years before. I guess it was a case of being grateful to be part of that whole thing.

At the time London was all R&B, which I didn't mind, although there was a lot of chart R&B and I wasn't interested in that – logs disco! After the creativity of the 1980s, London was getting up its own arse a bit, and the capital's big house music club, Ministry of Sound, came to sum that up.

I was the one of the first resident deejays at Ministry. When it first opened it was Paul Oakenfold, Danny Rampling and myself. Justin Berkman, who was one of the club's founders, also tried, but he was terrible! I'd known about the plans for Ministry for about five years before it opened, because Justin, the son of a peer, was one of my mates who I used to hang out with in New York – him, Jules, myself and around a dozen others would spend long summers there, the Nylon brat pack. We'd go to the Paradise Garage a lot, and Justin got the idea to build a club in London along those lines, with a sound system that amazing. He was friends with the property developer James Palumbo and the next thing I know they've sourced the location, got the lease and started building.

It was a fantastic place, totally dedicated to dancing and house music with a sound system that was pretty much perfect – the rumour was they'd spent half a million on that by itself. It was all going well, until about a year or so later when Cream opened up in Liverpool, which was being talked about as a rival to Ministry, although they were over two hundred miles apart! Naturally, all us deejays are interested, and Ministry tried to exert control by telling us if we play there we can no longer play at Ministry. *Fuck that!* We're free agents! This is what I meant about London having got a bit up itself, because this was a time when deejays had real power, and they were trying to pull a move that belonged in the old Funk Mafia days, or like when club owners used to tell us we couldn't bring the sound system in. It really got my back up, because this was 1992 and nobody told deejays you can't do this and you can't do that!

Paul Oakenfold was the first to go. He was a shrewd operator and always had his eye on the bigger prize. He went up to Cream where they gave him a residency and five large in cash every Saturday. Straight away he's telling me I need to get up there, but I said it's Liverpool and they don't book black deejays up there. Also, the previous year the guy who was running Cream had brought me up that way to play a little jazz/funk night and he'd never paid me. I didn't get dark on him, I just thought, 'Typical scally.' But he was a businessman and Paul had obviously endorsed me, so he made me an offer to come up and play Cream. £1,500 for a two-hour set (about £3000 in today's money). In my hand! *What?!* I was playing Ministry, but we were doing that for kudos rather than cash, so these guys up north had got my attention. Then he said he'd pay all he owed me from the year before, my fee and my hotel bill, he'd send it down. In a few days he was as good as his word, I was shocked!

I went up there and it was amazing! When I'd gone up to that area the previous year, there was nobody about and was sure my car was going to get broken into. This time when I pulled up I could hardly believe it, there were coaches from all over, as far away as Glasgow – it reminded me of the Northern soul nights at Wigan twenty-five years earlier. The excitement outside was tangible, none of your London too-cool-for-school, and when I walked into the club it was absolutely banging! It's rammed, three and a half thousand people, and it's going off! I just thought *whoa*!! I'm coming on after Paul, who is really glad to see me. I thanked him for bringing me up there, went behind the decks and the crowd went mad!

This was 1992 and it showed me the potential that scene had – these white kids were staying put in queues to get in and then they're feting us deejays like footballers! They follow deejays like they'd follow football teams and they were that loyal – we follow Sasha . . . we follow Jon Dickweed . . . It reminded me of how black kids always followed sound systems. And once these kids accepted you they made no secret of how they loved you – as I said before, we were their superstars.

A lot of deejays made their names on that scene and because of what I'd been through for years and years, building up an understanding of what made kids tick on the dancefloor, it was relatively easy for me to get into it. Once I did I actually loved it and for over ten years I was part of that very lucrative, exciting scene, playing to the biggest indoor crowds I'd ever played to. Getting into it wasn't an issue – getting out of something like that and remaining credible, that's the problem!

chapter forty-three: on the bbc

I left Kiss in 1993, of my own volition. I'd achieved what I wanted to there, I could see the direction the station was heading in, and I didn't want to be part of that future. I'd been out of radio for a few years when somebody I knew who was a producer at Radio London took me to lunch and asked me if I'd like to come and do a show. My immediate thought was 'Hmmmm!' I wasn't at all sure about going to the BBC because of the way it had ended quite acrimoniously for a few presenters on Kiss – I foresaw that Night of the Long Knives, which is why I got out – and I didn't think the BBC would necessarily be any better.

I told him I wasn't really interested in going back on the radio, but I knew they were really keen because Radio London was essentially talk radio and this would be one of only two music shows on there. He asked me what it would it take, and I was pretty militant in my demands: I would only do Sunday and I wasn't interested in a BBC-style show where you have a pre-approved playlist and a producer telling you what to do. My only concession was to allow a producer, but to *assist* me, because I'd always produced myself at Kiss and I wasn't having anybody controlling my content. While I'll be the first to acknowledge the value of a team – it can bring out the best in all of you – I've been successful as a deejay because I know what'll work. This show was to be a mixture of what I played in the clubs and my record collection; it was going to be about my experiences in clubland and I didn't need any help getting that across – I lived it, they weren't there! Fortunately I had enough of a way with words to get that across, and without being patronising I gave them an insight into how and why certain records worked. This is not something every deejay does, because so many, especially in radio, don't know themselves.

They agreed, but on my first Sunday they were so unprepared for another music show, or one like mine at least! They didn't have a set-up for me, no double decks, nothing! I had to load my own kit into my car and arrive an hour before my show, where an engineer had to hook it all up. Then he'd take it all down when I finished, I'd put it back in the car and go home! It worked like that there for about a year. But I wasn't really complaining, as they gave me a three-hour show on a Sunday, seven in the evening until ten, at a time when nobody anywhere across the whole BBC network was doing a three-hour music show. So I was really grateful for that, and even when they cut it down to two hours after three or four years, I didn't mind.

It was only after they wanted to shift it from Sunday that I began privately thinking I'd best be considering an exit strategy, because I was only interested in the radio on a Sunday night. Friday and Saturday I'm in the clubs, I'm up all night, I'm hyper and loving it. Sunday was for relaxing, my chill-out time. It was a time to get deeper into the music, to play a little bit of what I played the night before, but mostly more thought-provoking stuff. It worked too, because this was a time when Radio London's listening figures were going down steadily, but once they factored in my Sunday night audience it came back up to a respectable level.

I did really enjoy it for about seven or eight years, but then after that they started to play around with DAB, digital audio broadcasting. The BBC wanted to try out the digital platform on Radio London before they officially launched it, and they used me because mine was the music show. I always had my reservations about it: I knew from friends working in the BBC's technical departments that they couldn't make up their minds about which platform they were going to use. They'd compared it to the early days of VHS and Beta, implying that the BBC were choosing the wrong one. In the first few weeks of them putting my show on DAB, I bought a digital thing and put in in my Mini to see if would work, hoping it wouldn't! It was terrible, it kept cutting out! They could have asked any soundman at the time and they would have been told, 'This platform's shit, it's never gonna work!' But the BBC persisted with it and soon put my show on the platform. Almost immediately I had people ringing me saying, 'Norman, what's up? We can't get you on FM, we can't get you on this digital thing either!' I was on terrestrial and DAB for about a year, a kind of incubation period, then I was moved as they trialled it for this two-month period, but it never really worked. There were too many technical glitches and I was seriously unhappy about being made a guinea pig, so I thought I'm off.

I had told them right from the beginning that I didn't need to do radio, that I'd do it for as long as I was enjoying it, but once I wasn't I'd be walking out the door. By that time – mid-noughties – I was very comfortable with the notion that I was a live deejay and the radio was just a happy by-product. I was aware of how seductive a medium it could be, but at the same time I used to look at my mates who did radio and see how much shit they'd put up with. I wasn't prepared to. I understood how it gave you a reach to a great big audience, but I just thought it's simply not working for me. Of course I reconciled it in my own mind, thinking, 'OK, so only a few people will hear what I'm doing, but they'll be people who will *really* want to hear what I'm doing! They'll come out and support my live gigs!' I rationalised it by remembering that the only people who'd lose out were those who thought it was just an entitlement to turn on the radio and get my work for free! After that, my gigs had never been so full. It proved my view that you should make it special for those who can be bothered to come, those who have paid, they're the people you go out of your way for – it's like a duty of care, anyone else can go sing for it!

I am still really glad I did that time at the BBC, because compared with Kiss it was a different ballgame – it was like a finishing school for me in terms of presentation skills. It wasn't about music (music was secondary, because there was nothing they were teaching me about our music), but it let me learn how to articulate my passion to somebody with no interest. How do you hook someone in who isn't going to love everything you do unconditionally? The skill is in winning a new audience from the left field or wherever, people who wouldn't ordinarily give our music the time of day. That's what the BBC taught me: to entice that undecided audience, to make it about the *show* rather than just the records. Incidentally, this is what infuriates me about their handling of black music these days – they only seem to see it as 'street' and all their presenters talk street too. The point of building a radio audience is that not everybody who wants to listen will be that same street – how are people from Devon or the north of Scotland going to understand you? They're the people you want, you've already got the others. The most important thing I took away from the BBC was proper diction and proper grammar; I didn't have to sound posh, but didn't have to sound like an idiot either.

When I look back on my time at the BBC, I never really had a problem with them – by and large I was happy because I was in there on my own terms, I came in when it suited me and left when it suited me.

chapter forty-four: where i am as a deejay

I'm really content with where I am as a deejay now, and I have been for many years because I know what works for me. I'm busier than I've ever been and I put that down to the acceptance of the value of heritage – like what they call 'heritage rock acts', I'm a heritage deejay. I know I'm not appealing to sixteen- and eighteen-year-olds, I don't play grime or drill, but there's a generation of people that have been schooled in black music for fifty years, supplied by the likes of me. They're still out there and they still enjoy themselves. You don't so much see them in clubs, but they still go out – two gigs I've just got are supporting Sister Sledge and later in the year supporting Stevie Wonder. I've done a few of these *big* gigs with these *big* black acts, and it's like I'm accepted as the right fit: if you want a deejay to open for Stevie Wonder, you need to get Norman!

On an obvious level, it's brilliant, but at the same time there's a deeper cultural relationship going on there, as there were times when acts like Sister Sledge and Stevie were completely out of vogue and no one touched their music, but I always championed it – I never let go. As this is our musical heritage I'm never going to not play it: even though I'm into all the current electronic music too, I'll interweave a Marvin tune, a Stevie tune, a James Brown tune. As long as I'm deejaying my crowds will always be reminded that this is where all that stuff they love comes from, this is its DNA. These days I see my role as demonstrating the joining of those dots. I would never forsake the shared history of black music – it's too rich, it's too varied to just be able to jump on the next fashionable thing and run with it. Yes, I'm abreast of new music, but not because I have to be, because I want to be. I've still got an interest.

Something I have to be grateful to Carnival for is opening the door for me to play at the big music festivals, as I'm sure that was the only way they could have heard about Good Times. We were never promoted in any music press or covered by the music media; in fact, the mainstream never gave us props for anything. That used to make me so angry, but I mellowed out pretty quickly as soon as I realised we didn't need any of that, we always had more people at Carnival than they'd ever seen at their gigs. This was way before the big dance festivals, and by the time they came around I'd been playing for crowds of *thousands* of people for years – the first time I was asked to play a dance festival was 1995 or 1996, and I'd been playing Carnival since 1980. So I'd been preparing for fifteen years, because what is Carnival other than a rough-and-ready dance music festival for us!

Doing these few dance music festivals brought us on to the mainstream radar, along with offers to play festivals with bigger crowds than I'd been getting. The Big Chill was the first big one I did, but it wasn't that big when I first went there! It had been moving around different locations for quite a few years, then it settled at Larmer Tree Farm in Wiltshire in 1998 and I did the second one down there, which was amazing: a couple of hundred people and wild pheasants and tame peacocks wandering about all over the place! Very, very chilled and 'OK, yah!' I used to go back every year, and within five years it had moved again to a castle in Dorset, grown so much that there were several stages, and I'm playing on the main one to thirty thousand people. As the Big Chill always fell in early August, I would feed it into the Carnival by constantly telling the biggest crowd I'd ever played to that I'd be at the Notting Hill Carnival in two weeks' time and it would be free. I'm sure most of them had never been to the Carnival before, but would come to Good Times there and it would help to swell our numbers, so I was getting the best of both worlds out of the Big Chill.

It was out of this that I got to do Glastonbury, at a time when Glastonbury never used to entertain the idea of deejays as entertainment! If I'm perfectly honest, I don't really enjoy Glastonbury as much as I might, because unlike my gigs with Good Times or Shake and Fingerpop, and as with any massive festival, the crowd weren't there for me, they were just there for the event. I was just one of the many names on the flyer, which was what I always avoided when I was doing my own parties. That doesn't mean I didn't do my best to make the people dance and enjoy themselves and the music, but basically I was just another deejay and I fell in line with all the others they had on the bill, doing my job. I never used a mic when I was at these things, so there was probably not that much to tell me apart from the others from the crowd's perspective – you could take any of us out and it would make no difference. I wouldn't let anybody down at an event like that, but it couldn't be further removed from Carnival.

By the middle of the noughties, I was doing all the major music festivals, which was keeping my profile so high that pretty soon I had become a stand-alone event on the festival calendar, which suited me much better. I had moved away from the dance music ones because they'd all got a bit young and druggie, and I had already established myself at the Big Chill with a more mature audience, who were cooler and more diverse – black, white, Asian, gay . . . I realised that this was, in fact, an audience that had grown up with me, because it was twenty years since I had been doing the warehouses, twenty-five years since Good Times first played Carnival, and my original crowd were in their forties and fifties by that point – I was hitting my half century!

As I did more events like that, I discovered that there were quite a few of them I just enjoyed being at and hanging out, away from deejaying. One of those was Festival No 6 in Portmeirion in north Wales, because I was big fan of the cult 1960s TV series *The Prisoner*, which did its entire exterior filming there. I did the second Festival No 6 – 'Number Six' was the only name of the TV series' main character – because when I heard about the first one taking place there, I was all over my manager: 'Get me on there! . . . Talk to them! . . . I wanna do the next one! . . . Do a deal! . . . Get me in there!' I did it and I was bowled over to be deejaying in that environment, but like so many festivals it was losing money and now it's no more.

*

I went through a phase in the '90s and the '00s when I was getting invited to play at private functions all over the world, and there was a period when it seemed like I was the go-to man for film premieres and I was playing every one. I will admit I didn't really enjoy the corporate events and private parties, because it was all about media, not about me playing music to make people dance. My name was merely part of the entertainment, but once I understood my position I was happy to do them, it was just something else I did – club deejay, radio deejay, festival deejay, corporate deejay ... it kept me interested. My role is pleasing people with whatever music they will accept, and I feel blessed even to this day because I know I'm unique: I'm the only one who comes from that early era of black clubs and black music in London who's accepted on every scene – I can play on the northern scene, the jazz scene, the house scene, the hip-hop scene, and all with credibility. I'll never be out of work!

A real big deal for me as a deejay came just before the 2012 London Olympics, when I was asked to deejay at Jamaica House for the whole of the games. I'm not Jamaican, and there are so many deejays in London of Jamaican heritage that I thought it was a massive honour. I played there three or four times and I know everybody enjoyed it.

In terms of crowd size with these festivals, I've probably become about as big as any deejay could hope to get. I'm travelling all over the world and have enough status to be able to play what I like. But it was still about doing it in London, among my own crowd, and I would probably get more enjoyment out of doing gigs like the Prince of Wales pub in Brixton on a Sunday afternoon, in front of people that have followed me since the 1980s, than I would playing in front of a festival crowd of fifty thousand in Brazil. And, of course, taking Good Times to the Notting Hill Carnival up until 2013.

I never thought I'd have a career that lasted this long. I never took things for granted because you can't – the fickleness of the music business, the flavour of the month things, 'Who are you?' next year ... it can all cut your legs off at any time. People ask me 'What about retirement?', and I can only reply, 'Retirement from what? You retire from work, I don't consider what I do *work*.' I'm pleasing myself, mostly. I love the life it's afforded me, as a black working-class kid, child of the Windrush, I never imagined I'd be going to all these fantastic places just to play records.

For the last twenty-odd years, every January and February I've been to Australia and New Zealand on tour, chasing the sun. There's no reason for me to be in the UK – I get good gigs down there, stay out of the worst of the cold. The most important thing to me is that the desire's still there and I hope it never wanes. I hope my health holds up and it enables me to do it for the foreseeable future. I'm totally comfortable in my skin, because I know it works for me. I understand fundamentally why people go out, why they dance, why they enjoy it, and why they come back – as long as I don't forget that I'll be OK.

chapter forty-five: over and out

Personally, I'm in a very good place and have been for a while. I'm very happily married, I get great joy out of my grandson Rory, I've got a great relationship with my sons, who I see regularly and speak to practically on a daily basis. I have no contact with their mother, but that suits us both. I'm trying my best not to turn into a grumpy, miserable old bastard, but increasingly I find things irritating me, which is probably part of the job description of getting on in years.

My relationship with my mum and dad is perhaps stronger now since the passing of my brother and my sister. I see them a great deal too, and I'm really pleased they're both in reasonably good health and have still got their faculties, because they really are getting on a bit. I still tease them, I call them the pensioners, and I tell them one day I'm going to get my notification to send them back! I tease them about me being born in England, but I also thank them most profoundly because had the course of their lives taken them along a different path, I'd have been born somewhere else doing something else. We're all aware that life is a lottery and as far as I'm concerned, I realise I won the lottery! All my cards are stacking up and I'm eternally grateful to my parents and my family for that. I mean that really deeply, and I would do *anything* for them. Fortunately I'm now in a financial position where I can take care of them and they don't want for anything, although they never really *want* anything! They're pretty uncomplicated compared to my generation.

I'm not a Spurs season ticket holder any more, and when I went to a couple of games at the new stadium I was reminded why. I'm not averse to change, but when I went to the opening game with my eldest son Mark and my Rory, who was nine, it was like a total loss of control on our part. Stewards told us where to stand, where to walk, where to wait ... it was like being kettled! But I realised this was the new normal and I had to put up or shut up. It was not my idea of football, and I accept maybe I'm some old relic from a bygone era. I'm happy to admit and acknowledge that, but if this is the new modern way of going to sport, it's not for me.

One of the proudest moments in my life happened in 2002, when I got made an MBE for services to music. I was the first deejay to get one for deejaying work and not for charity or community work, and my citation read: 'For services to deejaying and black music.' Of course there were quite a few people telling me I shouldn't have accepted it because of the British Empire's connotations, but my reaction was 'Fuck it! I can't do anything about slavery hundreds of years ago. All I can do is hopefully influence tomorrow.' I figured I could do more good with it than without it, and I used it positively – when I went to give lectures in schools, or went to speak at young offenders' units, it meant the people in authority there took me a bit more seriously than they might have done otherwise. I am completely aware of history, but for ages after that when I was out in the community people were congratulating me – people who would never go to one of my gigs. For me, it was about being recognised by the highest authority in the land for doing what I do very well – it meant a bit more than winning a *Mixmag* Best Deejay Poll!

I almost missed getting it, because I was on tour in Scandinavia when I got a call at my hotel at about four o'clock in the morning from somebody claiming to be the Controller at BBC radio, saying he'd been trying to get hold of me for a few days. I'd just got in from a gig, I wanted to sleep and I was like a bear with a sore head, I wouldn't talk to him. He called back the next day and told me that 10 Downing Street was trying to get in touch with me – now I was sure it was one of those TV show wind-ups and I didn't want to play. I just told him I'd be home on Monday and I'd call him back then. I was a little intrigued, suppose he's telling the truth? He's my ultimate boss at the BBC! So I called him back and he didn't tell me anything about what it concerned, he just gave me a number and an access code.

I rang the number, put the code in, and it gets through to 10 Downing Street, or so it said. I said, 'This is Norman Joseph.' ... 'Oh, we've been trying to reach you. Did you get our telegram? You've been made an MBE.' I just stopped there and said, 'Listen, didn't I tell you guys I really wasn't up for this joke thing?' The guy said, 'No, this is serious.' And he said it so seriously that I thought before I completely shot myself in the foot, I'd engage with him. He told me they sent out a telegram with a royal seal on it but were unable to deliver it, so I asked for another one because I knew you couldn't fake the royal seal. He said they would but there wasn't much time, because I now had less than forty-eight hours to accept or knock it back.

The next morning, bright and early, there's a knock on the door, 'Mr Joseph, telegram.' Royal seal! I opened the thing up, 'You've been made an MBE.' That's when I believed it. Up until then I had thought it was a hoax, some game show. I went berserk, then later that day I got myself together and signed the forms to formally accept it.

Six months later I had to go to Buckingham Palace to be given the medal, and I was so paranoid about being late that I didn't go to sleep the night before! My mum and dad were so excited for me, everybody in the community had been congratulating me, and the well-wishing from my friends was fantastic – JK, Jamiroquai, lent me this very rare vintage Mercedes from his car collection so I could arrive at the Palace in style, and when we rocked up in it we stopped the show because nobody had ever seen a car like that. I was only allowed to take in Maria and the boys, and I went in a full morning suit and top hat, carrying this little wooden cane with a lion's head on it that I'd been given by a chieftain in Namibia a few years before. He had told me it would be my guidance, and it gave me the greatest pleasure to hand it to the footman in the cloakroom along with my top hat. Because there are lions everywhere you go in Buckingham Palace, and everybody knows lions don't come from England, lions come from Africa, it gave me great pleasure to tell him, 'Here's a real lion, this one came from Africa.'

It was an unbelievable day. I was especially pleased because the Queen was presenting the awards that day, not Prince Charles, or her husband – thank goodness it wasn't him! Up until then I was neither pro-royalist nor anti-royalist, but at that moment I felt really honoured and my mum and dad still talk about it. I always use it, Norman Jay MBE, because I earned it. I thought, 'Why should I be typically English and coy? No, I want it on *everything*!' I put the title to work immediately, as at my afterparty in a club under the flyover just off Portobello, I passed my top hat round in aid of Sickle Cell Anaemia and it was totally filled up, nearly two grand! The perfect end to that day.

Another honour bestowed upon me was when I was invited to go to Sigma Sound Studios in Philadelphia, where Gamble & Huff recorded all those TSOP hits, plus there were a load more soul classics made there. The place had been a museum for several years, but was by then closed. They opened it up especially for me and gave me a tour, a goody bag and a plaque acknowledging the contribution I made to Philadelphian music in England. This dated from my early days on Kiss, when my playlist was about 90 per cent Philly influenced, and I let everybody know there was a bit more to music from that city than Gamble & Huff. So much of what we danced to came out of that studio's MFSB orchestra, which was also the Salsoul orchestra and loads of other different things – same players, all classically trained.

Just to show how ridiculously varied my life has been, I have also appeared on BBC One's *Question Time*. This was in 2004 and while it was fantastic it was also daunting – a black deejay from the street, now I'm on *Question Time*? I was both flattered and intimidated. I'd been asked three times and always turned it down because I'm not trained in debate like all those other guests – I didn't go to university. I'm a barroom orator, you put me in front of a bar and I'll talk football or politics with anybody, but I'm not going to make myself look stupid in front of a television audience. This time, the presenter David Dimbleby took me to lunch and told me that I didn't have to answer any questions; I was only there to give an opinion. He was lovely and put me at my ease so much that I couldn't refuse.

On the night itself, everybody was in the green room having a stiff drink to steady their nerves before they went on, and because I'm a teetotaller I didn't know what to do! I was just standing there thinking, 'Norman, don't panic!' I was sitting on the end and I wasn't nervous at all – in fact I was so engrossed I felt like I was watching it from a front-row seat. I was mesmerised, then suddenly this thing about legalising cannabis landed in my lap like a hand grenade! Immediately I'm like, 'Fuck!! What do I say?' Then I thought, just be honest: 'The government makes enough money out of legalising cigarettes – tobacco's a drug – should cannabis be treated any different?' And the whole room applauded me. Amazing! I didn't really get warmed up until five minutes before the end, when some Tory woman made some stupid condescending remark, and in the moment I forgot I was on television and the street took over! I steamed into her, 'Well wadda you know? Were you there?', and then the programme ended! I got the last word but it was just as well it ended, because I'm sure I would have started cussing and embarrassed myself.

After the broadcast she came up to me in the green room, and I admitted how nervous I was at the beginning. She said they were all nervous of meeting *me*! This Labour guy from Scotland said he was nervous about meeting me after he'd researched me, which left me thinking *what*!?!?! You lot researched me? I hadn't prepared anything, but they'd all done their homework! No wonder they can debate, this is how they do it! After that my motto was 'you can never be over-prepared'.

Preparation came in handy in 2018, when the British Library did this two-week exhibition of photographs and archival material for the Windrush celebrations and I was booked to deejay it. I went up there for a meeting with them, and I thought this is fantastic, but I'd have to do my research. I spoke to my mum, my dad and people of that generation about it – what was the music like? Where did you go and buy records? And thanks to the wonders of the internet, I found them all, so I could curate it and compile a relevant set. There were about three hundred people there and they absolutely loved it. I got so much pleasure from it because I was playing music from 1952 to 1969, music that I distantly remember my dad or my uncle or somebody playing when I was a kid. I had an hour and played calypso, bluebeat, jazz R&B and reggae, all records I dug out. I played American records I could remember my granddad, who was living in America in the late 1950s and early '60s, bringing over for my dad when he visited England every year. Things I remembered as a tiny boy, and I was able to draw from all of that experience. People of my mum and dad's age were coming up and saying, 'Nice! Really enjoyed the music!' . . . 'Dat took me back to when I came here in 1956!' . . . 'How you know all dat music?'

That made me feel special, and like I'd come full circle: I was back playing the tunes from nearly sixty years ago, music that would remain in my consciousness for ever and would get me started on this journey.

acknowledgements

To my lovely amazing wife, JANE. Thank you for enriching my world through your punky creative attitude towards our life, our love, our marriage.

My sons MARK and RUSSELL who I love dearly and of whom I am especially proud.

My multi-talented little 'lion-cub' grandson, RORY, who continues to make Grandad even more proud.

Mum and Dad: thank you for your continued guidance, inspiration and life-long support. I hope I continue to make you both very proud.

BIG SHOUT to my surviving brother JOEY JAY for being there in the begining providing the initial inspiration with Great Tribulation Sound System.

FAMILY SHOUTS to sisters PATSY, CAROL and GLORIA. Luke and Olivia. Love you guys!

Special thanks to LLOYD BRADLEY for revealing our often shared musical past back in the day and without whom this book simply couldn't have been writtten. I salute you sir!

My brilliant management team, DAN G, DAVIDE B, ELISA M and LYDIA M @ Gray Matter Management Ltd.

Special thanks to top photographer DEAN CHALKLEY

for the amazing cover shot. Her Majesty the Queen Elizabeth II for my MBE.

Lifelong shouts to:

My man Ricky Pryce (BIG!)
DJ Rudy Ranx
Ryan 'Huggy' Lewis
Davy 'DMX' Garrard
Notting Hill Carnival
Bryan Webb RIP
Lou and Algie Webb
Ernie Baptist
Dan de Sausmarez
Dan Benedict
Mark Gregory
Pete Glass RIP
Kay Glass
Claire Martino
Robin & Tara Knight
Paul 'Trouble' Anderson RIP
Terry Farley
Judge Jules
Gilles Peterson
David Rodigan
Jazzie B, Soul II Soul
Carl Cox DJ
Andy 'Muz' Murray
Papa Scooby

Don Letts
Dave Swindells
Robert Elms
Chelsea Phipps
The Big Chill
Katrina Larkin
Pete Lawrence
Vibes on Summer's Day
Original Kiss FM DJs
Talkin Loud
Tottenham Hotspur FC
Cratediggers
Young Disciples
DJ Melvo
Patrick Lilley
Dele Fadahusi
Ernie Gadsby
Sharmaine Lovegrove and the whole brilliant crew at Dialogue Books
Dave Daniel
Adam Powley for the book inspiration in the first place

Bringing a book from manuscript to what you are reading is a team effort.

Dialogue Books would like to thank everyone at Little, Brown who helped to publish *Mister Good Times* in the UK.

Editorial
Sharmaine Lovegrove
Thalia Proctor
Sophia Schoepfer

Production
Narges Nojoumi
Nick Ross
Mike Young

Contracts
Anniina Vuori

Publicity
Hayley Camis

Sales
Andrew Cattanach
Ben Goddard
Hermione Ireland
Hannah Methuen

Marketing
Emily Moran

Copy Editor
Lydia Cooper

Design
Sean Garrehy
Jo Taylor

Proofreader
Anne O'Brien